ADOPTION

A Reference Handbook

Selected Titles in ABC-CLIO's
CONTEMPORARY
WORLD ISSUES
Series

Capital Punishment, Michael Kronenwetter
Chemical and Biological Warfare, Al Mauroni
Childhood Sexual Abuse, Karen L. Kinnear
Conflicts over Natural Resources, Jacqueline Vaughn
Domestic Violence, Margi Laird McCue
Energy Use Worldwide, Jaina L. Moan and Zachary A. Smith
Euthanasia, Martha L. Gorman and Jennifer Fecio McDougall
Food Safety, Nina E. Redman
Genetic Engineering, Harry LeVine, III
Gun Control in the United States, Gregg Lee Carter
Human Rights Worldwide, Zehra F. Kabasakal Arat
Illegal Immigration, Michael C. LeMay
Intellectual Property, Aaron Schwabach
Internet and Society, Bernadette H. Schell
Mainline Christian Values and U.S. Public Policy, Glenn H. Utter
Mental Health in America, Donna R. Kemp
Nuclear Weapons and Nonproliferation, Sarah J. Diehl and
    James Clay Moltz
Policing in America, Leonard A. Steverson
Sentencing, Dean John Champion
U.S. Military Service, Cynthia A. Watson
World Population, Geoffrey Gilbert

For a complete list of titles in this series, please visit
www.abc-clio.com.

Books in the Contemporary World Issues series address vital issues in today's society such as genetic engineering, pollution, and biodiversity. Written by professional writers, scholars, and nonacademic experts, these books are authoritative, clearly written, up-to-date, and objective. They provide a good starting point for research by high school and college students, scholars, and general readers as well as by legislators, businesspeople, activists, and others.

Each book, carefully organized and easy to use, contains an overview of the subject, a detailed chronology, biographical sketches, facts and data and/or documents and other primary-source material, a directory of organizations and agencies, annotated lists of print and nonprint resources, and an index.

Readers of books in the Contemporary World Issues series will find the information they need in order to have a better understanding of the social, political, environmental, and economic issues facing the world today.

ADOPTION

A Reference Handbook,
Second Edition

Barbara A. Moe

CONTEMPORARY WORLD ISSUES

A B C ☰ C L I O

Santa Barbara, California
Denver, Colorado
Oxford, England

Library of Congress Cataloging-in-Publication Data

Moe, Barbara A.
  Adoption : a reference handbook / Barbara A. Moe.— 2nd ed.
    p. cm. — (Contemporary world issues series)
  Includes bibliographical references and index.
  ISBN 978-1-59884-029-2 (hardcopy : alk. paper) —
ISBN 978-1-59884-030-8 (ebook) 1. Adoption—United States—
Handbooks, manuals, etc. I. Title.

HV875.55.M645 2007
362.7340973—dc22

                                                    2007001714

11 10 09 08 07   10 9 8 7 6 5 4 3 2 1

ABC-CLIO, Inc.
130 Cremona Drive, P.O. Box 1911
Santa Barbara, California 93116-1911

This book is also available on the World Wide Web as an ebook.
Visit www.abc-clio.com for details.

This book is printed on acid-free paper ∞
Manufactured in the United States of America

*To all those whose lives
have been touched by adoption.*

Contents

Preface

In late July 2006, while thousands of U.S. citizens rushed in panic to get out of war-torn Beirut, a prospective adoptive American parent of a Lebanese boy refused to leave. Interviewed on radio, she planned to stay with "her" child, not yet formally adopted. "What mother would leave her son behind?" she asked. "I don't know anyone here. If I go, I'll never see him again."

Chris, adopted at age six into a family with older birth children, is now twenty-six. In a discussion with his father, he stated (or did he ask?): "I suppose you love your birth children more than the adopted ones."

Adoption is a complicated entity. Anyone who has gone through the process as an adopted person, an adoptive parent, or as a birth parent knows this is true. The process can be so complex and filled with so many "potholes" that the subject could fill several books. While keeping much in common with adoption processes of the past, changes are constantly occurring. Keeping up with the changes in adoption can be challenging. Another area of complexity is the connection among members of the adoption triad, a relationship that for many (in the recent past) has become more open. In addition, support for all triad members is a must, but there is never (it seems) enough support to go around.

Adoption is an "affair of the heart." But as much as adoption fills a need for love, there is much more involved. There are legal issues, psychological issues, emotional issues, financial issues, sometimes medical issues, and much paperwork.

Adoption: A Reference Handbook is intended for anyone who wants to get more informed about the many "faces" of adoption. This one-volume reference work can answer some—maybe many—of the questions that students of adoption ask. If it cannot provide all of the answers (and it can't), it can at least point readers in the right direction for finding the answers they need.

A goal of the book is to present in an objective way the many facets of adoption. People who "know" adoption (and even some who don't) have strong and differing opinions about what is "right" in adoption. This book will present some of these differing views on various aspects of adoption and let the reader decide.

Chapter 1, Background and History, offers a starting point with the history of adoption. Where and how did it originate? In what directions does it seem to be going? The chapter includes information on who adopts children, how families are screened, the types of children available for adoption, the various adoption "programs," and the types of adoption. Chapter 1 also includes information on the Hague Convention and possible emotional or psychological issues some adopted children display. It includes the threats posed by substances such as alcohol, HIV/AIDS, and methamphetamine. Also discussed are laws and policies, postlegal services, costs of adoption, the role of attorneys, and what happens when an adoption does not succeed.

Chapter 2, Issues and Controversies, takes an objective look at some of the issues in adoption, and controversies over such questions as "Which is best—open or closed adoption?" "What about open records?" "Are transracial/transcultural adoptions good for children?" "Should single people adopt?" "What about same-sex couples?" "Should the government provide more or less regulation of adoption?" "Are infant abandonment laws—so called 'safe havens'—useful or not?" "What about the concept of adoption itself?" Chapter 3, Adoption Around the World, explores how people in selected countries outside the United States handle adoption.

Chapter 4, Chronology, presents a timeline of adoption "milestones"—the founding of national organizations and adoption movements, the dates of important adoption legislation, significant conferences, and publication dates of important books (to name a few). It provides a context for understanding how the practice of adoption has evolved over the years. Chapter 5, Biographical Sketches, presents thirty brief biographical sketches of adoption "pioneers," those whose actions, writings, or both have changed adoption.

Chapter 6, Facts and Data, presents figures and tables that answer some commonly asked adoption questions. The chapter also includes important federal laws related to adoption, excerpts from testimonies of people whose experiences have influenced adoption policy, Supreme Court verdicts regarding adoption cases, and a concept model for postadoption services.

Chapter 7, Directory of Organizations, gives listings of important adoption organizations for adopted persons, birth parents, and adoptive parents. Some of the groups have education as their main focus; others are set up to support the specific members of the adoption triad. Some have many purposes. Chapter 8, Selected Print and Nonprint Resources, provides an annotated and selective list of books, journals/magazines, websites, videos/DVDs, CD-ROMs, databases, and software, all useful in learning about various aspects of adoption.

I appreciate all of the willing helpers I have used so freely in the preparation of this second edition. Mary Sullivan and her colleagues, especially Phyllis Charles and John Vogel, at the Child Welfare Information Gateway have provided invaluable assistance along the way. Likewise, numerous staff members of the Denver Public Library and Adoption Alliance have helped. Also, many thanks to Ellen Herman of the Adoption History Project and Randy Comfort of Our Place. I am grateful for the help of my family, especially Paul and David Moe, and technical advisors, such as Jim Esten and Peggy Roberts, and to the adoptive families who allowed me to tell their stories. Last, many thanks to editors Mim Vassan, Dayle Dermatis, and Alisha Martinez who cheerfully and promptly answered many, many questions and never wavered in their support.

1

Background and History

Adoption of children, in one form or another, is as old as human history. Most people are aware of at least one legendary adoption: that of the pharoah's daughter rescuing the baby Moses from the bulrushes.

The Babylonian Code of Hammurabi (approximately 1780 BC) was found in what is now southern Iraq; it contains the oldest written law on adoption. One section of the code discusses risks and concerns about the experience of adoption—that parents may treat the adopted child differently (from their birth children), that the child will suffer from changes in caregivers, or that the family and the adopted child may not be a good match. Ancient Greece, Rome, Egypt and other countries in the Middle East, and Asia all practiced some form of adoption.

Adoption law was not part of English Common Law, from which many other U.S. laws evolved. (England did not even have adoption laws until 1926.) Much of the adoption law of the United States evolved from Napoleonic code or from early Roman laws having to do with inheritance. The purpose of adoption was not necessarily to promote the welfare of the child but to give the adults an heir. Modern U.S. adoption law came into being in the late 1800s as a way of helping orphaned and neglected children. In the recent past, however, adoption laws and policies have changed more than ever before. Most experts agree that two principles have emerged to guide adoption practice: decisions should be made in the best interests of the child, and a permanent home for every child is the primary goal of adoption.

Lifelong Issues in Adoption

Most adoption workers agree with this statement: adoption is a lifelong issue. In other words, adoption presents ongoing "work" for everyone concerned. The late Marshall Schechter, MD, a nationally known psychiatrist, counseled adopted adults. He believed that many of his patients shared such issues as feelings of loss and abandonment, questions of identity, and low self-esteem (Brodzinsky and Schechter, 1990).

Since 1988, two adoption professionals, Deborah Silverstein and Sharon Kaplan Rozsia, have worked to help the three parties in any adoption (birth parents, adoptive parents, and the adopted person) understand the lifelong implications of adoption. Their "seven core issues of adoption" are loss, grief, rejection, guilt and shame, identity, intimacy, and mastery and control.

Meeting with a therapist knowledgeable about adoption will help some. Others may access support groups through local organizations or national groups. The Child Welfare Information Gateway has a fact sheet, "Impact of Adoption on Adopted Persons: A Factsheet for Families," available at http://www.child welfare.gov/pubs/f_issues.cfm.

Who Adopts Children?

Although adoption laws vary from state to state, most states allow any "fit" person to adopt. In theory, there are few restrictions on who can become an adoptive parent. In actuality, agencies or courts may limit who adopts.

Those who adopt may be family members or may be unrelated to the child. Because the adoption of family members is often unofficial, estimates vary as to the frequency of this type of adoption (referred to as kinship adoption). Most experts agree, however, that stepparent and relative adoptions make up the largest percentage of adoptions in the United States today. An attorney familiar with adoption law can formalize a stepparent or kinship adoption in most states, but some states (and some judges) require a social worker to first do a home study. Although simple in a legal sense, stepparent adoptions maybe be complicated in an emotional sense, as is often the case with blended families. But because of blood ties, a child may feel more comfortable with relatives. Nonrelative adoption, however, is the primary subject of this book.

Those who adopt may have problems with infertility and be unable to have children by birth. Or they may have children by birth but believe they have room for another child (or two or three or more). Some couples who adopt older children do so because they want to help in some way; they may still have "parenting energy" left but choose not to add to the world's overpopulation and so decide to become parents to a waiting child. Some choose to adopt as single parents. Some are same-sex couples. (Who is permitted to adopt can become controversial and will be discussed in the next chapter.)

How Agencies Screen Prospective Parents: The Home Study Process

Regardless of what social workers and adoption agencies decide to call this getting-to-know-you experience, the home study process has remained at the center of the adoption experience for many years. Because the term *home study* connotes a physical inspection of a family's living quarters, efforts to rename the process continue. Some agencies have decided to call this evaluation a "family assessment."

Before taking a child into their home, a family must "pass the test" of suitability for adoption. The formal application process usually includes all or some of the following: the submission of fingerprints for FBI clearance, a check of the child abuse registry, physical examinations, letters of reference, the submission of a marriage license and/or divorce decrees, and proof of health insurance. A home inspection is actually a small part of the home study. More important for the social worker to explore with the family are questions such as: What are their motivations to adopt? What type of child will they consider (e.g., age, race, handicapping conditions)? How will they deal with emotional or physical disabilities? How were they disciplined? What is the status of their relationships with family and friends? How strong is their marriage? What hardships have they overcome? If they have not yet parented, what do they know about parenting? What do they know about adoption? Other areas for exploration are employment, finances, religious and ethical beliefs, lifestyle, expectations, and flexibility.

Training for prospective adoptive parents is mandatory in most agencies. Training gives credence to the belief that although raising an adopted child is in many ways similar to raising *any* child, there are different issues, and different skills may be required.

Types of Children Available for Adoption

Adoptive families face challenges and choices. Prospective adoptive parents may sometimes pick the sex of their child, but in an infant adoption this is not usually possible because adoptive parents often do not know the sex of the child to be born to them. However, those adopting an older child or a child from another country often do state a preference. An interesting paradox is that larger numbers of those expecting their first birth child would choose a boy if they could, while more adoptive couples and single women prefer girls.

Methods (Styles) of Adoption

In deciding how to go about finding a child, families have even more choices to make. Sorting adoption methods into categories helps explain these choices, but in reality categories overlap. Although federal laws are important, state laws govern the intricacies of adoption, and the content of these laws vary from state to state.

Domestic (In-Country) Adoption

Infant Adoption.   Infant adoption is both a *type* of adoption based on the age of the child (usually under one year of age, although some allow up to two years) and a *method* of adoption based on the procedures involved. The steps that prospective adoptive parents must take in order to adopt an infant from the United States are different, for example, from the procedures involved in adopting an older child from the United States or a child from another country.

In addition to completing the home study, couples interested in being considered for an infant usually make a profile of themselves for the adoption agency to present to the birth mother; they also write a "Dear Birth Parent" letter telling the birth mother (or birth couple) why they would be interested in the child, often not yet born. In many cases the birth parents want to meet the prospective adoptive parents and "choose" them; in other cases the birth parents want the agency to make the decision. (In general, when birth parents choose, they tend to pick young married couples with no children or only a few other children.) Often the birth parents request pictures of the child once a year on the child's birthday; the agency usually coordinates the exchange. In some cases, there is ongoing contact between the two families; in other cases, there is none.

Today there is a swing toward more openness in infant adoption and more involvement of birth parents in the process. The placement of domestic infants occurs on a continuum of openness and ranges from very open to totally closed, with most infant adoptions falling in the middle of this range.

Special Needs Adoption.   According to the Child Welfare Information Gateway and the Child Welfare League of America, there are approximately 114,000 special needs children waiting in foster care for adoptive families.

When a couple (or single person) decides to adopt a child with "special needs" (sometimes called a "waiting child"), they may go either through the county or state agency that has custody of the child or through a private agency. (Not all private agencies work with public agencies to place special needs children, but many do.) Although the designation of "special needs" varies, social workers tend to put the following "types" of children in the special needs category:

—Any child over the age of seven (or eight)

—Children of color, especially those over the age of four

—Siblings to be adopted together, especially more than two siblings

—Any child born to a mother who has used alcohol and/or drugs during her pregnancy

—Children who have a positive result from an HIV antibody test

—Children who have been physically, emotionally, or sexually abused

—Children with physical, intellectual, or emotional disabilities

—Children who have had multiple moves (these children are at high risk for attachment disorder, which we will discuss later in this chapter under the heading "Reactive Attachment Disorder")

Coparenting.   Coparenting is a community-based alternative for families adopting children with developmental disabilities. In some places the project is federally funded through a grant from the U.S. Department of Health and Human Services. The goal of the program is to strengthen families through "planned sharing." Volunteer caregivers, who have no legal rights, come into the families' lives to help when needed. Because research has shown that children with developmental disabilities wait ten times longer than other children for an adoptive home, a special effort is being made to preserve these placements. In this project, coparents help reduce stress on the adoptive family by sharing some of the workload. Coparents receive up to six weeks of specialized training.

Adoption Exchanges.   No discussion of special needs adoption would be complete without a mention of adoption exchanges. These organizations, usually regional in scope, are not adoption *agencies* but referral sources (networking units) for hard-to-place children. Their role does not duplicate that of agencies; exchanges do not usually do home studies and do not work directly with children, except to film them for photo books, the Internet, or television. Exchanges function as intermediary organizations in linking waiting children with waiting parents.

Laws and Policies Relating to Domestic Adoption.   When parents in one state adopt a child from another state, they are subject to the conditions of the Interstate Compact on the Placement of Children (ICPC). The compact is not a national law but an agreement to which all of the states, as well as the District of Columbia and the U.S. Virgin Islands, subscribe. Its purpose is to assure safe placement of children across state lines and to make sure the requirements of the "sending state" and the "receiving state" are in agreement and being complied with by all parties.

Each state has a compact administrator who reviews the paperwork, including the home study of the prospective adoptive parents, before the child is placed. Until the administrator gives permission, the adoptive parents may not travel with the child to their home state.

The Interstate Compact on Adoption and Medical Assistance (ICAMA) helps provide medical and other services to adoptive families and children in placement across state lines or in the case of a parental move to a different state before the adoption is finalized. Currently most of the states belong to ICAMA. The compact provides for consistent policies and procedures in programs such as Medicaid. For children covered by Medicaid, the "receiving state" may issue a new Medicaid card to the child who has moved.

Intercountry (International) Adoption

The terms *intercountry* and *international* adoption are used interchangeably. According to the Evan P. Donaldson Adoption Institute, citizens of the United States began adopting children from other countries in substantial numbers after World War II. Many of these children were war orphans from various countries of Europe and also Japan. Following the civil war in Greece (1946–1949), the Korean War (1950–1953), and the Vietnam War (1954–1973), international adoptions continued to increase. Other factors driving these adoptions in recent years have included poverty and social upheaval in Latin America, Eastern Europe, and the former Soviet Union. In China, government controls on population have led to the abandonment of infant girls and overcrowded orphanages. As a "scarcity" of available infants developed in the United States, more couples looked to other countries to find young children to adopt. Altruistic motives also motivate some parents to pursue intercountry adoptions.

Citizens of the United States adopted more than a quarter of a million children internationally between 1971 and 2001. Between 1991 and 2001, international adoptions more than doubled, with 19,237 immigrant visas issued to orphans coming to the United States in 2001. In the decade between 1995 and 2005, intercountry adoptions climbed from 8,987 in 1995 to 22,728 in 2005.

Those who would like more information on intercountry adoption statistics can visit the U.S. State Department website at http://travel.state.gov.

Intercountry adoption continues to change. Throughout the 1960s and 1970s, most internationally adopted children came from Korea and Vietnam. Thrust into the world spotlight during the 1988 Olympic Games, South Korea began to reconsider the loss of many of its children to overseas adoptions, and the number of adoptions from that country dropped. With the breakup of many Communist-bloc nations in that same era, international adoptions began to shift focus. The early 1990s saw a surge in adoptions from Romania; in the late 1990s there was an increase in adoptions from Russia and China.

Many single parents, mostly women, have found the international adoption process more hospitable to them than either domestic infant or special needs programs. An intercountry adoption may be the only way a single person can adopt a very young child. (Almost 9 percent of internationally adopted children are younger than five years old; 46 percent are under one year of age.) In the United States, a birth mother may be a single parent herself and want her child to have a two-parent family. Single persons can also pursue an intercountry adoption of a child with "special needs." Nevertheless, the process of adopting a child from another country can be challenging.

Because of the complexity of the intercountry adoption process, many people choose to work with a licensed child placement agency. Some are able to find an agency in their area that has its own adoption program in a certain country. At other times, the local agency links up with a different agency in another part of the country. Adoption Alliance, a nonprofit agency in Denver, Colorado, opened its doors in 1989, and has since found homes for children in Latin America, Jamaica, the Dominican Republic, China, Romania, Vietnam, and other locations throughout the world.

The countries themselves decide what the requirements, such as age, marital status, or religion, will be. For example, Adoption Alliance's work with Jamaica requires adopting parents to be practicing fundamentalist Christians.

In addition to the rules of the other country's government and the laws of the adopters' own state, the U.S. government has regulations. U.S. Citizenship and Immigrations Services (USCIS) requires that at least one person in an adoptive couple be a citizen of the United States, and one of them must be at least twenty-five years old.

Other rules apply. Under immigration law, the definition of an orphan (from the Immigration and Nationality Act) is a long one. An orphan is

> a child, under the age of sixteen at the time a petition is filed in his behalf to accord a classification as an immediate relative under section 201(b), who is an orphan because of the death or disappearance of, abandonment or desertion by, or separation or loss from both parents, or for whom the sole or surviving parent is incapable of providing the proper care and has, in writing, irrevocably released the child for emigration and adoption; who has been adopted abroad by a U.S. citizen and spouse jointly or by an unmarried U.S. citizen at least twenty-five years of age, who personally saw and observed the child prior to or during the adoption proceedings; or who is coming to the United States for adoption by a U.S. citizen and spouse jointly, or by an unmarried U.S. citizen at least twenty-five years of age, who have or has complied with the preadoption requirements if any, of the child's proposed residence: *Provided,* That the Attorney General is satisfied that proper care will be furnished the child if admitted to the United States: *Provided further,* That no natural parent or prior adoptive parent of any such child shall thereafter, by virtue of such parentage, be accorded any right, privilege, or status under this Act. (U.S. Department of Justice, September 2000, revised, 35)

The child, living in either an orphanage or a foster home, may be represented by an attorney, physician, judge, or social worker.

Rosemary and Sam Wilber of South Carolina have one birth child, Ben, age ten. The Wilbers wanted to complete their family by adopting a younger girl. For a while, they considered adopting a child with special needs from the United States. Although their social worker told them about several girls over the course of a year, they didn't hear about one that seemed right for their family. Ultimately, they decided to try an intercountry adoption, which involved a whole new set of paperwork and a home study addendum. During the second process, the social worker realized that Rosemary had at one time taught Spanish in an elementary school. Now Rosemary is brushing up on her language skills while the family waits for the go-ahead to travel to Guatemala to pick up their newly assigned daughter, Maria, age seven.

After a couple receives a referral of a particular child and they accept the child, they may, for a variety of reasons, have a long wait before they can parent that child. Changes in country policies and procedures may lead to delays in the process. Once the paperwork is complete, depending on country and/or agency policies, either the prospective adoptive parents will travel to the country (sometimes twice) to finalize the adoption and bring the child home or, as is the case with many Korean adoptions, the child may travel with an escort to the United States.

People often believe that adopting from another country will be an easy way to get a healthy Caucasian infant. Often they are wrong. In the first place, intercountry adoptions are rarely easy. Second, most children adopted from other countries in the past fifty years, beginning with Pearl Buck's Welcome House in the 1940s and Holt International Children's Services in the 1950s, have been children of color. According to adoptive parent and publisher Patricia Johnston, "many couples who would not even consider adopting an American black child adopt internationally from Asia, India, or South America without considering it a transracial or transethnic placement." (This is one of the controversial topics we will consider in Chapter 2.)

Laws and Policies for Intercountry Adoption.   In addition to the requirements all adoptive parents must meet, those adopting from out of the country have special requirements. For most countries, the family must put together a notarized dossier and follow the guidelines set forth by U.S. immigration law, found in the Immigration and Naturalization Act. These guidelines not only determine if a particular child may enter the United States but also mandate adherence to state laws and the laws of the child's country.

Most often the first form prospective parents see from the U.S. Citizenship and Immigration Services (USCIS) is the I-600 A, the Application for Advanced Processing of an Infant. To be approved, families must submit such documents as a positive home study, fingerprint forms, proof of citizenship, and marriage and divorce decrees. Adopters then file the I-600 Petition to Classify and Orphan as an Immediate Relative, most often in the other country. This form allows a child to enter the United States. In addition to giving information about the prospective parents, the I-600 Petition must also include information about the child to be adopted, particularly the status of his or her parents.

Much of the immigration paperwork is done before the parents travel to meet their assigned child or before the child is escorted to the United States. Usually parents legally adopt the child in the child's country of birth. After the child comes to the United States to live with his or her adoptive family, the adoption agency may do six to twelve months of post-placement supervision, which may be followed by a court validation or finalization. Later the child must be "naturalized," a separate process.

The Hague Convention on Intercountry Adoption is a multilateral treaty designed to protect children, birth parents, and adoptive parents by developing uniform standards and safeguards for intercountry adoption. After three years of work, sixty-six nations took the first step toward making the convention a reality and approved the treaty at the Hague. Before this time, rumors of child abduction and organ stealing had surfaced in many countries, which then closed or reduced their international adoption programs.

In September 2000 the United States ratified the treaty. The Intercountry Adoption Act of 2000 (IAA), enacted on October 6, 2000, provides implementing legislation for the convention. In August 2005 the U.S. Department of State submitted regulations on accreditation and approval of international adoption services to the Office of Management and Budget (OMB). This is the final step before the regulations become final. Accreditation of agencies to conduct adoptions under the Hague Convention must be finished before the United States can *officially* ratify the treaty. The United States is expected to implement the treaty by 2007–2008.

Types of Adoption and Care

Agency Adoption

Those who would like to adopt a child must travel down many "streets" on their way to adoption. If potential adoptive parents take the agency route, they have to decide between a private and a public agency. To support their work, public agencies receive tax money from the federal government and/or state, county, or municipality in which they are located. Because these agencies generally place children within their jurisdictions, they do not get involved in intercountry adoptions, nor do they place infants unless the child has special needs or has been in foster care.

The private agency is another route to adoption. Private agencies may be nonprofit or for-profit; they may be denominational or nondenominational. Because private agencies do not receive tax dollars, they usually have to charge fees for their services. Fees and policies vary from state to state, but in each state they are governed by state laws.

People may choose an agency for the services they hope to receive, such as training about adoption, assistance in communicating with birth parents, and/or support during and after the adoptive placement.

Independent Adoption

Another route to adoption is the independent or private one. In a private adoption (not the same as a private *agency* adoption), a couple legally adopts a baby directly from the birth parents without the involvement of an adoption agency. An intermediary (attorney, physician, member of the clergy, social worker, or "adoption consultant") may act as a "facilitator," making sure all of the legal requirements have been followed. Several states prohibit independent adoptions.

Jean Warren Lindsay, author of *Open Adoption: A Caring Option* (1987), says she always favored agency adoption because of the expectation that a good agency would provide the all-important counseling for birth parents as well as counseling and training for adoptive parents. The disadvantage (years ago) to an agency placement was that absolute secrecy prevailed. Things have changed. Nowadays more and more agencies are not only providing counseling but are also insisting on some degree of openness in the infant placement. At the same time, says Lindsay, some independent adoption services offer counseling and education similar to what was formerly available only through an agency. Distinctions have blurred.

Designated Adoption

A designated adoption (also called a "targeted" or "identified" adoption) falls somewhere between the two aforementioned adoption styles. In a designated adoption, prospective adoptive parents locate a birth mother, or a birth mother finds the adoptive parents, sometimes through an intermediary. Together they locate a licensed child placement agency from which they can receive the needed services, such as a home study for the adoptive family and counseling for the birth mother (as well as for the birth father, if he is involved).

Parent-Initiated Adoption

A parent-initiated adoption is a style related to designated adoption in which prospective adoptive parents and/or birth parents take an active role in the pre-adoption process. Either party may send out letters and resumes or place classified advertisements in newspapers and on the internet. When the two sets of parents match up, there is an assumption that the birth parents will go through with an adoption plan. No one is obligated, however, until court involvement has taken place. Sometimes a parent-initiated adoption occurs when a family has found a child free for adoption in another country.

Foster-Adoption

There are many differences between foster care and adoption, but the two sometimes interface when a foster-care situation "turns into" an adoption. The state (or county) and the courts work together to try to keep children safe. Children are placed in a foster home when birth parents have been unable to care for them; in many cases, the children have been neglected or abused.

Foster-adoption is sometimes called fost-adopt, fos-adopt, legal-risk, or concurrent permanency planning. Not too many years ago, foster parents were not considered for the adoption of children placed in their home. These days, the current foster parents usually become the family of choice for a child when that child becomes "free" for adoption.

Because foster parents and adoptive parents may have the same goal (providing permanence for a child), many child placement agencies screen, educate, and "study" adoptive and foster families together. More and more often, caseworkers (especially those who work with young children) ask prospective adoptive parents who have not been foster parents if they would consider a legal-risk (foster-adopt) placement because this arrangement could spare the child another move. Nevertheless, some prospective adoptive parents are hesitant to accept a child who is not legally free for adoption.

While adoption is "forever," and the adoptive parents have the same rights and responsibilities as if the child had been born to them, foster care may be temporary. If the birth parents succeed in following through with the treatment plan ordered by the court (e.g., to be free of drugs and alcohol, to have a means of earning a living, and to have a safe place to live), the child may go home. This is the goal.

However, if the birth parents are unable to follow through with the court orders, the court may terminate the parental rights of the birth parents, and after an appeal period, the child becomes legally free for adoption. In these cases, the current foster parents may be allowed to adopt them. This works out well for many children, who have already begun to think of their foster parents as their "forever" parents.

Baby Tonya was born to Martha, a patient in a mental hospital in Ohio. Caseworkers believe Martha's ex-husband, who came to the hospital for visits, was the baby's father. Martha had six other children she had not been able to parent. Authorities believed that a family in California had adopted the older four; the workers were looking for a home together for the younger two, who had been badly burned by the birth mother during one of her psychotic episodes. Tonya, the seventh child, was placed with the Fletchers at two days of age. They were the only couple at the time willing to take two risks: a history of mental illness in the mother, and the risk that Martha might get well enough to eventually parent her baby. In this case, the court terminated the birth parents' rights, and the Fletchers became Tonya's permanent parents.

Kinship Care

Kinship care refers to a situation in which relatives by blood or by marriage, or others with close family ties, take care of children who are unable to live with their original parents. Sometimes the birth parents ask these relatives to take in the children; sometimes social service agencies recruit them so that the children will not have their birth links completely severed. Kinship care may lead to a formal adoption.

Travis, eight, and Katie, six, have the same mother but different fathers. Their mother left them with a number of her boyfriends, who sexually abused them. As a result, these siblings act out sexually when they are together. In addition, each requires a tremendous amount of individual attention. Two years ago Lisa, the birth mother, left Oregon for Texas, and no one in town has seen her since. Lisa's older sister is taking care of Katie, a compliant child, and wants to adopt her. Travis is anything but compliant. He has temper tantrums that last for hours; he lies, cheats, and steals; he has no friends. The foster father in the home in which Travis has lived for the past two years is the cousin of Travis's father. This family has offered to take legal guardianship of Travis but believes his problems are too severe for them to adopt him. (Legal guardianship is an arrangement under which the law allows a person who is not the child's adoptive parent to take responsibility for the daily care and financial management of the minor child.)

A recurring question in kinship care is whether relatives caring for children are entitled to the same financial and other supports as nonrelative foster parents, or whether relatives should instead care for "their own" without financial assistance.

Stepparent Adoption

Although the exact numbers are not known, stepparent adoption is considered the most common type of adoption in the United States. In order for a stepparent to legally adopt a child, the child's birthparent (who is not living in the home) must consent to the adoption or a judge must terminate his/her parental rights.

Depending on the state and/or the circumstances, a judge may order a home study and criminal and child abuse background checks. If the child is over a certain age (for example, ten, twelve, or fourteen, depending on state requirements), the child must also consent to the adoption. In many cases, the child will want to (and be able to) continue to have a relationship with the biological parent.

Possible Emotional and Health Problems

No one knows how many adopted children develop special problems, but those who do often end up in the spotlight. For example, if an adopted teen drinks, drives, and causes an accident, a newspaper headline may say, "Adopted Youth Causes Accident." A similar mishap caused by the parents' birth child is unlikely to say, "Birth Child Causes Accident." Thus, the expectation of some that adopted persons are either less or more responsible for their own actions *because* they are adopted may compound any existing issues the child may have.

Reactive Attachment Disorder

One condition in adopted children that can be difficult to diagnose and treat is reactive attachment disorder (RAD). Attachment is a child's emotional connection to his primary caregivers. If a consistent figure meets a baby or young child's needs when he cries, he develops a secure attachment, which leads to a feeling of well-being. Many people believe that a child's future emotional health, including his ability to form healthy relationships, has its basis in the quality of attachment during the child's first one or two years. (Some people use the word *bonding* to describe this process.)

RAD is a psychological diagnosis describing children who, on a continuum of seriousness, have not bonded to their current caregivers. (Students of this condition will find a more thorough description in the *Diagnostic and Statistical Manual of Mental Disorders* (the *DSM-IV*), published by the American Psychiatric Association.) Abuse and/or neglect, alcohol and drug exposure in utero, illness or separation from the primary caregiver—all break attachments and may cause the child to lose (or never develop) the ability to trust, which is the underlying cause of attachment problems.

Although any child, such as a premature infant placed in an incubator, can develop attachment difficulties, some people *expect* to see this condition in children adopted at an older age. And yet, not all "special needs" children develop RAD, especially if they have not moved from place to place and have bonded to a caregiver, such as a foster mother or father. In the preface to the second volume of his trilogy on attachment and loss, John Bowlby writes, "What is believed to be essential for mental health is that the infant and young child should experience a warm, intimate and continuous relationship with his mother (or permanent mother-substitute) in which both find satisfaction and enjoyment."

In 1988 a county department of social services placed David, age eight, for adoption with Bill and Lisa Burns. Bill is an attorney; Lisa is a registered nurse. The couple had three almost-grown birth children and an eleven-year-old daughter named Carrie, who was adopted as a six-year-old. Carrie was doing well, and the family believed they had "room for one more." The ink on this family's home study had barely dried when the county asked Bill and Lisa if they would consider adopting David. The social worker suggested that David might be a wonderful addition to the family, and a psychologist had found him to be highly intelligent.

David had a troubled background. When he was six, his birth mother, an alcoholic with drug problems, had threatened to take him to the social services building and leave him there; on another occasion, she did. David had witnessed domestic violence, having seen his birth mother's boyfriend pull a knife on her husband (not David's father). When David was two, a policeman had found him, teddy bear in hand, running away from home. Furthermore, he had been shuttled back and forth between his birth mother in Texas and his grandmother in Oklahoma. Although the social worker also mentioned the possibility of sexual abuse in David's background, as well as some of the symptoms of RAD, she hoped a loving home could help David overcome these difficulties.

For some reason unknown to them, Bill and Lisa did not receive any financial help for the overwhelming psychological problems that developed after David's formal adoption. With two older children in college and one a senior in high school, Bill and Lisa could not afford $6,000 a month (the cost at the time) to maintain David in a residential treatment center for children with attachment problems. By age seventeen, David, who at one time seemed to have the potential for a promising future, had no friends, did not work or go to school, and spent most of his time watching television.

Adoption professionals who place older children know the symptoms of RAD. They include some or all of the following:

—Crazy lying (lying about the obvious)

—Stealing

—Preoccupation with fire

—Cruelty to animals

—Absence of conscience or poor conscience development

—Unusual food habits, which may include gorging, stealing food, hoarding food, getting up at night to eat, or refusing to eat

—Lack of impulse control

—Abnormal speech patterns

—Learning problems

—Superficially charming behaviors but lack of real friends

—Overabundance of affection with strangers and/or lack of affection with parents

David displayed some of the above behaviors. His parents were afraid to leave the house for fear they would come back to a pile of rubble; David loved to burn incense and was addicted to cigarettes.

Ten years later, David shows increased developmental maturity, conscience development, and attachment. He lives independently with an occasional "infusion" of financial help from his parents, has a job working with developmentally delayed adults, has a few friends, and is considering going to a community college to become a nurse. Although he has never said "I love you" to his adoptive parents, he solicits their advice and often thanks them for their help. In spite of some misgivings along the way, David's parents now consider his adoption a success.

Members of the adoption community generally support the concepts of bonding and attachment, but some professionals are skeptical about current views on the subject. Psychology professor Diane E. Eyer (1992) says that people use the term *bonding* to suggest that parents can mold children like clay. Not so, says Eyer. There are too many other intervening factors, such as the influence of genetics, the child's unique temperament, and other people in his world.

Even though the majority of those in the community *do* support the concepts of bonding and attachment, much is still unknown, including how to best treat RAD. Specialized therapists often attempt to treat the assumed absence of attachment with various types of holding therapies. Therapy of some kind is almost always essential to the healing process for children who have experienced neglect and abuse, but it must be therapy specific to the problems and by a therapist familiar with adoption. (For an excellent description of the types of therapy that have helped adopted children, see chapter 10 in *Adopting the Hurt Child: Hope for Families with Special Needs Kids* (1995), by Gregory C. Keck and Regina Kupecky.

Fetal Alcohol Spectrum Disorder (FASD)

No level of alcohol consumption is safe during pregnancy. Fetal alcohol spectrum disorder (FASD) is an umbrella term used to describe a range of conditions that may affect a person whose birth mother drank alcohol at any time during her pregnancy. The effects are irreversible and may include physical changes, mental or behavioral difficulties, and learning disabilities. Conditions under the umbrella are fetal alcohol syndrome (FAS), alcohol-related neurodevelopmental disorder (ARND), and alcohol-related birth defects (ARBD). Some people still use an older term, fetal alcohol effects (FAE), but the Institute of Medicine replaced that term with FASD in 1996.

A diagnosis of FAS, which was first described as a syndrome in the early 1970s in the United States, is based on (1) abnormal facial features, (2) growth deficiencies, and (3) central nervous system difficulties. Children may have difficulties in school and in getting along with other people. Those affected may also have problems with vision and/or hearing, communicating, paying attention, remembering, and learning. Children with FAS tend not to put together cause and effect, which makes taking care of them frustrating for their caregivers. As they become teenagers and older, they are at risk for noncompletion of their education, unemployment, psychiatric disturbances, and even criminal behavior. Protective factors include early diagnosis and interventions as well as a stable family life.

A child whose birth mother drank alcohol during her pregnancy may have some, but not all, of the clinical signs of fetal alcohol syndrome. The terms ARND (alcohol-related neurodevelopmental disorder) and ARBD (alcohol-related birth defects) refer to less serious levels of involvement. Experts believe these disorders occur three times as often as FAS.

Fetal alcohol spectrum disorder is a potential problem in

children adopted from anywhere in the world, including the United States. If a birth mother does not drink alcohol during pregnancy, the condition is entirely preventable.

HIV/AIDS

HIV (the human immunodeficiency virus) progressively damages the body's ability to protect itself from disease organisms. It is transmitted by sexual contact or the sharing of needles. AIDS (acquired immune deficiency syndrome) is the chronic condition the virus causes. Without treatment, pregnant women may transmit the virus to their babies.

Since the introduction of new antiviral therapies in the mid-1990s, the death rate (and transmission rate to newborns) from HIV/AIDS in the United States has greatly decreased. Unfortunately this is not true in some other parts of the world, such as Africa.

Currently in the United States if a pregnant woman's infection is identified and she receives up-to-date treatment, the transmission rate of the virus to her baby is less than 2 percent. In mothers who do not receive treatment, approximately 28 percent of babies will be infected.

Carol Salbenblatt, RN, MS, is the HIV program coordinator at the Children's Hospital in Denver, Colorado (interview with the author, November 23, 2005). She says that if a young woman in the United States has HIV infection and gets "state-of-the-art" treatment that she complies with, she may live a relatively normal life span (similar to a person with diabetes). Two factors, however, may change this optimistic outlook: (1) if the disease for some reason progresses quickly and aggressively, and (2) if a person continues to use intravenous drugs, does not take her medication, and/or has multiple sexual partners.

In these situations (or in the case of a parent with a terminal illness from any cause), a guardianship arrangement can be important. Every state allows the transfer of guardianship authority from a parent to another adult. A potential problem is that there are no guarantees. If challenged by another person with legal standing, the sick person's wishes may not stand up in court.

A relatively new type of legal arrangement is more friendly to birth parents with HIV infection, another disability, or a terminal illness. In *standby guardianship,* a person the parent chooses "stands by" until, or if, needed. This type of legal guardianship allows the parent to give testimony in court as to the child's best interests as she knows them. The parent can then feel comfortable that her chosen plan will actually happen—if she becomes incapacitated.

Methamphetamine

Methamphetamine is a relatively new substance on the substance abuse scene. "Meth," as it is usually called, is an addictive central nervous system stimulant, most often available as a powder that dissolves in water. Sometimes it comes in clear crystals, hence the name "crystal meth." It is also referred to as "ice," "speed," "crank," "biker's coffee," and "chalk."

Although methamphetamine can have legitimate medical uses, it is the illegal use that worries agencies of the federal government, local governments, and child welfare workers. At the ninth hearing (July 26, 2005) on methamphetamine abuse held by the federal government's Subcommittee on Criminal Justice, Drug Policy, and Human Resources, chairman Mark Souder said, "Meth is one of the most powerful and dangerous drugs available, and one of the easiest to make. It can be 'cooked' using common household or agricultural chemicals and simple cold medicines, following recipes easily available on the Internet. The drug is highly addictive and has multiple side effects, including psychotic behavior, physical deterioration, and brain damage. Death by overdose is a significant risk."

It doesn't take a big leap, then, to realize that when parents spend their time getting high, struggling to recover from the "crash" (sometimes by using alcohol or other drugs), they may neglect and/or abuse their children. In fact, having children in the same house where meth is being made constitutes abuse because of the potential harm to the children.

Souder went on to tell about two reports that detailed the effect meth abuse is having on law enforcement agencies and child welfare services. "Criminal Effect of Meth on Communities" and "The Impact of Meth on Children: Out of Home Placement" came from surveys of hundreds of counties across the country. The surveys showed that children are increasingly becoming the primary victims of methamphetamine abuse. Forty percent of child welfare agencies reported an increase in "out of home placement because of meth in the past year." This abuse included physical and mental trauma, as well as sexual abuse. Sixty-nine percent of county social service agencies reported that they had to provide additional training for staff to be able to address the specialized needs of children affected.

At the same hearing, Nancy K. Young, PhD, director of the National Center on Substance Abuse and Child Welfare and director of Children and Family Futures, observed that although the population of children in out-of-home care had actually *decreased* since 1999, the percentage of children in foster care because of their parents' substance abuse had probably increased. Anecdotal estimates ranged from 40 to 80 percent. In its report to Congress in 1999, the U.S. Department of Health and Human Services (DHHS) estimated that between one-third and two-thirds of children in the U.S. child welfare system are affected by substance abuse disorders.

Health Problems That May Occur in Children Adopted Internationally

As a result of poor economic conditions, children from developing countries may have health problems when they first arrive in the United States. Dr. Dana Johnson started the first International Adoption Clinic at the University of Minnesota in 1986. Since then, many international adoption clinics have sprung up across the country. Parents, with the help of health professionals, can usually correct or mitigate the presenting problems with improved nutrition and health care. Among the most common health issues are intestinal parasites, earlier exposure to tuberculosis, hepatitis B or C, dental caries, lactose intolerance, incomplete immunizations, parasitic conditions such as scabies or lice, emotional or behavioral problems, and visual or hearing impairments. A standard screening protocol usually includes a review of immunizations, a complete blood count and urinalysis, and screening tests for hepatitis B and C, HIV, intestinal parasites, tuberculosis, and syphilis.

Thoa is a fourteen-month-old girl adopted from Vietnam. On the way home in the plane, Thoa had a seizure, perhaps from a high fever. At the same time, she had chicken pox, impetigo, eczema, a runny nose, a cough, an ear infection, and conjunctivitis. On arrival in the United States, she seemed slow in her development. Doctors did routine screening tests, which were all normal. It is still too early to tell if Thoa's developmental delays are the temporary results of orphanage life, or if her delays will be permanent.

Laws and Policies

Laws and policies are important parts of the adoption picture. Those who do not abide by the rules of a particular state may end up with a failed adoption and much heartache. Although state laws govern most adoption policies, certain procedures are common to most adoptions. These procedures can be looked at from two different perspectives—that of the birth parents, and that of the adoptive parents.

For Birth Parents

Consent. The first step in any adoption is the birth parents' written consent. Parental rights must be terminated (or relinquished) before finalization of an adoption. This part of the process may be done before the adoptive parents meet their new child. The Consent for Adoption, sometimes called the Petition for Parental Termination or Relinquishment, must be signed before a judge, notary public, or other witnesses. Details vary from state to state. Some state laws specify that seventy-two hours must pass before consent is given. States also vary as to whether or not persons under the age of eighteen may give consent to an adoption without their parents' knowledge or approval. The purpose of these laws is to protect birth parents' rights. Since 1972, unmarried fathers must also give consent to an adoption; disregard for a father's rights can cause disaster for the adoptive parents. If a known father's name is on the child's birth certificate, the father will have to sign a consent form. A common way of trying to find an unknown birth father (if his consent is required by law) is to place a notice in the newspaper. A birth father has parental rights even if he is prison, is not married to the child's mother, or is married to someone else.

Exceptions to the above are circumstances in which a court terminates parental rights because of neglect, abuse, abandonment, mental illness, or other conditions making the birth parents unfit. Termination of parental rights is a long and involved court process in which the petitioning party (usually the social service agency that has custody of the child) has the burden of proving the birth parents unfit.

Consent Revocation. When may a birth parent "break a promise" and revoke his or her consent to the adoption? Certainly if they have signed nothing, birth parents have every right to change their minds. State laws differ, but a birth parent may always revoke his or her consent if it was obtained by fraud or under duress. Most states allow the revoking of consent only with court approval. A few states allow birth parents to withdraw consent (for any reason) before the judge issues the final decree of adoption. Courts try to balance the interests of all triad members and usually rule in favor of the "best interests of the child" combined with birth parents' rights.

Available Resources.   As part of making the difficult decision that may result in an adoption plan, birth parents need counseling. Some states require a certain number of hours of birth parent counseling; other states "suggest" an amount. Adoption agencies often prefer ten or twelve hours of counseling, but usually it is up to an individual judge or magistrate to decide how much is acceptable.

The cost of birth parent counseling is most often paid by the adoptive parents whether or not the birth parents decide to place their child for adoption. The work should be done (before and after the child's birth) by a knowledgeable, impartial birth parent counselor. When the birth parents believe they have had enough counseling and are ready to go to court, a relinquishment hearing is scheduled. The judge will usually ask the birth mother if she feels she has been coerced into making her decision and/or if she has received enough counseling to help her make an informed decision. In states where there is a requirement for birth parent counseling, a birth father involved in the process must also be offered counseling.

For Adoptive Parents

Placement.   Placement day is an important date in the life of an adopted child, especially if he or she remembers that day. Some families celebrate this date as an adoption birthday because it is the true beginning of the adoption. An agency may make arrangements for a placement, or in the case of an independent adoption, birth parents or an attorney may arrange the placement date—the day the child moves in to stay. A court must then approve the placement, often with the recommendation of a social service agency.

Petition to Adopt and Adoption Hearings. One of the tasks of prospective adoptive parents is to file paperwork, such as proof of marriage, a financial statement, the results of physical examinations, letters of reference, and fingerprint cards. Agency policy rather than state law usually sets standards of placement. A home study is the standard proof that a family is suitable for a particular child or category of children.

After the child is placed in a home, the adoptive parents file a Petition to Adopt and may go to court for a preliminary or "interlocutory" hearing, at which time the judge gives his or her consent to the placement. At the final hearing, usually six months to a year from the date of placement, the judge issues the Final Decree of Adoption. The judge has determined that the adoption is in the child's best interests based on recommendations of the guardian ad litem (the court-appointed attorney for the child) and the social service agency involved.

Along with the adoptive parents, the child is usually present in court, especially if he or she needs to consent to the adoption. (In most states a child of age twelve or older must add his or her consent.) The Final Decree of Adoption gives children new legal parents, a new last name, and a new birth certificate. At this time adoption records may be sealed or not sealed, according to state law.

Postadoption Services. Even after adoptive families finalize an adoption, they are likely to need help in the form of support groups and/or possible referrals to special services and therapists. In recognition of the fact that adoption is a lifelong process, some states have begun to fund such services for parents and their children. One of the purposes of the Promoting Safe and Stable Families Amendments of 2001 was to admit to the need for postadoption services.

Costs of Adoption. Citing the average cost of an adoption is impossible because costs range from virtually nothing to more than $30,000. State or county agencies will charge the lowest fees for the adoption of a waiting child, who may also receive a monthly government subsidy. The main thing for adoptive parents to keep in mind is that judges often look carefully at costs to make sure adoptive parents are paying only for *services rendered* and are not "buying" a baby. Typically, adoptive parents of infants do pay for birth parent medical expenses related to the pregnancy and delivery, for authorized living expenses, and for birth parent counseling, attorneys' fees, and agency fees. A special report in the February 2006 issue of the magazine *Adoptive Families* analyzes costs of various types of adoptions and how some families have dealt with these costs.

The Attorney's Role

The role of the attorney varies with the type of adoption. In an independent adoption, an attorney may be the major player. He or she may have several roles, not only of handling legal details but also of dealing with financial and social matters. In fact, because of the possibility of a conflict of interest, a single adoption may have two attorneys involved, one representing the birth parents and the other representing the adoptive parents. On the other end of the scale, some adoptions, such as special needs adoptions through an agency, may not require an attorney. The agency may be able to prepare all of the forms and documents needed for court.

Probably the most important thing for clients to know is that not all attorneys are knowledgeable about adoption law; adoptive parents who need suggestions about a competent attorney can contact an adoptive parent support group, the local bar association, or the American Academy of Adoption Attorneys.

Black-Market Adoptions

Not a sanctioned type of adoption, black-market adoption occurs when birth parents or intermediaries of some kind profit illegally from the adoption. One method used to control black-market adoption is to have adoptive parents and all other parties involved report to the court any payments made or received. Financial help given to birth parents should be for pregnancy-related expenses and nothing else. Any other monies given to birth parents could be construed as "baby buying" or "baby brokering."

Disruption and Dissolution

If a child is placed for adoption but proper legal proceedings have not been followed, a birth parent or other intervener may challenge the adoptive placement. The objecting person could be a birth father whose rights were ignored. Or, if a supervising case-worker discovers a child is not being properly cared for in the adoptive home, he or she could remove the child. Both are examples of involuntary disruption.

In a voluntary disruption, the child may not want to leave the home, but his behaviors may be so disturbing to the adoptive parents that they ask to have the child removed.

Joan and Jim Welch had an approved home study and, in their search for a child, had "fallen in love" with the picture of thirteen-year-old Emily on the Internet. A social worker arranged to bring Emily along with Joel, another thirteen-year-old from Nevada, to an Adoption Exchange picnic in Colorado. At the picnic, the Welches, a childless couple in their mid-thirties, got acquainted with both of the children. As caring people, the Welches could not bear the idea of adopting one child without the other; eventually both Emily and Joel came to live with them.

After five months, Emily, who expressed overwhelming homesickness for birth relatives in Nevada, went back to her former foster home. Although the children and parents had received family counseling and support from their agency, the Welches believed their marriage was about to collapse from the strain of Emily's lying, stealing, and fighting. Three months after Emily left, the Welches, in cooperation with the various agencies, arranged for Joel to return to his home state. He had run away several times after the Welches had put limits on his activities; they decided they couldn't parent this child either.

Involuntary and voluntary disruptions are those that take place in the first six months to a year *before* the adoption is finalized. Although most adoptive placements are successful and go on to finalization, research has shown that for older children the disruption rate is between 8 and 16 percent.

Dissolution is the term used for an adoption that dissolves *after* it is finalized. Dissolution is a difficult court process; the adoptive parents relinquish the child after they have had enough counseling to satisfy themselves and/or the court. Probably the most common cause of a dissolution is the parents' claim that the agency deliberately deceived them as to the health or background of the child. For this reason, most agencies give the prospective parents before placement *all* of the information known about the child. Some agencies even record this "presentation." Experts estimate that 3 to 6 percent of special needs adoptions result in dissolution. No agency can foresee the future, and neither can the adoptive parents, which is why a strong commitment to the child is essential.

Disruption or dissolution can be devastating to all the parties involved. Most adoption professionals do anything they can to avoid it.

Funding, Financial Assistance, and Other Aid for Adoptive Parents

In addition to the obvious benefits of adoption, financial resources are sometimes available to help with adoption costs. These include loans, grants, adoption tax credits, subsidies, and employer-provided benefits.

For the year 2005, some adoptive parents were able to take a tax credit of up to $10,630 for qualifying expenses paid to adopt an eligible child. Internal Revenue Service "Qualified Adoption Expenses," Publication 8839, gives details at www.irs.gov/pub/irs-pdf.

In addition, children with special needs may be eligible for a monthly subsidy. The Adoption Assistance and Child Welfare Act of 1980 was the first federal law to make subsidies ("adoption assistance") available for children adopted from the foster care system. The two major funding sources of adoption assistance are (1) the Federal title IV-E program under the Social Security Act, and (2) various state subsidy programs. Those interested will find information on all of the above at the Child Welfare Information Gateway website, http://www.childwelfare.gov.

Employers may also provide benefits, some financial and some "other." Over the years, the number of employers willing to offer benefits to adoptive parents has grown. A survey by Hewitt Associates in 1990 found that 12 percent of the employers surveyed offered some type of adoption benefits. At the time of the 2004 Hewitt survey, the number had increased to 39 percent. The average maximum reimbursement was $3,879 for adoption-related expenses.

Employers may offer financial assistance to adoptive parents in the form of a "lump sum" reimbursement for costs related to the child's adoption. Or, employees may get reimbursed for specific expenses such as the home study.

Other possible benefits from employers include information such as referrals to support groups, adoption specialists, and licensed agencies, to name a few. A third possible employee benefit is parental leave. Federal law requires employers with fifty or more employees to offer mothers and fathers up to twelve weeks of unpaid leave after the birth or adoption of a child. Also, employees must be able to return to the same job (or an equivalent position) with the same health benefits. Those interested in learning more about the Family and Medical Leave Act can find this information at http://www.dol.gov/esa/whd/fmla.

Other Information of Interest

Available Resources

Similar to birth parents, adoptive parents need advice, education, and support. For couples who have experienced infertility, RE-SOLVE, Inc., a national organization begun in 1974 by Barbara Eck Menning, may be helpful. RESOLVE members are more than 15,000 couples dealing with infertility problems. Grieving and resolving infertility issues are important so that adoptive parents and their adopted children can develop a sense of entitlement, the feeling that each belongs with the other.

Education is another enormously important part of preparing *all* prospective parents for adoption. In many ways parenting an adopted child is the same as parenting *any* child. There are, however, significant differences. Acknowledgment of differences is important. Similarities are obvious—all babies need to be fed, bathed, and changed; all older children need rules and structure, as well as flexibility from their parents. All need unconditional love. To help with issues common to all parents, first-timers may find parenting classes helpful. To help with the differences, support groups and/or educational classes such as those offered by agencies or groups of experienced adoptive parents may be helpful. Common topics include the effects of physical, emotional, and sexual abuse and how to anticipate and deal with the resulting behaviors; the use of psychological therapists; attachment disorder and what do about it; parental expectations; the importance of genetic influence; and how parents can take care of themselves.

Groups of parents may support each other in informal ways. An example is the friendship of the Trenton family with the Stanley family. By most standards the Trentons are a large adoptive family; they have five children with special needs and would like to add two more. Their friend Miriam Stanley is a single nurse who had planned on adopting an infant with Down syndrome. Instead, the agency offered Miriam eight-year-old Francesca, a child with developmental delays from abuse she had suffered in her birth family. When the two families began attending monthly support group meetings at their agency, they discovered they lived only a mile from each other. They now carpool to meetings and have an occasional family picnic together. The Trentons have a ten-year-old daughter named Melissa who has a hard time getting along with peers, but she and Francesca have become friends. All nine members of this informal support group have helped families new to the adoption process, and the three parents have spoken at the agency training sessions about their adoption experiences.

Assisted Reproductive Technologies

Before 1978, when the first "test-tube baby" was born by in vitro fertilization, couples with fertility problems had two choices: remain childless, or adopt. Today's infertile couples face a confusing array of choices—too many choices, some say. These "solutions" may cause other problems—moral questions and ethical dilemmas, as well as related adoption issues.

In the most common option, in vitro fertilization (IVF), ova and sperm from the couple, who may have a problem such as blockage in the woman's fallopian tubes, meet in a laboratory dish. When fertilization occurs, the embryos are placed in the woman's uterus. An advancement in the treatment of male infertility is intracytoplasmic sperm injection. This procedure aims to place one sperm in the right place in the egg for optimal growth of the embryo, which is then placed in the woman's uterus.

Another variation is gamete intrafallopian transfer (GIFT), in which the woman's eggs are combined with the husband's sperm, then surgically injected into the fallopian tubes. If fertilization occurs, it will happen inside the woman's body.

ZIFT stands for zygote intrafallopian transfer. In this procedure the eggs and sperm are mixed in the laboratory, and after fertilization occurs, the doctor places the embryo in the fallopian tubes.

In many cases, one (or both) of the prospective parents will not be the child's biological parent. If the husband is infertile, sperm donation (referred to as artificial insemination through a donor, or AID), may solve the problem. A single woman or a woman in a lesbian relationship may choose this option. Most commonly, the sperm donor is not known to the parents. Similarly, if the wife is infertile because she no longer produces viable eggs, a female donor may provide the eggs. If the procedure is successful, the wife becomes the baby's birth mother but is not the biological mother.

Another procedure offers embryos for "adoption." Premade frozen embryos result from a mixture of donated eggs and sperm.

When a woman is unable to produce a child or to carry a baby to term, the couple may pursue surrogacy, in which another woman is selected to receive the husband's sperm (or the mother's fertilized egg), carry the baby, and then at birth, allow the infertile couple to adopt the baby. This process may cause problems, as in the famous 1986–1987 "Baby M" case, in which the surrogate mother, Mary Beth Whitehead, decided she wanted to keep the child she had given birth to. After a long court battle, Mary Beth Whitehead lost her parental rights. A year later, however, the court granted her visitation rights.

Samantha's single mother worried about how to tell five-year-old Samantha that she had been conceived by donor insemination. The longer she waited, the harder the task seemed, so Samantha's mother said nothing. "Where's your daddy?" asked Sam's friend one day when she visited. (There were no pictures of Sam's daddy on the mantle.) "I never had a daddy," said Samantha. "Yes, you did," said her friend. "Everyone has a daddy." Tears rolled down Sam's cheeks. "No, I don't." Samantha's mother might have gotten some help with the task of explaining the scientific facts about conception to her daughter. Instead, her silence caused Samantha much emotional pain. One helpful book is *Choosing Assisted Reproduction: Social, Emotional, and Ethical Considerations,* by Susan Lewis Cooper and Ellen Sarasohn Glazer (1998).

Positive Adoption Language

In 1972, Marietta Spencer of the Children's Home Society of Minnesota brought up the importance of using positive and constructive expressions when discussing adoption. Over the years, various types of "politically correct" terminology have come and gone. The bottom line remains the same: positive adoption language shows respect for the joining of persons in a family by a legal process. Indifference to language can be irritating at best and demeaning at worst. For example, the absence of respect for the adoption process could cause birth parents to avoid making an adoption plan for their child when adoption might be in the best interests of the child and the parents.

This book takes its cues from adoption professionals currently at work in adoption. While it is not possible to cover every error here, it is possible to highlight some outstanding stereotyped responses and misusages (i.e., negative, thoughtless, or unconstructive adoption language).

The word *adoptee* may seem harmless, similar to the word *divorcee* used to describe a divorced person. However, the phrase *adopted person* is preferable because adoption does not define a person's entire being.

In the past, people might have said that a birth mother "gave up" her child for adoption, or she "gave away" her child. Preferred language includes the terms *making a plan* for a child and *choosing* or *deciding on* adoption, suggesting that the well-being of the child is of the utmost importance. Similarly, the terms *adopted out* or *put up for adoption* take us back to the Orphan Train Era, a time in which children were "put up" on the platform at the train station to be chosen by adoptive families. The terms *natural parents* and *real parents* are objectionable because *all* parents are "natural" and "real." The terms *birth parents, first parents,* or *genetic parents* are preferable.

Finally, it is important to remember that those introducing or discussing an adopted person need not mention "adoption" any more than they would say, "This is Mrs. Miller's *birth child.*"

Adopt-A-What?

Adopt-A-Pet, Adopt-A-Tree, Adopt-A-Whale, Adopt-A-Highway, Adopt-A-Park, Adopt-A-Bus Stop—the list goes on. As noble as these causes seem, the image they project may be confusing to adopted children. For example, if a person adopts a pet and discovers after a week or so that the animal bites, it can be returned for another. *Will the same thing happen to me?* Also, in the aforementioned programs, the "adopted" object is not taken home and cared for; in most cases it exists for the person who adopted it only on a piece of paper. Adoption activists argue that Adopt-A-Whatever media campaigns trivialize the serious and life-changing nature of the adoption of a child.

Adoption Month

Every year adoption organizations invite those with adoption connections to celebrate November as Adoption Month. During this time, posters feature waiting children from the United States with some of these children participating in national media events. The goals of Adoption Month are to increase the public's awareness of adoption, to increase positive media coverage of adoption, and to find more permanent homes for waiting children.

Adult Adoption

Adoption of a person over the age of eighteen is not common but is possible in some states. The prospective adoptive parents and the adult person must both consent. One of the more common reasons for such an adoption is that a person has reached the age of eighteen without being eligible for adoption. That person may now want his foster parents to adopt him. Another reason is to establish legal inheritance rights. Those interested should find out the adoption laws in their state.

Summary

Adoption is a many-faceted entity. Whatever happens in an adoption affects three groups—the birth parents, the adoptive parents, and the children. All of these parties have something to gain, but they share the issue of loss. Loss requires grieving, and grieving takes time—in some cases, a lifetime.

In order to understand adoption, sorting it into various categories may help, but in reality categories overlap, and confusion sometimes results. No matter how we approach it, adoption is a sensitive topic touching the hearts and souls of all those involved.

References and Further Reading

Ashe, Nancy. "Interstate Adoption: ICPC and ICAMA." Accessed at http://www.adopting.org/adoptions/interstate-adoption.html.

Ashe, Nancy. 2005. "Politically Correct Adoption Language, Part 3: Talk the Talk." Accessed at http://www.adopting.org/adoptions/politically-correct-adoption-language–2,3.html.

Benet, Mary Katherine. 1976. *The Politics of Adoption.* New York: Free Press.

Brodzinsky, David, M., and Marshall D. Schechter, eds. 1990. *The Psychology of Adoption.* New York: Oxford University Press.

Child Welfare Information Gateway. 2004. "Adoption Assistance for Children Adopted from Foster Care: A Factsheet for Families." Accessed at http://www.childwelfare.gov/pubs/f_subsid.cfm.

Child Welfare Information Gateway. 2004. "Impact of Adoption on Adopted Persons: A Factsheet for Families." Accessed at http://www.childwelfare.gov/pubs/f_issues.cfm.

Child Welfare Information Gateway. 2005. State Statutes Series. "Standby Guardianship." Accessed at http://www.childwelfare.gov/systemwide/laws_policies/statutes/guardianshipall.pdf.

Child Welfare Information Gateway and U.S. Department of Health and Human Services. 2005. "Post-Legal Services for Children with Special Needs and Their Families." Accessed at http://www.childwelfare.gov/pubs/h_postlegal/index.cfm.

Committee on Government Reform, Subcommittee on Criminal Justice, Drug Policy, and Human Resources. July 26, 2005. "Fighting Meth in America's Heartland: Assessing the Impact on Local Law Enforcement and Child Welfare Agencies." Accessed at http://reform.house.gov/CJDPHR/Hearings/EventSingle.aspx?EventID=31114.

Cooper, Susan Lewis, and Ellen Sarasohn Glazer. *Choosing Assisted Reproduction: Social, Emotional, and Ethical Considerations.* 1998. Indianapolis: Perspectives Press.

Evan P. Donaldson Adoption Institute. 2005. "International Adoption Facts." Accessed at http://www.adoptioninstitute.org/FactOverview/international.html.

Eyer, Diane E. 1992. *Mother-Infant Bonding: A Scientific Fiction.* New Haven, CT: Yale University Press.

Freundlich, M., and L. Wright. 2003. "Post-permanency Services." Seattle: Casey Family Programs. Accessed at http://www.childwelfare.gov/pubs/h_postlegal/index.cfm.

Frievalds, Susan. 2001. "A New International Treaty on Adoption." *Adoptive Families* (January/February): 29–30.

Johnston, Patricia I. 1995. *Adopting after Infertility.* Indianapolis: Perspectives Press.

Keck, Gregory C., and Regina Kupecky. 1995. *Adopting the Hurt Child: Hope for Families with Special Needs Kids.* Colorado Springs, CO: Pinon Press.

Lindsay, Jean Warren. 1987. *Open Adoption: A Caring Option.* Buena Park, CA: Morning Glory Press.

Melina, Lois R., and Sharon Kaplan Roszia. 1993. *The Open Adoption Experience.* New York: HarperCollins.

National Center on Birth Defects and Developmental Disabilities, Centers for Disease Control and Prevention. 2005. "Fetal Alcohol Information." Accessed at http://www.cdc.gov/ncbddd/fas/fasask.htm.

"News and Notes." 2005. *Adoptive Families* (September/October): 12–13.

Powell, Dwight A. 2005. "The Challenges of Making Health Assessments on Foreign Children." *Pediatric Directions* 28, Columbus (OH) Children's Hospital: 2–5.

Salbenblatt, Carol. 2005. Children's Hospital, Denver, CO. Discussion with the author, November 23.

Silverstein, Deborah N., and Sharon Kaplan Rozsia. 1982. "Lifelong Issues in Adoption." Accessed at http://library.adoption.com/parenting-and-families/lifelong-issues-in-adoption/article256.

Sorosky, Arthur D., Annette Barron, and Reuben Pannor. 1978. *The Adoption Triangle: The Effects of the Sealed Record on Adoptees, Birth Parents, and Adoptive Parents.* Garden City, NY: Anchor Press/Doubleday.

Streissguth, Ann. 1997. *Fetal Alcohol Syndrome: A Guide for Families and Communities.* Baltimore: Paul H. Brookes Publishing.

Substance Abuse and Mental Health Services Association, U.S. Department of Health and Human Services. Fetal Alcohol Spectrum Disorders Center for Excellence. 2005. Accessed at http://fasdcenter.samhsa.gov.

U.S. Department of Justice. September 2000, revised. "The Immigration of Adopted and Perspective Adoptive Children." Glossary/Definitions, 35. Available at http://uscis.gov/graphics/lawsregs/handbook/adopt_book.pdf.

2

Issues and Controversies

That there are two sides (or more) to every question is no less true in adoption. Many of the controversies of the past are still providing material for debate. This chapter will examine some of these controversies, including the following:

—Open or closed adoption? Which is best?

—What about open adoption *records?* Should records be open or closed?

—Do transcultural and/or transracial adoptions "work"?

—Should single people be allowed to adopt?

—What about adoptions by same-sex couples?

—Should the government provide more or less regulation of adoption?

—What about infant abandonment laws? Are they "safe havens" or "baby dumps"?

—What about adoption itself? Is it valuable?

Open versus Closed Adoption

Those who like an argument along with a state of confusion will enjoy the debate over closed versus open adoption. There is little agreement (even among professionals) as to the meaning of these terms. Although we can try to define the terms, in reality, each adoption is unique and "open" or "closed" along a continuum.

Closed Adoption

In most closed or confidential adoptions, there is no sharing of identifying information. In most open adoptions, children may have ongoing contact (e.g., letters, e-mails, telephone calls, or visits) with their birth family. The parties involved decide how often they want to have contact. Within these two categories, many variations of openness exist. Adoption professionals often call the middle ground "semi-open" or "mediated" adoption. In this type of adoption, a mediator, such as an attorney or agency caseworker, relays information from one party to another.

Closed adoption, also called "confidential," "traditional," "classic," or "anonymous" adoption, became the norm in the early part of the twentieth century because of increased regulation of adoption that sought to protect single birth mothers from the scorn of society. As E. Wayne Carp points out in *Family Matters: Secrecy and Disclosure in the History of Adoption* (1998), birth mothers originally demanded secrecy. At the same time, married women who couldn't biologically produce offspring because of infertility were also stigmatized.

In the twenty-first century, those who favor confidential adoption argue that birth parents can have *some* choices, which may include choosing the race or religion of the prospective adoptive parents. Sometimes birth mothers in a closed adoption can actually meet the prospective parents and have an exchange of first names.

The proponents of closed or confidential adoption argue that in some cases, birth parents may choose *not* to make an "adoption plan" for their child unless they are promised confidentiality. Another argument for confidentiality is that openness may be disruptive to all members of the triad (or adoption circle) because it impedes the ability of the birth parents to "move on" with their lives. Also, ongoing contact may be disruptive to the daily routines of the entire adoptive family. "Bonding" between the child and the adoptive parents may be impaired; the child may feel "caught in the middle" between two sets of parents.

Adults who were adopted as infants in a closed adoption often feel the urge to search for their birth parents. They want to "see someone who looks like me," or they have a desire for genetic information. One young adult woman of Mexican heritage adopted by a Caucasian family often dreamed about a search but eventually commented, "It would be like finding a needle in a haystack." Still, she wondered if her health plan would allow her to have an early mammogram because "I have no medical history."

Most adopted persons would like to know their history, especially their medical history. And, according to the American Academy of Pediatrics, there is ample evidence to suggest that this need to seek one's ancestry is an important one.

The search may affect all members of the adoption triad; confidential adoption proponents sometimes give the following arguments for their point of view. For example, the searcher may worry about rejection by the birth parent or about rejection by his or her adoptive parents, who may feel threatened by a search. The adoptive parents may feel that they have done something wrong in their child rearing. Otherwise, why would their child need to search? (However, most experts agree that if the child is willing to discuss a search with the parents who raised him, the parents have probably done something *right*.) The birth parent who is "found" will also probably deal with strong, mixed emotions. Nevertheless, say most experts, the results of a search (even if the adopted person experiences rejection) will likely have many positive aspects. One of these aspects is that the searcher usually experiences satisfaction, a sense of accomplishment, and a feeling of completeness.

Until recently, there was little documented evidence about the results of searches. But results from a five-year study in Great Britain showed that such reunions had generally positive outcomes: 80 percent of adoptive parents were pleased about the search, 97 percent of those adopted said that the reunion did not change their feelings for their adoptive families, and 66 percent of birth families and adoptive families became friends.

The Child Welfare Information Gateway (CWIG) offers many resources for those interested in a search. "Searching for Birth Relatives" is a factsheet that also provides a state-by-state listing of local and national adult search and support groups in the United States. CWIG provides referrals to adoption experts (psychotherapists and other counselors) who specialize in working with those touched by adoption. In addition, it has an online library of more than 48,000 documents at www.childwelfare.gov/library. More than 130 informational publications are also available at www.childwelfare.gov/search/pubs_search.cfm. For further information on the Child Welfare Information Gateway, see the complete listing under Resources in Chapter 8.

Open Adoption

Those in favor of open adoption also have many reasons for their strongly held views. Brenda Romanchik, a proponent of open adoption and a triad member herself, emphasizes that a truly open adoption is one in which the adopted child is free to develop an ongoing, one-on-one relationship with his or her birth family.

Beginning in the 1970s and 1980s, societal changes made open adoption more popular. In the 1990s and onward, the open adoption concept began to gain momentum. Reasons include the increased empowerment of women (who usually bear the "brunt" of an unintended pregnancy because they are carrying the child), greater acceptance of single parenthood, more openness about the subject of adoption in general, and more valuing of diversity, including acceptance of different types of families.

Romanchik argues that although adoption professionals may advise prospective adoptive parents to do "what they are comfortable with," the level of contact should not be about the adults' comfort level but about what is best for the child. Some of the goals of open adoption are to minimize loss for the adopted child, to help children resolve the losses they feel with reality instead of fantasy, and to maintain and celebrate the child's connections.

On July 19, 1997, Metropolitan Adoption Services placed a three-month-old girl, Jessie, in the home of Bob and Linda Maitland. Linda's fourteen-year-old son by a previous marriage was very involved in the adoption process. The birth parents chose the Maitland family for Jessie when they decided they could not raise her. Both birth parents, who are young and unmarried, have visited Jessie at the Maitland home. So have the baby's birth grandparents on both sides and even one great-grandmother. The Maitlands were willing to have these visits because they believe the contact will be good for Jessie, and because they want the birth parents to feel as if they've had some "say" in Jessie's life plan.

Open adoption requires not only the respect of all parties for each other but also clear communication. After some time, the two families became such good friends that the grandparents began to drop in often and unannounced, interrupting the adoptive family's life. When Linda requested that visits be scheduled at least three days in advance, the drop-in visits stopped.

Those who favor open adoption maintain that it benefits all members of the triad (adoption circle). First, the child benefits. An open adoption takes away much of the mystery, secrecy, and taboos connected with a closed adoption. A child will have less need for fantasies and, as an adult, will have no need to search. In addition, adopted persons have the right to know their health history, which should be available in an open adoption. In addition to medical knowledge, children need knowledge of their origins to help with identity formation. Further, children need to know that they weren't "rejected," but that their birth families care about their welfare.

Second, proponents of open adoption say an open adoption benefits the birth family. (Birth fathers are less likely than birth mothers to be involved in ongoing contact, but this is not always the case. There may also be interested grandparents, uncles, aunts, or cousins.) Knowing where their children are and being able to relate to them on an ongoing basis helps birth parents "move on" with their lives. In fact, say proponents of open adoption, unless birth parents have an opportunity for an open adoption, many will choose *not* to make an adoption plan for their child.

Finally, there are many reasons why adoptive parents benefit from an open adoption. First, this is *their* child. (Research has shown that birth parents do not pose a threat to a child's *legal* adoption. If the court has issued a decree of adoption, the birth parents no longer have legal rights to the child.) Whatever benefits the child also benefits the legal parents of that child. Adoptive parents tend to feel more entitled when they receive "permission" from birth parents to be the child's "real" parents. Family relationships in general are more healthy when they exist in a climate of openness rather than in one of secrecy. (For example, the adoptive parents do not have to fear an accidental meeting with the birth parents at a restaurant or at the mall.)

Mimi is friends with a young couple who is in an open adoption process through Lutheran Family Services. They are adopting a six-month-old girl. Mimi reports that the process is going well even though the adoptive mother says she is sometimes tired from being the arranger of visits, or, as she called herself, "social chairwoman."

In their book *The Open Adoption Experience* (1992), Lois Melina and Sharon Roszia discuss a problem common to both birth parents and adoptive parents: the feeling of loss of control. Birth parents' feelings of loss of control may come from an unplanned pregnancy and the need to make a decision that will affect them and their child forever. In addition, the birth parents may feel that the adoptive family is offering an open adoption as a "carrot" and will change their minds about contact later.

The adoptive parents may feel a loss of control because of their inability to produce a birth child no matter how hard they try, that they are being scrutinized by an agency and by birth parents, that they may never be "chosen" by birth parents, and that if chosen, they will have to proceed or perhaps never be chosen again. They may prefer a closed adoption but feel that they "must" choose openness.

However, a feeling of loss of control (although in a different way) is also common in a confidential adoption. In a closed adoption, birth parents must give up control to the agency and/or to the adoptive parents. Adoptive parents may also feel a loss of control because of an inability to connect with the child's history and lack of knowledge about the child's origins.

Bruce Rappaport, PhD, executive director of the Independent Adoption Center in Pleasant Hill, California, takes the concept of open adoption to a new level. Writing in the September/October 2005 issue of *Adoptive Families*, Rappaport says he believes the term "open adoption" is outmoded. Twenty years ago, a distinction between two controversial types of adoption ("closed" and "open") made sense. But now, Rappaport thinks there are few truly closed adoptions in the United States, and that the trend toward openness has even spread to international adoptions. He proposes that members of the adoption community no longer need to say "open adoption" but simply "adoption."

Cooperative Adoption

Cooperative adoption (sometimes called "adoption with contact") is a relatively new concept that involves postadoption contact between adoptive families and certain members of the child's birth family. Adoption of older children from the foster care system is different from infant adoption and may be confidential in some ways, but older children are likely to know their last names and may remember much about their birth parents. In some cases, keeping healthy connections (after finalization) with birth relatives may be beneficial to the children, to the birth parents, and to the adoptive parents. For example, adoptive parents may find that birth family members have valuable medical information about the child. Arrangements can be informal or formal (as in written contracts). The parties usually figure out what will work and sign the contract before finalization.

Cooperative adoptions work well in many cases. In other cases, problems may arise. If the agreement is not formalized with a contract, adoptive parents could change their minds about contact after finalization. More and more often today, adoption professionals are looking to state legislatures to provide enforcement for cooperative adoption arrangements.

In 1999 the Children's Bureau of the U.S. Department of Health and Human Services convened a group of experts who recommended certain key provisions in cooperative adoptions that include the following:

—The birth parent cannot "set aside" a voluntary relinquishment.

—The court will approve the agreement only if all parties, including children twelve and older, agree. The court must also agree that the arrangement is in the child's best interests. (A relationship with a birth parent may not be in a child's best interest in cases where there has been violence directed at the child and/or when birth parents cannot maintain appropriate boundaries with a child because of emotional or mental illness.)

—Parties to the agreement may petition the court for changes to the agreement or to terminate the agreement.

Fewer than half of the states currently have legislation allowing written and enforceable cooperative adoptions. Some states allow contact only with birth parents; other states may include grandparents, aunts, uncles, and siblings in the agreement. Information on the states that have this legislation, as well as information on laws related to cooperative adoption and access to adoption records and mutual consent registries, is available through the Child Welfare Information Gateway website: http://childwelfare.gov/systemwide/laws_policies/statutes/infoaccessapall.pdf.

An easy-sounding solution to the debate over closed vs. open adoption would be to hope that all of the adults (although not all birth mothers are legally adults) involved in an adoption would be able to find an agency that works well for them and with them. After all, the child has no choice.

In his book *The Realities of Adoption* (1997), Jerome Smith reports on the results of his interviews with five adoption authorities, several of whom had worked in the field of adoption when closed adoptions were the norm. Most took a cautious but hopeful approach to open adoption while at the same time saying there is no "one size fits all" in adoption. The goal is to find the approach that works best for the child.

Neither closed adoption nor open adoption is without difficulties, but in spite of some difficult issues that must be worked out between the parties, open adoption seems to be in the ascendancy; societal changes have forced the issue.

Open versus Closed Records

The debate over closed versus open adoption *records* is different from the previous controversy over closed versus open *adoption*. The issues, however, are related, and some overlapping occurs. For example, the same reasons that made open adoption more popular beginning in the 1970s also increased the pressure for open records.

"A Short Personal History of Adoption Reform," by Mary Anne Cohen (August 2000), begins with a look at Jean Paton and her organization, Orphan Voyage. Beginning in the 1960s, Paton, an adopted person and a social worker who had gotten access to her own birth records, fought for open records for all adopted adults. Florence Fisher, an adopted person from New York City, founded the Adoptees' Liberty Movement Association (ALMA) in 1971 and wrote *The Search for Anna Fisher* (1986) about her own search for her birth mother. In addition, the 1970s saw the publication of *The Adoption Triangle: The Effects of the Sealed Record on*

Adoptees, Birth Parents, and Adoptive Parents (1978), written by Arthur Sorosky, Annette Baran, and Reuben Pannor, who argued that adoption laws should be changed to allow adult adopted persons access to their own birth records. Also in his book *Shared Fate* (1984), adoptive parent David Kirk supported the adopted person's right to know his or her heritage.

More individuals and organizations followed with similar (though sometimes also differing) agendas. Members of the Concerned United Birthparents (CUB, organized in 1976) testified at early hearings for open records legislation. The American Adoption Congress (AAC), begun in 1978, promised to be an umbrella organization for adoption reform.

Bastard Nation, born on the Internet in 1996, has as its goal to restore the right of adults adopted as children to access their birth records. When asked if open *records* is the same as open adoption, Bastard Nation says "no." In an open adoption the birth parents, adoptive parents, and the minor child have an ongoing relationship. But even in an open adoption, the adult adopted person cannot necessarily access his or her birth and adoption records. Access to open records means the adopted person should be able to get his own legal documents, including the original birth certificate and the adoption decree, and ultimately, the right to contact birth parents if he chooses.

At the other end of the spectrum is the National Council for Adoption (NCFA), based in Washington, DC. The stance of NCFA, founded in 1980, is that states should have to use "extraordinary" measures before records are opened to an adopted person. In 2005 the organization, which believes strongly in closed records, laid out (on its website) why it was upset with the governor and legislators of the state of New Hampshire. NCFA's president and CEO, Thomas Atwood, scolded the state, which allowed an open records law to become a reality. "The failure of New Hampshire's legislature and governor to keep the promises made to birthparents and to preserve and protect adoption is an egregious violation of trust and common decency," he wrote. He went on to state that the policy of open records would "deny women and teens with crisis pregnancies the perfectly valid option of confidential adoption."

The Massachusetts Adoption Act of 1851 initiated the first adoption court records in the United States. A small start in the regulation of adoption, the law required that judges investigate the suitability of adoptive parents (the first "home studies"), and that adoption should serve the best interests of the child. Closed adoption records began with the Minnesota Act of 1917, the first state statute to seal adoption records. Many states followed with similar acts, and by the 1920s sealed adoption records were the standard because of the dictates of society—out-of-wedlock births were supposed to be hidden. Today, advocates of confidentiality argue that the opening of birth records violates a promise made to birth parents and also to adoptive parents. Birth parents may not have told others, such as the children they are parenting, that they placed an earlier child for adoption. Adoptive parents may fear that the birth parents will "find" them and interfere with their parenting.

Thinking for the adopted person, proponents of sealed adoption records say that in the case of a "search and reunion," the adoptee may experience a devastating rejection. Also, many adopted persons do *not* search and apparently feel satisfied with any nonidentifying information they have received from the agency or from their adoptive parents. (Nonidentifying information is anything that would not help the adopted person in finding the birth parents, such as date and time of birth. Identifying information, such as a last name, is information that might enable the adopted person to find his or her birth parents.)

Those in favor of strict confidentiality add that if the adopted person desperately needs medical history in a life-threatening situation, he can petition the court to open the records. In "Whose Rights Rule in Adoption?" Marianne Means (2000) writes that "illegitimacy may no longer be the devastating scandal it used to be, but the decision to make it public should be the mother's alone." She argues that "opening old records meant to be closed creates trouble and turmoil." She describes the conflict as "explosive on many levels."

Those who favor closed records in adoption offer mutual consent registries (sometimes called "passive registries" or "mutual consent voluntary registries") as an alternative to openness. Jean Paton's book *The Adopted Break Silence* was published in 1954, just a few years after she began operating the first voluntary registry from her home. ALMA had an early nongovernmental registry, and in 1975 Emma Mae Villardi started the International Soundex Reunion Registry in Carson City, Nevada. CUB also established a mutual consent registry. Soon afterwards, some states began their own registries. In 1981 Senator Carl Levin of Michigan introduced the idea of a voluntary national computerized clearinghouse in the Adoption Identification Act. But the proposed federal registry did not become law because of opposition from some members of the public and groups such as the National Council for Adoption.

Registries provide another topic for disagreement. Although the earlier registries helped many adoptees and their birth parents find each other, the state registries that came later had problems. Mutual consent registries (in the states that have them) offer central repositories where adopted persons, birth parents, and sometimes birth siblings who have had involvement in an adoption can indicate their willingness to disclose identifying information. The registries are based on the concept that if birth parents and adopted persons want to meet, both parties may have the opportunity to do so by signing up with a state agency. Currently about half the states have some form of mutual consent registry. Interested persons must register in the state in which the adopted person was born or adopted. Some states employ "confidential intermediaries," who act as objective third parties between the adoptee and the birth parent. One problem with registries is that some states will not release the requested information if the other party has died.

State legislatures began offering mutual consent registries to adoptees eager to access their identifying information in the late 1970s. The American Adoption Congress (AAC) surveyed twenty-one of these registries in 1993, 1996, and 1998. Based on these contacts, the AAC reached the conclusion that the state registries (in general) are understaffed, underfunded, and underpublicized. Budget restrictions are one of the causes.

Proponents of open records give many reasons for wanting access to their records. Kate Burke, a former president of the American Adoption Congress, summarized some of these reasons in 2004. First, adoptees have a civil and human right to see their own vital statistics and court records, just as every other citizen has that right. They are not asking that adoption records be open to the general public.

Second, opponents of open records argue that opening adoption records breaches a contract made years earlier with the birth parent or parents. Proponents of open records agree that "civil codes" may have implied confidentiality at the time. But times have changed, and confidentiality is not necessarily considered desirable in the present day. Even if a birth parent wants confidentiality at the time of placement, the adopted person should have the right to see records at a later date.

Third, even if only 2 percent of adopted persons search annually, it is a different 2 percent each year. Besides, say proponents of open records, why should the minority (those who search) be denied their rights just because they are in the minority?

Fourth, what if birth parents do not want their adopted children to find them? Those in favor of open records say that gaining access to vital records and court files is not the same as searching for a birth parent. Although it is possible that gaining access to records may lead to a search, a birth parent, if found, has the right to say "no." (A note in the May/June 2003 issue of *Adoptive Families* says that nearly 15,000 adult adoptees asked for their original birth records in the four states that had opened those records in the preceding four years.) In addition, the *Washington Times* reported that more than 80 percent of birth parents in Alabama, Delaware, Oregon, and Tennessee said it would be okay for an adoptee to contact them.

Fifth, proponents of closed records say that open records laws will encourage abortion. Burke points out an important difference: abortion is a decision not to *have* a child; adoption is a decision not to *parent* a child. Informal studies have shown that one reason a birth parent may choose abortion is because of "secret" adoption practices.

Finally, proponents of closed records argue that the "threat" of open records will keep birth parents from considering adoption. This does not seem to be the case, however, as open adoption and open records have gained in popularity in the past twenty-five years.

Because of increased interest in open records, in 1980 the U.S. Congress considered the Model State Adoption Act and Model State Adoption Procedures. At the time, Congress was trying to fulfill a mandate from Public Law 95–266, the Child Abuse Prevention and Treatment and Adoption Opportunities Act of 1978. The latter was the first statute to lay out a role for the federal government in adoption of children in foster care.

As proposed, the Model State Adoption Act would have opened adoption records to all members of the adoption triad. However, public comment, along with opposition from the Child Welfare League of America, caused changes in the act. By 1981 the renamed Model Act for Adoption of Children with Special Needs became an entity that recommended changes for adoption of children with special needs without the force of law and without the open records provisions.

In 1994, in spite of opposition from groups such as the Child Welfare League of America, Concerned United Birthparents, and the American Adoption Congress, the National Conference of Commissioners on Uniform Laws decided that adoption records should be sealed for ninety-nine years.

As E. Wayne Carp points out (1998), trends come and go. No one can predict the future. Some birth parents and some adoptive parents will undoubtedly work out agreements for openness, and this group may join with adults who are products of donor insemination in demanding open records.

On the other hand, even some birth parents and some adoptive parents prefer secrecy. Perhaps, Carp writes, in the future, adoption may again become illegal, birth mothers may again feel stigmatized, and more infants may be available for adoption. In such a new world, the trend may shift again. Will more members of the adoption triad want secrecy in adoption records, or will more adopted persons demand the right to see their vital statistics and court reports? Only time will tell.

Do Transcultural and/or Transracial Adoptions Work?

Transracial (sometimes called interracial, transcultural, or transethnic) adoption is the joining together of racially or ethnically different parents and children in an adoptive family. These terms may apply to adoptions within the United States, such as when a Caucasian family adopts an African American child, or to an international adoption, such as when Caucasian parents adopt Asian children or children from Latin America. Technically, the term could refer to African American parents adopting a Caucasian child, but this situation is uncommon.

Transracial adoptions were not common until after World War II, when they began in significant numbers. Between 1946 and 1953, Americans adopted close to 6,000 children from Greece, Germany, and Japan, countries that had suffered from war. As a result of the Korean War, Harry Holt and his wife began a program now called Holt International Children's Services. Between 1953 and 1981, approximately 38,000 Korean children were adopted, primarily by Caucasian citizens of the United States. Another spurt of transracial adoptions came with the Vietnam War. And before Native American opposition put brakes on the practice, Caucasian families adopted Native American children. More recently, in addition to adopting transracially from many other countries, families in the United States have adopted children in significant numbers from Central America. The number of adoptions from Guatemala, for example, has grown from 1,609 in 2001 to 3,783 in 2005 (U.S. Department of State). Federal government data shows that the overall rate of transracial adoption from the foster-care system rose from 10.8 percent in 1995 to 15 percent in 2001 (News and Notes, 2006).

In the liberal climate of the 1960s and 1970s, "racial matching" gave way to more transracial placements, such as the placement of black infants in white homes. Before the 1960s, some states prohibited transracial adoption. But eventually child welfare workers began to see a need for more parents to give permanent homes to children who were trapped in permanent foster care. The number of black-white placements continued to rise throughout the 1960s, and peaked in 1971 with more than 2,500 such placements (Silverman and Fiegelman, 188).

Meanwhile, black social workers had begun to rise up against this trend. In 1968, they founded the National Association of Black Social Workers (NABSW) and protested what they considered racist social welfare policies. For example, they criticized traditional screening practices, which emphasized marriage stability, financial security, and youthfulness, as discriminating against black parents. Further, the NABSW pointed out that more often than not, Caucasian families were not adopting older black children from foster care but were seeking the same black infants for whom there were already enough black families. At its third annual conference in 1972, the group came out strongly against transracial placements: black children, its members stated, belonged in black families. In the next year, transracial placements dropped by half, and by 1975 the number had shrunk to around 800.

Approximately 60 percent of the children in foster (or out-of-home) care in the United States are racial and ethnic minorities. African American children make up 46 percent of this group (but African Americans make up only 15 percent of the U.S. population).

Because the U.S. government stopped collecting adoption

data (such as total number of children adopted) in 1975, the quoted numbers of transracial/transcultural adoptions are educated guesses. One source estimates that Caucasian families adopt 1,000–2,000 African American children each year. Taking into account data from the U.S. Citizenship and Immigration Services regarding intercountry adoptions, the Child Welfare Information Gateway estimates that about 14 percent of all adoptions are transracial or transcultural.

Experts expect the number of transracial/transcultural adoptions to continue to rise. According to some estimates, approximately 60 percent of children adopted internationally are nonwhite. Laws and financial incentives initiated in the mid-1990s are encouraging people to adopt from the U.S. foster-care system, and intercountry transracial adoptions continue.

Authorities on the subject tend to lump all transracial/transcultural adoptions into a single category. But if a single white woman adopts a black six-year-old boy from the foster-care system, the issues they face are likely to be different from those of a Caucasian couple who adopt a two-year-old girl from Korea.

Two laws that deal with the subject of transracial/transcultural adoption in the United States seem to reach different conclusions about what is best in the transracial/transcultural debate. The first, which became law in 1978, is the Indian Child Welfare Act (ICWA), the first major national act legislating adoption in the United States. The law was designed to prevent nontribal public and private agencies from removing Native American children from their birth tribes. Government and private institutions had developed "boarding schools" for Native American children. As late as 1974, approximately 34,000 native children still attended these schools away from their homes.

Native Americans also lost children through adoption and foster care. During the 1950s and 1960s, welfare agencies placed hundreds of Native American children with Caucasian families. The Association on American Indian Affairs undertook a study in 1976 that showed 25 to 35 percent of Native American children were not living in their own homes. Of that figure, 85 percent of those children lived in non–Native American homes. Those who proposed the act had concerns about the survival of Native American tribes.

The Indian Child Welfare Act is complicated. It requires adoption agencies to make a concerted effort to find Native American families for Native American children. Under provisions of the act, anyone involved in the placement of a Native American child must first notify the Bureau of Indian Affairs or the child's tribe, so that the tribe can make custody arrangements. Tribal courts have jurisdiction over children living on reservations and some rights over Native American children living off reservations. If a Native American birth mother wants to place her infant for adoption, she must first go through the process and receive the tribe's permission. Placement preference is given first to members of the child's tribe and last to persons of another culture.

Federal and state laws together govern a child of Native American heritage. According to the Indian Child Welfare Act, termination of parental rights may be held before a tribal court. If a state court hears the case, the child's tribe has the right to intervene and object to the placement preferences of the child's birth parents or those of an adoption agency. A birth parent who initially agrees to the placement of a Native American child has a chance to withdraw consent until a decree of adoption is entered in court. If the consent to adoption was obtained by fraud or under duress, the birth parent has at least two years to get the adoption nullified. Prospective adoptive parents who have had a Native American child in their home for months, or in some cases for years, may have their adoption petitions denied. The Indian Child Welfare Act trumps all other laws.

Donald Standing Bear (not his real name) and his wife, Betsy, had no children; they came to a private nonprofit agency in their home state of Colorado, hoping to adopt young children. Although he was not registered with a tribe, Donald had Native American heritage through his father and participated in celebrations and rituals within his community. Betsy was not Native American but participated in tribal activities with Donald. They had many Native American friends.

Through a photo listing on the Internet, the couple found in North Dakota two Native American boys, ages two and four, that they hoped to adopt. The social services department that had custody of the boys visited the Standing Bears in Denver. After months of back-and-forth visits, two social workers brought the boys to stay in their new home in Colorado. A letter from a tribal judge in North Dakota had given permission for the boys to be moved. Agencies of both states followed proper procedures for an interstate placement.

The Colorado agency carefully supervised the boys' placement, doing regular home visits during which its caseworkers got to know the children in order to support the new parents and give them parenting tips. The agency also provided contact with other adoptive parents, as well as a support group. The boys, who had been somewhat developmentally delayed at placement, made much progress, especially in signs of attachment and in speech development. Donald, who worked from home, was the primary caregiver.

Approximately five months into the placement, the two social workers from North Dakota who had brought the boys to Colorado came (on short notice) to pick them up. A distant relative had intervened and, backed by the Indian Child Welfare Act, had gotten permission to take the boys to live on the reservation. Devastated by the loss of the boys, Donald and Betsy never again attempted to adopt.

Some ICWA supporters say the act does not go far enough in addressing the wrongs of the past. Those who have had problems with it, they say, are mostly doing independent adoptions or working with people who do not understand the law. Opponents say the act impinges on the rights of birth mothers (for one thing) and gives too much power to the tribes, who may not understand adoption issues such as attachment. Although many in Congress have proposed amendments, the Indian Child Welfare Act has changed little since 1978.

The second controversial act is the Multiethnic Placement Act, passed in 1994, which requires that any entity receiving federal funds cannot delay or deny the placement of a child in foster care or adoption because of concerns over race or ethnicity. Its author, Senator Howard Metzenbaum (D-Ohio), believed that children should not languish in foster homes while black parents were being sought for them if there were Caucasian parents willing to adopt them. Frustrated that the act was not being implemented, Senator Metzenbaum went back to Congress in 1996 and pushed an amendment through. With the change of some wording, the 1996 amendment, the Removal of Barriers to Interethnic Adoption, made clear that discrimination on the basis of race would not be tolerated.

Two experts, Owen Gill and Barbara Jackson believe that arguments against transracial adoption fall into two categories: the first has to do with robbing the black culture of its most valuable resources, its children. Those who oppose transracial adoption point to the overrepresentation of African American and Latino children in the foster-care system as a failure of the system to help those families affected by poverty. Rather than encouraging transracial adoption, minority families need support to keep their children at home. Those who support transracial adoption would no doubt agree to the truthfulness of this statement. But what happens to the children while "someone" comes up with the funding to give the needed support?

In the second category, those who oppose transracial adoption say that some black children may do well in their Caucasian families during the elementary school years but will likely have racial-identity problems when they become teenagers and start dating. In response to this statement, Arnold Silverman and William Feigelman (in *The Psychology of Adoption*, 1990) prepared a report titled "Research Evidence on the Outcomes of Transracial Adoptions." They cite one study that found that the attitudes of the adoptive parents had an impact on their transracially adopted children. Parents who saw their children as African American and supported their children's identification with the African American community produced positive attitudes from the children toward their heritage.

Subsequent studies such as the one by Rita J. Simon and Howard Alstein found that young black children saw themselves as black and did not attach a negative evaluation to that assessment. Simon and Alstein did their study with a sample of 206 transracially adopting families, beginning in 1972 and continuing to 1983. The longitudinal nature of the study made it possible to evaluate the findings even after the adoptees had finished college, married, and had children of their own. Simon and Alstein reported that the adoptees—now older adolescents or adults—were firmly committed to their adoptive parents in spite of relationships that in some cases had been "rocky, accusative, and angry."

Those who believe in transracial adoption (if a same-race placement is not available) say that it's the length of time without permanence that is the main problem. The longer children wait for permanent families (of any race), the more damage is done to their sense of identity and self-esteem, and the less likely they will be adopted. Summarizing this point of view in an article in *Adoption Today* (June/July 2005, 22), Elizabeth Bartholet, a Harvard professor and adoptive parent of two transracially/transculturally adopted children, argues that there is no evidence in the research that transracial adoption hurts children. In fact, she says, "there is extensive, unrefuted, and overwhelmingly powerful evidence that delays in permanent placement do devastating damage to children." Researchers Simon and Alstein also found that a majority (63 percent) of the transracially adopting parents said that their children identified with the racial backgrounds of their birth parents as well as the racial backgrounds of their adoptive parents.

At the risk of sparking another argument, the authors of *The Complete Adoption Book* (Beauvais-Godwin and Godwin, 2005) ask whether there are really enough transracial adoptions to wipe out black culture. And even if there were, should the welfare of children be sacrificed to that end?

A November 2005 article in *Ebony Magazine* suggests that more and more African American families are coming forward to adopt black children. This is an encouraging trend. But the majority of African American couples want infants or young children, just as most other adopting parents do. (As mentioned earlier, children of all races tend to stay longer in foster care the older they get. And the older they get, the less chance they have of being adopted.)

No one would argue that all transracially adopted children are "well adjusted" or free of problems. All children have "issues," especially in adolescence. According to most studies, 25 percent of transracially adopted children do have adjustment problems. Beth Hall and Gail Steinberg of PACT–An Adoption Alliance say that although transracial adoption offers unique and positive outcomes for children, it also results in some "losses." Children have to work to deal with these losses; transracial adoption, they say, is not something to be "for" or "against," but a reality to be dealt with.

"Heritage starts at home," says Lisa Milbrand, editor of *Adoptive Families* magazine. In her article by that title in the April 2006 issue, Milbrand offers many ways for adopted children to connect with their heritage. Culture camps and heritage tours are one way, she says. But cultural activities should not be reserved for holidays and events; they must be a part of daily life.

Adoption research is hard to quantify. For example, if a black child is not well adjusted (and how can anyone define that term?) would a person conclude that the "maladjustment" has to do with the transracial placement? Perhaps that child in an African

American family would have similar problems. Unfortunately for research purposes, adoption is not an assembly line with the "product" turning out the same each time it goes down the belt. Each adopted child and each adopted family is different.

Margaret is a single Caucasian adoptive parent of four African American children. Years ago when she was married, Margaret and her husband had adopted two biracial siblings, who are now adults. As she contemplated the adoption of a second sibling group, Margaret made it clear to her agency that although she had many contacts with the African American community and could handle the transracial part of the adoption, she did not want children who had been sexually abused. Margaret found the children she wanted on a website; the agency in the other state assured Margaret that there was no sexual abuse in the children's background. After a couple of months of back-and-forth visits, the children, Tasha, 5, and Aaron, 4, moved in. Soon afterward, Tasha apparently felt comfortable enough with her adoptive mother to reveal that she had in fact been sexually abused in her former foster home. In addition to therapy, Margaret used her connections with her African American church congregation and a local support group for transracially adopted families to support herself and her new daughter. Tasha is now a sophomore in high school and doing well.

The preceding discussion has concentrated mainly on domestic adoptions. But much of it, such as skin color, also applies to children adopted from another country. When families adopt from China, Korea, or Guatemala, for example, their children will be both transracially and transculturally adopted. While these programs continue to thrive, there are many who take a negative view.

Arguments against transracial or transcultural adoption include the reasoning that intercountry adoption is a "one-way street" in which rich adopting parents from Western nations pay large sums of money to take away a country's most precious resources. Second, because children in families beset by poverty and lack of resources get "whisked away," the supplying countries do not have a chance to develop their own social service networks, which might be able to prevent out-of-home/out-of-country adoptions. Third, opponents of transethnic adoption (as practiced in intercountry adoption) see some parallels to slavery: children are stripped of their identities, separated from parents and siblings, and forced to fit into the dominant white culture. Although some adoptive parents take their adopted children back to the places of their birth, the children return to their country of birth as foreigners. Fourth, although adopted children may have received special attention and privileges in their adoptive homes, when they become adults in the "real world," strangers may treat them as if they were "just another immigrant." Fifth, unscrupulous adoption "facilitators" in other countries may bribe poor, uneducated women to part with their infants and then turn around and charge high prices to foreign (e.g., American) lawyers and agencies.

In the June/July 2005 issue of *Adoption Today*, Jinny Jordan, adopted as an infant from Korea by American parents, has compiled comments about some of life's challenges (low points and high points) from four transracially/transculturally adopted children, now adults. Christopher C. Brownlee (formerly Tran Quoc Tuan), adopted from Saigon, Vietnam, talks about being discriminated against "from all sides." Asian Americans accuse him of not being "Asian enough" while white Americans think he should be good in math and science, accomplished in kung fu, and experienced in "eating dog." Kim Winn, adopted from Seoul, Korea, believes she has been "shamefully blessed," but hopes that transracially/transculturally adoptees and their adoptive parents can "confront, combat and educate against . . . harmful stereotypes and prejudices."

Is transracial/transcultural adoption a good idea? Many experts agree that given the powerful role of race in U.S. society, those contemplating transracial/transcultural placements must think deeply, be carefully screened, and be *more* than adequately prepared. To help in this effort, social workers and adoption trainers can ask prospective adoptive parents some basic questions. Many variations are available, including questions asked by Holt International and available through the Child Welfare Information Gateway. Adoption Alliance, a private nonprofit agency in Denver, Colorado, has for years asked its parents to carefully think about answers to these questions when considering a transracial/transcultural adoptive placement.

1. What is their motivation? What made them consider parenting transracially/transculturally?
2. Are there people of other races in their family? If so, what experiences have they had with these family members?

3. Have they discussed their interest in parenting transracially/transculturally with their nuclear family, extended family, and neighbors? What was the reaction?
4. Do they have friends or neighbors who are of the same race as the child they wish to adopt? Do they socialize with those of other races and cultures?
5. What is the racial composition of their neighborhood, including schools and churches, childcare centers, and organizations the child would become a member of?
6. What do the applicants know about the music, entertainment, and eating preferences of the child's race or ethnic group?
7. What do the applicants know about the skin/hair care, dietary, and health needs of the child?
8. How will the children in their home learn about the new child's race/culture history and customs?
9. How will they involve people of the child's race and other races in the child's life?
10. How do the applicants feel that their decision to parent interracially will benefit the child? How will it benefit themselves?
11. How may their decision to parent interracially negatively affect them? How about the child? How will they handle negative effects and the hurt for the child and for themselves?
12. How will they teach coping skills to a child of a different race?
13. What problems do they think might come up in school and in the neighborhood? How will they handle social situations, such as dating?

According to Silverman and Feigelman, transracial adoption appears to result in "children whose self-esteem is at least as high as that of nonadopted children and whose adjustment seems more than satisfactory." They go on to state that for the most part, nonwhite children raised in white homes identify with both white and nonwhite communities. "Though they are afflicted with some degree of doubt and discomfort, there is every evidence that most transracial adoptees have a positive evaluation of their nonwhite backgrounds" (199-200).

Should Single People Be Allowed to Adopt?

Until about thirty years ago, departments of social services and adoption agencies rarely considered single persons as possible adoptive parents. Some states even had laws prohibiting singles from adopting. Now, singles adopt more than 25 percent of children with special needs. Experts estimate that single people are responsible for about 5 percent of all other adoptions. Today, some adoption professionals may still look at single people as a last resource and then only for the most hard-to-place children, but the picture seems to be changing. And yet, prospective single parent adopters may have to "prove" themselves even more than couples do. Singles can make themselves more desirable and feel more prepared if they try to answer some of the following questions suggested by Jane Mattes, founder of the organization Single Mothers by Choice, Inc.

1. Have you accomplished all of the personal and career goals that are necessary for you to feel good about yourself? How will you feel if you are not able to achieve some of these goals?
2. How will you feel about others' criticism of your decision to be a single parent?
3. Are you able to support yourself and a child emotionally and financially?
4. Do you have elderly parents who may need your assistance at the same time you will be devoting yourself to a baby or young child?
5. Are there particular reasons why you are not with a partner, and will these reasons affect how you parent your child?
6. If you date often, can you manage working, dating, and caring for a child? How will a child affect your likelihood of finding a mate? Can you make a distinction between which needs can be fulfilled by a child and which ones can be fulfilled only by a spouse?
7. Do you have a good support system involving friends,

family, a religious community, or work to help you during stressful times?

8. Is your job flexible enough so that you can meet your child's needs when he is sick, has a special event, or needs extra attention?

9. How do you handle stress? Will you be able to meet the challenge of caring for a child while working?

10. If you are considering adopting an older child, are you prepared to meet the child's special emotional needs and issues? Do you have time to take your child to a therapist in addition to Girl Scouts and other school and community activities?

(These questions were condensed from a list published by Laura Beauvais-Godwin and Raymond Godwin, *The Complete Adoption Book*, 2005, 120–121.)

After a long wait, Amy was chosen to parent Bryan, age six; some professionals considered him "unadoptable" because of his behavioral disturbances. (In reality, most adoption professionals agree that there are no "unadoptable" children.) Most single parents work outside the home, and Amy was no exception. Although she found it difficult to respond to the frequent calls from school, she "hung in there" with Bryan, who is now twelve and still has some hard-to-manage behaviors. A year ago, Amy and Bryan moved to the East Coast so that Amy could be closer to her sister and brother-in-law, who could give her support. Bryan has enjoyed getting to know his uncle, a new male role model.

Another single woman, Carol, a nurse, was selected to parent Becky, an eighteen-month-old girl exposed to methamphetamine in utero. Carol figures she got Becky because no one else wanted her. Fortunately, at age four Becky shows few developmental delays. Carol's mother and father, both retired, take care of Becky when Carol works twelve-hour shifts at the hospital. Becky's adoptive grandparents think she's wonderful. Now Carol wants to adopt again. According to Vic Groze, assistant professor at the University of Iowa School of Social Work, studies have shown that support from extended family is a huge factor in making a single-parent adoption successful. (Groze defines single parents as those who choose to become a parent while single, not those who lose a spouse because of death or divorce.)

In both of the above situations, the chosen single moms, receiving children from the foster care system, turned out to be excellent choices. But birth mothers usually choose a two-parent family and are unlikely to choose a single mom for several reasons:

—Birth mothers who decide to make an adoption plan may be young, needing more education, and struggling financially. They may "buy into" the stereotype of a single parent being in the same situation, not realizing that with their older age, prospective single mothers and fathers may be better educated, have more support, and be financially stable.

—Birth mothers may think there is "something wrong" with a person who remains single instead of getting married.

—Birth mothers may worry that a single parent will not have enough time to devote to the child.

—Birth mothers tend to favor younger parents (in their twenties and thirties) rather than people in their forties or older, the age of many singles considering adoption.

Because the odds in domestic adoption seem stacked against them, prospective single mothers often turn to intercountry adoption—if they can afford it.

If single mothers have more difficulty adopting than two-parent families, single men have even more difficulty. The same questions, such as "Will the adoptive parent have enough time for my child?" persist, but additional questions arise. Men are generally considered less nurturing and less communicative than women. Birth mothers and agencies tend to question a single male's motivation to adopt: is he perhaps a pedophile, someone who preys on children? Agencies tend to "study" single men extensively (if they consider them at all), often doing psychological testing, asking for extra references, and requiring them to take parenting classes. Agencies often encourage single men to apply to adopt an older male child. Many international programs rule out men completely.

Those who argue against the idea of single-parent adoptions point out that even an older single person may find a "significant other," and a child who has adjusted to the single parent will have a hard time accepting another person in the home. Another argument against adoption by single parents is the question, "What if that parent dies?" For that reason agencies tend to be extra careful in asking the parent if he or she has a will and/or plans for a guardian.

Research shows that single-parent adoptions dramatically increased between 1970 and 1986. One study showed that although single parents had a lower level of income than dual-income families, single parents, who are mostly female, had a high level of emotional maturity along with a high frustration tolerance, and did not let the opinions of outsiders upset them.

On the positive side, the disruption rate of children placed with single parents was not significantly higher than those placed in two-parent families. Groze admits that many single parents have difficulty in the immediate post-placement period. Apparently the anxiety any new parent feels is compounded by the fact that single parents usually have an "intense" relationship with the child, and additionally have to deal with any difficulties by themselves.

Sara, forty-three, had overcome many difficulties in her life (usually a sign of the emotional strength necessary to raise an older "special needs" child). However, a month after the placement of Kayla, age eight, in Sara's home, she asked to have Kayla removed. "It's too much togetherness," she said. "She even follows me into the bathroom." Sara's agency had prepared her with classes and a preadoptive support group, but obviously better preparation, perhaps mentoring a child, might have helped. Groze concludes, however, that based on his studies, single-parent adoption turned out to be a workable plan for many children.

What about Same-Sex Couples?

One of the most hotly debated current issues has to do with the rights of same-sex couples. In *Single Parents by Choice* (1992), Naomi Miller writes that because the word *homosexual* has a long history of pejorative use, many in the gay community disdain its use. They prefer the words *lesbian* and *gay*. The latter term can refer to males or females, whereas *lesbian* refers only to women. The debate over whether gays and lesbians should be allowed to adopt is part of the debate over whether same-sex persons should be allowed to marry. Before the debate begins on these pages, it's important to note that proponents and opponents on both sides of the debate point to what they consider reliable data to back up their claims. Each says that the other is selective, biased, or just plain incorrect. Those who are members of conservative religious and/or political groups often speak of the negative effects; those who support gay rights and/or are themselves homosexual are likely to point to the positive effects. Adoption adds a new variable, and the true number of same-sex couples who have adopted is not known.

According to the Child Welfare Information Gateway, defining the structure of a gay family can be difficult. For one thing, the most common kind of homosexual family is a stepparent or blended family. One or both of the parents may have had birth children in a former heterosexual relationship. Or the parents may have used various types of reproductive technology. Finally, the couple may have adopted their children.

Sexual orientation (or an ongoing romantic attraction to same-sex individuals) is usually evident by early adolescence to the person who has these feelings. But because of the shame connected with homosexuality, many individuals with this type of sexual orientation do not "come out" until much later, if ever. Sexual orientation, referring to a person's innermost feelings, is not the same as sexual behavior. What causes homosexuality is for many people a matter of debate. Some believe in a genetic cause; others believe in environmental factors, such as early childhood experiences. Some experts believe in a combination of factors.

Experts still debate the number of homosexual persons in the United States. Some say gays make up 5 to 10 percent of the population. Others have revised that number downward to 1 or 2 percent. Another estimate is that up to 14 million children have a gay or lesbian parent, and up to 10 million children are being raised in a gay or lesbian home.

So what about same-sex couples? Should they be allowed to adopt? While the debate rages, homosexual couples *are* adopting children. However, most states do not allow gay couples to adopt as a unit. Commonly only one member of the couple can adopt the child; if the other person also wants custody of the child, that person has to apply for "second parent" or "coparent" adoption status. Courts in only about half of the states grant second-parent adoptions. Second-parent adoption offers benefits for children, including health benefits, social security benefits, and the ability of both parents to consent to medical treatment. Most important, it guarantees that the second parent will have custody rights if the first parent dies or becomes incapacitated.

State laws tend to govern the intricacies of adoption, and states have different laws. If a homosexual couple wants to adopt from the *public* child welfare system, they should look into their state's laws. For example, both California and New York have laws against discrimination. Therefore, social workers in these states cannot reject applicants because of their sexual orientation. It is possible, though, that a social worker who has her own ideas about homosexuality might find another reason to reject the potential adoptive parents. And what if there really was another reason to reject them? A judge will make the final decision based on "the best interests of the child."

A private agency will "study" a family but may have different policies on working with gay clients. Keeping in mind the best interests of available children, the home study worker will use references and other measures to recommend or not recommend her clients for adoption. As for the prospective parents, it is illegal to lie during the home-study process. However a same-sex couple may present themselves in a variety of ways.

Stacey, a high-school math teacher and girls' basketball coach, was a card-carrying member of a Native American tribe. In retrospect, her single-parent adoptions (at different times) of two Native American infant boys were a "piece of cake." Stacey's spacious residence on acres of land was also home to several horses that the boys would learn to ride. By the ages of three and five years, her boys were happy, healthy, and "attached."

Several years later, the private agency that had worked with Stacey on those two adoptions recruited her for the adoption of eight-year-old William, a Native American special needs child from Alaska. But what had not been an issue in Stacey's two previous adoptions suddenly reached epic proportions in the run-up to the third. In the earlier home studies, Stacey's agency had included Tara, Stacey's housemate, in the study. They had interviewed Tara and had gotten references and child abuse and FBI clearances. Tara, who had her own bedroom, played a significant role in the upbringing of the younger boys.

But questions initiated by the placing agency that had custody of William became intense. Was the relationship between the two women a lesbian relationship? "No," said Stacey, and her agency took her at her word. Her home-study worker's experience with Stacey had been 100 percent positive. Her sexual orientation was not an issue with her agency. Eventually, they were able to persuade the placing agency that Stacey was "okay." William came to stay, "but not," said Stacey, "until Tara and I had jumped through more hoops than two dogs in a circus."

In an *independent* adoption, a facilitator, such as an attorney or a physician, brings the adoptive and birth families together. (This type of adoption is illegal in some states.) Although some birth parents may be reluctant to pick a nontraditional couple, getting picked and having an open adoption situation with birth parents might work well for gay parents who won't have to worry that someone will discover their "secret."

If they are totally forthcoming about their relationship, an *intercountry* adoption will probably not work for a homosexual couple. Some foreign countries prohibit homosexual adoptions. For example, in 2002, in a probable effort to stem the tide of homosexual adoptions, China reduced the quota of single-parent adoptions from 40 to 8 percent. Currently, only heterosexual couples and single females can legally adopt Chinese children.

In an interesting development on December 30, 2005, the countries of England and Wales gave gay couples, as well as unmarried couples, the right to adopt a child together. The *News Telegraph* called the Adoption and Children Act, which had been on the drawing board for three years, "the biggest shake-up in adoption law for 30 years."

In the United States the debate rages on. Those against gay adoption often base their arguments on religion or morality. Tim Dailey, a senior fellow in culture studies at the Family Research Council—a conservative organization that promotes public policy based on Judeo-Christian values and traditional definitions of marriage and the family—attacks the methodology of research showing that children raised in homosexual households fare no worse than children raised in traditional families. He says that "children raised in traditional families by a mother and father are happier, healthier, and more successful than children raised in non-traditional environments" (2005, 30). He adds that children need a mom and a dad, and that "homosexual or lesbian households are no substitute for a family" (39). Robert H. Knight, also of the Family Research Council, agrees. According to the *CQ Researcher,* Knight commented after newborn twins from Texas were adopted by two Washington professional women that placing the babies in a lesbian household would deliberately deprive the children of a father's love.

Dailey believes that same-sex households expose children to harmful situations resulting from the homosexual lifestyle. Among these are promiscuity, health hazards, family violence, incest, substance abuse, greater risk for suicide, and sexual identity confusion. Activists in favor of the homosexual lifestyle, Dailey adds, are out to undermine marriage "by attacking monogamy, commitment, and chastity," and that children do better in traditional families "where they receive appropriate discipline, attention, and moral and spiritual guidance" (29).

Even in committed, monogamous homosexual relationships, says Dailey, "there is a magnum order of difference between the lifetime fidelity rate cited for homosexuals and the 75 to 90 percent cited for married couples" (33). Homosexual relationships, he says, are unstable and incapable of providing children with security. Evidently *committed* means something entirely different in a homosexual relationship than in a heterosexual marriage.

Dailey mentions AIDS as one of the "bacterial and parasitical sexually transmitted diseases" that are the result of unhealthy sexual practices common among homosexuals (34). Domestic violence, he states, is higher in homosexual relationships than in traditional marriages. He cites studies showing that homosexual relationships are far more violent than traditional relationships and notes that this fact is not often reported.

Dailey says there is a high incidence of mental health problems among homosexuals, and points to a national survey of lesbians published in the *Journal of Consulting and Clinical Psychology* that shows that nearly 75 percent of the respondents had pursued counseling of some kind, many for treatment of long-term depression or sadness. A study published in *Nursing Research,* says Dailey, found that lesbians are "three times more likely to abuse alcohol and suffer from other compulsive behaviors" (35). He points to two simultaneous articles in the *Archives of General Psychiatry,* one of which discusses a higher incidence of suicide for those with same-sex partners.

The claim that homosexual households do not "recruit" children into a similar lifestyle, Dailey says, is refuted by growing evidence that children raised in these households are more likely to engage in sexual experimentation and homosexual behavior. He concludes that "no society has ceased to honor the institution of marriage and survived" (40). In his view, those who wish to live together without marriage are free to do so, but children should not be entrusted to those unions.

Paul Cameron is chair of the conservative Family Research Institute (FMI) in Colorado Springs, Colorado. The institute is a "non-profit scientific and educational corporation that believes the strength of our society depends on preserving America's historic moral framework and the traditional family." It welcomes those who would like to join the fight to "restore a world where marriage is upheld and honored, where children are nurtured and protected, and where homosexuality is not taught and accepted, but instead is discouraged and rejected at every level" (home page, Family Research Institute, http://www.familyresearchinst.org). Cameron takes issue with the findings of the American Academy of Pediatrics, which, in the year 2002, recommended legal and legislative efforts to allow children born to or adopted by one member of a gay or lesbian couple to be adopted by the homosexual partner. Cameron points to narratives by children living in homosexual households who mentioned one or more "problems" in these households. (The narratives are available on the FMI website.) Cameron states that gay-rights activists are adept at manipulating research to their own ends and describes the report of the American Academy of Pediatrics as "cooking the books" (2005, 54). He also says that homosexuals die earlier than heterosexuals; therefore, children with homosexual parents are more likely to lose a parent to death.

Another person against allowing homosexuals to adopt is Lynn Wardle. At the time of his presentation at the Marriage, Adoption, and the Best Interests of the Child Symposium, Wardle was professor of law at Brigham Young University. He observed that some individuals advocating for gay rights say it is unconstitutional for states or state agencies to prohibit or restrict gay couple adoption. Wardle states that homosexual couples do not have a constitutional right to adopt (Dudley 2004). Some experts might argue that no one has the *right* to adopt but that individuals interested in adopting should have the right to be "studied" or to be considered as adoptive parents.

A mini-debate, "Are Gay Parents Good for Children?," begins on the pages of the *Psychotherapy Networker* (January/February 2006) with President George W. Bush's announcement at a press conference a year earlier. "Studies have shown," said the president, "that the ideal is where a child is raised in a married family with a man and a woman" (22). After a review of research in 2002, Tufts University professor of pediatrics Ellen Perrin differed with the president. She concluded that "there's no good evidence that same-sex parents are any less fit than heterosexual parents, and some of them may provide subtle advantages" (22). The American Academy of Pediatrics based its stance that there should be no barriers to gay adoption and custody partly on Perrin's report.

In support of the other side, the American College of Pediatricians (ACP), a smaller organization that broke away from the American Academy of Pediatrics because of the latter's position paper, states that children of gay parents are at a risk for emotional problems (*Psychotherapy Networker*, January/February 2006). In the same debate, Perrin faced off with Paul Cameron of the Family Research Institute. Cameron accused Perrin of using "biased studies from homosexual journals." Perrin responded that her studies came from peer-reviewed journals, whereas ten of Cameron's studies have been published in only one journal, *Psychological Reports*, in which authors must pay to be published. Perrin concluded, "It isn't the sexual identity of the parents that matters: it's things like how well the parents get along, how integrated the children are in school—the same social factors that matter to all kids" (23).

Those who believe that homosexual individuals and/or couples have the right to be considered as adoptive parents maintain that the arguments and research from the "other side" is flawed or wrongly applied. These advocates believe same-sex couples *can* give good homes to children, and they agree with Perrin that all of the available research to date has concluded that children of homosexual parents grow up as successfully as the children of heterosexual parents. Some of the organizations in support of gay adoption, in addition to the American Academy of Pediatrics, are the American Civil Liberties Union (ACLU), the American Psychological Association, the Child Welfare League of America, the North American Council on Adoptable Children, the Evan B. Donaldson Adoption Institute, the National Association of Social Workers, the American Counseling Association, the American Academy of Child and Adolescent Psychiatry, and the Dave Thomas Foundation for Adoption.

Countering the arguments of those who do not want to see homosexuals as parents, the American Civil Liberties Union has drawn up a list of "myths vs. facts" (*Gay and Lesbian Families*, 2005). The first myth, according to the ACLU, is that the only acceptable home for a child is one with a married-to-each-other mother and father. Out of the more than 100,000 children in the foster care system available for adoption in 1998, only 20,000 found adoptive homes. The rest may never get a mother *or* a father if child welfare policies do not include nontraditional families.

The second is the myth that children need to have a mother and father to provide proper role modeling. Children in foster care may have mother/father role models in the foster home, but unless children have *permanent* parents, they may move to twenty different foster homes and end up with no parents at all. Additionally, children find role models not only in parents but in grandparents, uncles, aunts, teachers, religious leaders, family friends, and neighbors.

The third myth, argues the ACLU, is that gays do not have stable relationships and have no idea how to be good parents. The fact is that most lesbian women and gay men do have stable relationships, just as most heterosexual couples do. However, there are many divorces in heterosexual marriages, and there are breakups in homosexual relationships. The American Psychological Association has not found one study that shows children of homosexual families to be disadvantaged in any significant way relative to children raised in heterosexual families. The fact is, says the ACLU, that children are not placed with *any* parents who do not pass rigorous screening tests, including reference and background checks.

Fourth, states the ACLU, it is a myth to say that children raised by gay parents are more likely than other children to grow up homosexual. Studies have shown that the children of gay parents are no more likely than other children to become homosexual themselves. Some children of same-sex parents will become gay, but so will some children of heterosexual parents. Research has also shown that children of same-sex parents are more tolerant of diversity than many other children, which is not a bad trait. If indeed a child of a homosexual parent turns out to be gay, the child will have the advantage of being raised by a sympathetic parent. Charlotte Patterson, a professor of psychology at the University of Virginia, adds that the quality of a child's parenting is more important than a parent's gender, and that a parent's sexual orientation is not a predictor of how well the child will adjust.

Fifth, while it is true that children of homosexual parents may be subject to harassment and teasing, children endure teasing for many other reasons—being too fat or too thin, being too short or too tall—and survive. Besides, parents who themselves may have endured harassment will be well qualified to support the child. If the child grows up in permanent foster care and never gets adopted, he or she will certainly bear the brunt of teasing.

The sixth myth, says the ACLU, is that when gay men and lesbians adopt, their children will be living in an "immoral environment." One argument against this reasoning is that there is no general agreement as to what is moral or immoral. Some people believe that war is immoral or guns are immoral; others believe that dancing is immoral or that playing cards is immoral. If all of those willing to provide an adoptive home for a child are rejected because something they did is someone else's idea of "immoral," there will be no parents left to adopt children.

A seventh myth is that gays are more likely than heterosexuals to molest children. An adult sexual attraction to children or the molesting of children is pedophilia. Experts say there is no connection between homosexuality and pedophilia. Heterosexual men perpetrate 90 percent of sexual abuse on children. In a study reported in the journal *Pediatrics,* out of 296 cases of child sexual abuse, only two of the offenders were homosexual. In 82 percent of the cases, the alleged offender was a heterosexual partner of a close relative of the child. The study reports that a given parent's heterosexual partner is more than 100 times more likely to abuse a child than a homosexual or bisexual. The study concluded that "there is no support for . . . advocating (for) legislation limiting rights of homosexuals" (Jenny, Roesler, and Poyer, 1994, 44).

According to an article in the *National Law Journal,* a ban on gay adoptions hurts children. The author, Vivian Berger, takes aim at Florida, the only state in the United States that prohibits outright *all* gay and lesbian adoptions. Berger says, "sexual orientation has nothing to do with parental performance."

A report from the Evan B. Donaldson Institute states that "gay adoption is commonly accepted" (2005, 46). The institute, established in 1996, is an independent, nonprofit organization with no affiliation to any interest group. Its goal is to provide accurate research-based information leading to more ethical, effective, and informed policies, practices, and laws.

Some of those against the idea of homosexual adoption say that child-welfare agencies are biased *in favor* of same-sex couples. Candi Cushman is a writer for the *Citizen,* a publication of Focus on the Family, a conservative Christian organization. She says that "county governments' subtle antagonism to religious and conservative families . . . aggravates the backlog of homeless children" (2004, 194). Cushman quotes a social services investigator from Alameda County, California, as saying that certain counties will give preference to gay or lesbian families while putting "what I see as good religious families with good values on the bottom of the pile" (194). But Cushman concludes by writing that Christians who "pool their resources have conquered political pressure" (195). She urges Christians to stare down the state.

The Evan B. Donaldson Institute does not deny "that Americans' attitudes are evolving—as reflected in the fact that more and more agencies are allowing openly gay and lesbian clients to adopt" (2005, 47). According to the institute, solid research showing agency practices and results were lacking until a study done in 1999–2000. The institute mailed surveys requesting information on agency policies and practices to the fifty-one public (state) agencies in the nation. In addition, surveys were mailed to 844 randomly selected private agencies. The results confirmed that gays were adopting "regularly and in notable numbers, both at public and private agencies" (47). A clear majority, states the institute, or 60 percent, said they had accepted applications from self-identified lesbians and gay men in 1999–2000. The agencies most likely to work with same-sex couples were those who did special-needs placements (85.3 percent). Religious affiliation also affected the results. Almost all Jewish-affiliated agencies accepted gay clients, followed by public agencies (90 percent), private agencies with no religious affiliation (80.2 percent), and Lutheran agencies (66.7 percent). About 20 percent of all agencies reported that in one or more instances, they had rejected applications from prospective adoptive parents who were homosexual.

In different writings on the subject of scrutiny, prospective parents from both groups (homosexuals and Christians) believe they have received more scrutiny than other groups. The social services investigator from California (mentioned earlier) believes that Christian families are often "phased out through heavier screening processes and regulations" because of being religious. "If you're going to be religious," he said, "then they are going to hold you to a greater weight of certain rules. Like where the bed's located . . . Do they have their own separate bedrooms? . . . There's 100 different questions" (Cushman, 2004, 194–195). However, in special-needs adoptions, families must often be certified or licensed for foster care, which can involve a very long list of questions.

At the same time, according to the Child Welfare Information

Gateway, same-sex couples may be asked *extra* questions, such as those suggested by Denise Goodman, PhD, a consultant and trainer in Ohio. (Except for the first question, however, hetero-sexual couples are often asked the same questions.) Are they comfortable with their self-image and with being gay? What kind of family support do they have? How stable is their relationship? Do they have a will (or wills)? Do they share finances?

Should the Government Provide More or Less Regulation of Adoption?

Regulation of adoption—whether to have more or less government involvement—is a complicated subject that generates controversy. First, although state regulations govern much of adoption practice, federal legislation also enters in. Second, one must consider what type of adoption is being regulated—for example, domestic infant, the adoption of older children from the foster-care system, or intercountry adoption. The reasons people give for wanting more or less regulation often depends on the type of adoption they have experienced. If the person speaking feels he or others have been victimized by too much government interference, he may argue for less regulation. If the person speaking has had a negative experience with too little regulation, she may argue for more regulation.

Those who believe that *more* government regulation is necessary may have had a bad experience in an intercountry adoption. On January 8, 2006, National Public Radio aired part of a special program by American RadioWorks called "Finding Home: Fifty Years of International Adoption," which included information on difficult experiences. Internet scams are not uncommon, says Trish Maskew, president of Ethica, a group that lobbies for better rules governing adoption. For example, P. J. Whiskeyman and her husband lost thousands of dollars in an effort to adopt two Ukrainian girls they had seen on the Internet. After a trip to the country to pick up the girls, they returned "empty handed." Because federal regulation of adoption agencies in the United States is lacking and state laws vary widely, adoption fraud is difficult to prosecute.

The Joint Council on International Children's Services is the oldest and largest affiliation of licensed nonprofit agencies for intercountry adoption in the United States. However, in some states there are no laws to give "teeth" to the standards. Some agencies apply for accreditation through the private Council on Accreditation of Services for Families and Children, but the process is expensive and time-consuming.

Many adoption professionals argue for more regulation of intercountry adoption. When fully implemented, the Hague Convention on Intercountry Adoption should help regulate intercountry adoption by setting minimum standards and practices for those involved in intercountry adoption. Under regulations drawn up by the U.S. State Department, those providing adoption services will have to have government-approved accreditation, a written policy prohibiting child buying, and a fee schedule detailing each part of the adoption process. If they do not follow the rules, agencies could lose accreditation.

However, there are concerns about the Hague Convention. One concern is that the convention binds only the countries that have ratified it. And, according to Joan Hollinger, an adoption specialist at the Boalt School of Law at the University of California at Berkeley, some people worry that these regulations will hold U.S. adoption providers responsible for the misbehaviors of those in sending countries. For example, an agency could face criminal or civil liability for not disclosing vital medical information about a child to an adoptive family when the agency believes it has disclosed everything. Linda Donovan, international adoption coordinator at Adoption Alliance in Denver, says that there are many good agencies and some not-so-good agencies, but almost all agencies do release medical information if they have it. Sometimes, she says, they just don't have it. Hollinger says the problem is that agencies rely on attorneys, social service agencies, and local "facilitators" in the countries of origin. For this reason, U.S. agencies are reluctant to be held accountable.

Cindy Freidmutter, former executive director of the Evan B. Donaldson Institute, on May 22, 2002, testified for more regulation of intercountry adoption before the U.S. House Committee on International Relations. She suggested three ways she hoped the Hague Convention and the Intercountry Adoption Act would improve services for all members of the adoption triad, as well as ensuring more ethical international adoptions. Freidmutter recommended that (1) providers in the United States should be directly responsible for financial transactions, and that adopting families should not have to carry large amounts of cash to make financial contributions in other countries; (2) prospective adoptive parents should know ahead of time exactly what services they will receive, the fees they will pay, and the complaint resolution process—in other words, that they will receive legal consumer protections; and (3) prospective adoptive parents will have all the information they will need to make an informed decision about which agency to work with.

Another problem is that unscrupulous unregulated agencies sometimes have placed children with severe problems, such as fetal alcohol syndrome and attachment disorder, in unsuspecting homes. (Linda Donovan of Adoption Alliance says that these conditions are often difficult to diagnose even in the United States and are especially difficult to diagnose in young children who come from countries where medical resources are scarce.) However, say those wanting more regulation, a problem is that if the placement disrupts, the children end up in foster care or in expensive residential treatment facilities, and U.S. taxpayers foot the bill.

Intercountry adoption is not the only type of adoption that cries out for more regulation, say its proponents. According to Maureen Hogan, executive director of the National Adoption Foundation, many of those opposing more regulation think lawmaking should be left up to the states. Hogan argues for more federal regulation in domestic infant adoption. She says, "Adoption is big business and inherently interstate in nature" (Hogan, 2004, 88).

Hogan reports that as far back as 1955, the U.S. Senate looked into deceptive and even abusive adoption practices. In oversight hearings in the Judiciary Committee, Senator Estes Kevauver of Tennessee heard testimony about some of the unethical practices, which included kidnapping of babies by unscrupulous adoption agencies and placement of infants with life-threatening conditions with unsuspecting adoptive families.

In her 1993 testimony before the before the U.S. Senate Subcommittee on Children, Family, Drugs and Alcohol, Lynn Gabbard, an adoptive mother of seven special-needs children, called for a set of national standards for the care of children. Because of chronic abuse by some birth parents with their own problems, children sometimes suffer irreversible damage before they are removed from these homes. Gabbard, who also placed children as an adoption caseworker, did not presume to know how the government could implement such standards. However, the Adoption and Safe Families Act of 1997 and the Promoting Safe and Stable Families Amendment of 2001 were steps in the right direction, according to many child welfare workers. These acts call for "reasonable efforts" to move eligible foster children toward permanent adoptive placements (Gabbard, 1995).

Those *opposed* to more government regulation of adoption also come from various corners. Laura Cecere, speaking for the thousands of Americans who have happily adopted children from other countries, believes that minimal interference from the federal government has "worked" in intercountry adoption. If the federal government's role expands, Cecere fears that the process could become burdensome, bureaucratic, and even more expensive than it already is. Many people will not be able to adopt or will decide not to. In addition, smaller agencies giving personalized services could be forced to close their doors. Cecere does not believe there is a crisis in intercountry adoption and feels that attempts to "fix" what some see as problems will make the situation worse.

Based on his family's experiences in trying to adopt a three-year-old child, Jacob Sullum, a senior editor at the libertarian *Reason Magazine*, believes that "government regulations and procedures are too cumbersome" (2004, 88). Sullum writes that the "byzantine system" is biased against action (108). Workers and agencies are afraid to make decisions with which someone will later find fault.

Infant adoption, too, should have less government regulation, says Donald Boudreaux, a professor of law and economics at Clemson University. Boudreaux has proposed "a liberalized adoption market" in which birth parents would be allowed to contract freely (at mutually agreed upon prices) for the sale of parental rights of children up to the age of nine months. Adoptive parents who purchase the parental rights would have the same rights and responsibilities as if they had given birth to the child. The adoptive parents could not resell the parental rights. Some of the current regulations would still apply. For example, adoptive parents who contracted with birth parents would still need to have a home study, and courts would still approve each adoption.

One advantage of this arrangement, says Boudreaux, would be the end of the baby shortage. The supply of adoptable infants would increase when the birth parents sell their parental rights. Added benefits, he says, would include fewer abortions, greater wealth for birth mothers, increased prenatal care, less child abuse, fewer children in foster care, and a decrease in the cost of fertility treatments. Boudreaux anticipates objections to his proposal, such as the argument that human life should not be an object of economics. But he argues that the gains he foresees should not be forsaken because some people "are uncomfortable with the use of the language of economics and of commerce to explain how a liberalized market in parental rights will function" (120).

Although she offers different suggestions, Elizabeth Bartholet, author of *Family Bonds* (1993), believes we need to deregulate adoption. Current regulations, she writes, create obstacles, cause adoption to be costly and unpleasant, and degrade adoption as a way of building family, making adoption a "last resort." She suggests more financial incentives and reimbursements, as well as state and federal tax systems to provide credit for *all* adoptions.

What about Infant Abandonment Laws? Are They "Safe Havens," or "Baby Dumps?"

A newborn baby is left dead in a bathroom during the prom while its birth mother goes back to the dance floor. Babies in trash cans, Dumpsters, alleys . . .

Situations such as these inspired the first infant abandonment law in Texas, passed by the legislature on September 1, 1999. Since then almost all of the states have followed with their own infant abandonment laws, also called "safe haven" or "safe surrender" laws. Most of the laws consider up to three days the age limit, but some give the parent up to forty-five days.

What are these laws, and what is all the fuss about? Simply put, state legislators have enacted the laws to provide havens for newborns to be anonymously abandoned at "safe" places, such as fire stations and hospitals. Most of the laws grant immunity from prosecution for those who leave infants at the designated sites if the baby has not been harmed.

Popular support for the laws is strong. No one likes to think of puppies or kittens being abandoned, much less newborn babies. So the idea of offering a distraught parent a safe, legal, and confidential way of relinquishing an unwanted infant has much appeal. Those in favor of the laws say they will save babies' lives (a baby's last chance, say some), prevent crimes such as child abuse, and make more infants available for adoption.

Those who question the laws say that at least they call attention to the desperation women feel who have an unwanted child that they are unprepared to care for. But, they add, the laws offer a "simplistic" apparent solution to a complex problem. They say the laws were enacted too quickly. Because there is no national agency that tracks the states' programs and because many states are not keeping track either, the effectiveness of the law is hard to gauge.

Another problem is that (even now) not enough women have heard of their state's law. And yet, since 1999, states have tried various advertising campaigns, sometimes spending large sums of money on advertising. New Jersey tried a slogan, "No shame, no blame, no names." But a headline in the *New York Times* (March 20, 2004) announced: "Program Questioned after Another Dead Baby Is Found." The story says that critics worry that the program is not reaching enough mothers. Since the program began in New Jersey, sixteen mothers had used the program while fifteen others simply abandoned their babies.

A second problem is that young women who abandon their babies in unsafe places are usually in a state of denial about the pregnancy; they are unlikely to have weighed their options or to have thoughtfully considered possible outcomes. For example, Cynthia Dailard pointed out that in the year after Texas passed its law, twelve Texas infants were "illegally abandoned." Not one was abandoned under the terms of the law.

Many adoption advocates have other concerns about the safe haven laws. For one thing, if the laws protect the anonymity of the birth parents as most do, the children face a "closed book" when it comes to identity questions later in life. (Some state laws do provide for the parent to pass along medical information.) However, in many of the states, the babies are turned over to state or county departments of human services, which are prohibited from contacting the birth parents.

Professor of family law Joan Hollinger points out that in some cases the laws are unnecessary. Most states allow birth mothers to "walk away" from the hospital in which they have given birth without fear of prosecution. According to the *New York Times*, a 1998 federal survey of hospitals showed that 31,000 birth mothers (many with drug problems) had left infants in maternity wards.

Also, critics say, the laws may bypass the interests of birth fathers. She says safe haven laws create a disincentive for welfare officials to look for birth fathers, who may have family members interested in the baby. Hollinger also observed in a *New York Times* story (August 31, 2001) that the "practice of dropping your children by the wayside," formerly regarded with disfavor, has suddenly become "favored and promoted."

On March 10, 2003, the Evan B. Donaldson Institute issued a report that raised more questions about the effectiveness and consequences of safe haven laws. The report concludes that contrary to the claims made by safe haven law proponents, there is no evidence that the laws are working, mainly because they do not address the root causes of the problem. In addition to the objections already mentioned, the report pointed out several "negative consequences" of the laws: (1) that upset family members, or friends, such as boyfriends and others with no legal rights, can abandon the baby without the mother's consent; (2) that women who might not have abandoned their child may now do so because it seems easier than receiving counseling and/or making an adoption plan through an agency; (3) that biological fathers may be deprived of the legal right to care for a child, even if they have the desire and resources to do so; (4) that the possibility (in the future) of contact and/or the exchange of information between birth parents and the child may be precluded; and (5) that the laws may send a signal to young people that they do not necessarily have to assume responsibility for their actions, and that deserting one's child is acceptable.

But those in favor of the laws maintain that a flawed approach is better than no approach at all, especially when the lives of children are at stake. The laws, now passed, are unlikely to disappear anytime soon. (The Promoting Safe and Stable Families Amendments of 2001—federal legislation—allows states to use some of their federal dollars for safe haven programs.) Perhaps, as some suggest, state laws may be amended at some time in the future. If so, and even if not, the Evan B. Donaldson Institute recommends that the following elements be considered because they are important adoption policy: (1) research on the causes of abandonment to better tailor an effective policy response; (2) education for students, teachers, parents, counselors, and clergy about how to identify concealed pregnancies and enable affected teenagers and women to get help; (3) confidential counseling for at-risk pregnant teens and women about prenatal care and safe alternatives for their babies, such as care by other biological family members, or adoption if they cannot or do not want to parent; and (4) the use of educational materials and support services to help mothers, fathers, and other biological relatives raise infants if they wish to do so.

What about Adoption Itself? Is It Valuable, or Not?

Doesn't everyone agree that adoption is wonderful? A birth mother "makes a plan" for her child, a loving couple receives the baby, a child gets a "forever home." Isn't that a perfect arrangement?

No, say some individuals and groups who are not pleased with various aspects of adoption. In 1979, *Death by Adoption*, written by Joss Shawyer of New Zealand, condemned adoption as an alternative to abortion. Shawyer wrote that "adoption is a violent act, a political act of aggression towards a woman who has supposedly offended the sexual mores by committing the unforgivable act of not suppressing her sexuality, and therefore not keeping it for trading purposes through traditional marriage" (18).

Shawyer went on to state that unmarried mothers slide to the bottom of the social ladder. She called the birth mother the "real mother" and wrote that the adopted child has been denied the right to her natural heritage, her "birthright." Shawyer also pointed to the suffering of the natural mother over the years and postulated that for her, the actual death of the child might be preferable.

Those adopted also feel pain because in many cases they must hide their feelings in order to keep their adoptive parents from "hurting." Shawyer wrote that money spent on intercountry adoption would be better spent on improving conditions for the underprivileged in the foreign land. She concluded by saying that studies have shown the long-term psychological after-effects of abortion to be minimal, and that "restrictive abortion laws are not only dangerous to women's health, they are insulting to the entire female population" (23). She urged "prevention" of unwanted pregnancies and the "restructuring of society" to enable birth parents to keep their babies.

Writing in the 2002 *CUB Communicator*, the newsletter of Concerned United Birthparents, Darlene Gerow seems most upset about the commercial aspects of adoption. She states, "Adoption is a huge profit-driven industry where babies are the commodity." Gerow argues that "the business of infant adoption is out of control" because the affluent can buy whatever they want. Poverty, she says, is the main reason birth parents cannot raise their children.

James Gritter, author of *The Spirit of Open Adoption* (1997), agrees. However, he *disagrees* with the prevailing practice in which prospective adoptive parents pay the expenses (related to the pregnancy) of prospective birth mothers because the adoptive parents end up expecting a return on their "investment." In many cases this practice causes birth mothers to feel indebted to the prospective adoptive parents and coerced into a decision to relinquish parental rights.

Gritter also believes that infant adoption has become a lucrative business that attracts many nonadoption professionals such as attorneys. Adoption, he says, has become a "business model that aggressively recruits consumers on a buyer-beware basis" (254). Today, for many reasons, there are fewer infants to adopt. Society has become more accepting of single parenting and out-of-wedlock births, which allows more single mothers to parent their babies. Birth control and abortion also decrease the number of babies available for adoption. At the same time, says Gritter, infertility rates in the United States have increased, also for several reasons. Those who might have had birth children are not having them because of age and sexually transmitted diseases. Those adopting are more interested in infants than in older "special needs" children.

In an article in *Money* (April 2003), Gay Jervey agrees that money cannot be left out of the discussion on the value of adoption. Although adoptive parents consider their children "priceless," adoption does involve an exchange of money, sometimes a great deal of money.

Another who agrees is Adam Pertman, author of *Adoption Nation* (2000) and executive director of the Evan B. Donaldson Adoption Institute. Although Pertman definitely does not advocate doing away with adoption, he writes, "Big money threatens to undermine the confidence that prospective parents and the general public must have if adoption is to fit comfortably into America's cultural mosaic, without people developing a new set of negative values about the process" (51).

Concerned United Birthparents does not advocate the "overthrow" of adoption but *does* advocate for the preservation of birth families as a first choice. In a brochure prepared for birth parents considering adoption, the CUB brochure states, "The words that follow are not intended to be anti-adoption . . . but in order to be truly a good thing, it needs to be a well-considered decision."

It is not difficult to find those who believe that adoption, in spite of its faults, is a good thing. Elizabeth Bartholet is one of adoption's most outspoken champions. In her book *Family Bonds* (1993), Bartholet agrees that adoption is "often built on a foundation of human misery" (xx). But she looks at adoption in a way that is different from the way that those who oppose it see adoption. "In an ideal world," she writes, "we would eliminate the social ills that force some to give up the children they bear and that deprive others of their fertility" (xx). She offers that the argument of her book is "that in the world in which we live today and will live tomorrow, the social ills with which we are familiar do and will exist" (xx-xxi). Adoption works, says Bartholet, and "should be understood as a possible alternative to the blood-based family form" (xxi). She adds that although adoption has the potential to exploit, "it is not *inherently* exploitive" (xxi).

Another adoption champion is Jerome Smith, author of *The Realities of Adoption* (1997). Smith says the fact that he has changed his views about adoption does not alarm him. What does worry him are statements made by some experts who say that adoption doesn't work and should be abolished. Smith thinks that in the recent past, adoption has gone through more changes than any other part of social work. Adoption is not without difficulties, he writes. But unlike some foes of adoption, he still sees adoption as a solution to three interrelated social issues: child dependency, unwanted pregnancies, and infertility.

Adam Pertman, author of *Adoption Nation* (2000), is another of adoption's champions. Although he admits that adoption is fraught with controversy as well as aspects that call out for change, he writes, "The emerging new realities undeniably are replete with problems and paradoxes. They are raising new issues for families and creating new dilemmas for the country. But they also are more sensible, more humane, and more focused on children's well-being than the realities being left behind" (7).

Summary

Controversy in adoption is likely to continue for the foreseeable and not-so-foreseeable future. Each controversial topic represents a huge range of opinion. Perhaps if the student of adoption remembers only one phrase, it will be "in the best interest of the child," which is not a cliché but a working command.

Adoption is a complex subject and will not please everyone all of the time. But discussion is useful because from discussion comes change. The entity of adoption will respond to some, but not all, of the attempts to "fix" it. Every minute counts in the life of a child. The challenge is to find new and better ways to make sure that all children have safe and nurturing homes.

References and Further Reading

Adamec, Christine, and William Pierce. 2000. *The Encyclopedia of Adoption,* 2nd ed. New York: Facts on File.

"Adoption Controversies." 1999. *CQ Researcher* 9, no. 34. September 10.

American Civil Liberties Union. 1999. "ACLU Fact Sheet: Overview of Lesbian and Gay Parenting, Adoption, and Foster Care." Accessed at http://www.aclu.org.

American Civil Liberties Union. 2005. "Gay Parenting Does Not Place Children at Risk." In *Gay and Lesbian Families,* Kate Burns, ed. Farmington Hills, MI: Greenhaven Press, 41–45.

Amos, Deborah. 2006. "Finding Home: Fifty Years of International Adoption." American RadioWorks and National Public Radio, January 8. Accessed at http://americanradioworks.publicradio.org/features/adoption/j1.html.

Ashe, Nancy. "Legalized Abandonment." Accessed at http://www.crisis-pregnancy.com/birth-mother/legalized-abandonment-safe-haven-laws.

Ashe, Nancy. "Report on Safe Haven Laws Draws Criticism, Support." Accessed at http://www.adopting.org/adoptions/report-on-safe-haven-laws-draws-criticism-support.html.

Bartholet, Elizabeth. 2005. "Adoption and Race." *Adoption Today.* June/July: 21–23.

Bartholet, Elizabeth. 1993. *Family Bonds: Adoption and the Politics of Parenting.* Boston: Houghton Mifflin.

Bastard Nation: The Adoptee Rights Organization. Accessed at http://www.bastards.org.

Beauvais-Godwin, Laura, and Raymond Godwin. 2005. *The Complete Adoption Book: Everything You Need to Know to Adopt a Child,* 3rd ed. Holbrook, MA: Adams Media.

Berger, Virginia. 2005. "Ban Hurts Children." *National Law Journal*. April 4. Accessed at http://wf2la3.webfeat.org.

Bernstein, Nina. 2001. "Few Choose Legal Havens to Abandon Babies." *New York Times*. August 31: Al.

Boudreaux, Donald. 2004. "Infant Adoption Should Be Deregulated." In *Issues in Adoption*, William Dudley, ed. Farmington Hills, MI: Greenhaven Press, 109–120.

Brooks, Dorothy E. 1991. "Black/White Transracial Adoption: An Update." *OURS*. July/August: 19–21.

Burke, Kate. 2004. "Arguments against Opening Adoption Records Are Spurious." In *Issues in Adoption*, William Dudley, ed. Farmington Hills, MI: Greenhaven Press, 125–128.

Cameron, Paul. 2005. "Gay Adoption Should Not Be Accepted." In *Gay and Lesbian Families*, Kate Burns, ed. Farmington Hills, MI: Greenhaven Press, 51–54.

Carp, E. Wayne. 1998. *Family Matters: Secrecy and Disclosure in the History of Adoption*. Cambridge, MA: Harvard University Press.

Cecere, Laura. 2004. "More Federal Regulation May Displace Small International Adoption Agencies." In *Issues in Adoption*, William Dudley, ed. Farmington Hills, MI: Greenhaven Press, 93–96.

Child Welfare Information Gateway. 2000. "Gay and Lesbian Adoptive Parents: Resources for Professionals and Parents." Accessed at http://www.childwelfare.gov/pubs/f_gay/index.cfm.

Child Welfare Information Gateway. 2004. "Impact of Adoption on Adopted Persons: A Factsheet for Families." Accessed at http://www.childwelfare.gov/pubs/f_issues.cfm.

Child Welfare Information Gateway. 1994. "Transracial and Transcultural Adoption." Accessed at http://www.childwelfare.gov/pubs/f_trans.cfm.

Cohen, Mary Anne. 2000. "A Short Personal History of Adoption Reform." First published in the *Bastard Quarterly* (Fall 2000). Accessed at http://www.cubbirthparents.org/personalhist.html.

Cooper, Garry. 2006. "Are Gay Parents Good for Children?" *Psychotherapy Networker*. January/February: 22–23.

Cunningham, Ann Marie. 2004."More Regulation Is Necessary to Protect People from International Adoption Scams." In *Issues in Adoption*, William Dudley, ed. Farmington Hills, MI: Greenhaven Press, 79–83.

Cushman, Candi. 2004. "Adoption Workers Are Wrongly Biased in Favor of Gays and Lesbians." In *Issues in Adoption*, William Dudley, ed. Farmington Hills, MI: Greenhaven Press, 188–196.

Dailard, Cynthia. 2000. "The Drive to Enact 'Infant Abandonment' Laws—A Rush to Judgment?" *The Guttmacher Report on Public Policy* 3, no. 4 (August). Accessed at http://www.guttmacher.org/pubs/tgr/03/4/gr030401.html.

Dailey, Tim. 2005. "Gay Parenting Places Children at Risk." In *Gay and Lesbian Families,* Kate Burns, ed. Farmington Hills, MI: Greenhaven Press, 29–40.

Dudley, William, ed. 2004. *Issues in Adoption.* Farmington Hills, MI: Greenhaven Press.

Ethica. 2003. "Safe Haven for Whom? An Ethica Position Paper." Silver Spring, MD: Ethica. Accessed at http://www.ethicanet.org/item.php?recorded=savehaven.

Evan B. Donaldson Adoption Institute. 2005. "Gay Adoption Is Commonly Accepted." In *Gay and Lesbian Families,* Kate Burns, ed. Farmington Hills, MI: Greenhaven Press, 46–50.

Freidmutter, Cindy. 2004. "More Regulation of International Adoption Agencies Is Necessary." In *Issues in Adoption,* William Dudley, ed. Farmington Hills, MI: Greenhaven Press, 84–87.

Gabbard, Lynn. 1995. "Unnecessary Barriers to Special Needs Adoption Must Be Eliminated." In *Adoption: Opposing Viewpoints,* Andrew Harnack, ed. San Diego: Greenhaven Press, 279–285.

George, Jason. 2004. "Program Questioned after Another Dead Baby Is Found." *New York Times.* March 20: B5.

Gerow, Darlene. 2004. "The Infant Adoption Industry Should Be Abolished." In *Issues in Adoption,* William Dudley, ed. Farmington Hills, MI: Greenhaven Press, 49–65.

Gill, Owen, and Barbara Jackson. 1983. *Adoption and Race: Black, Asian, and Mixed Race Children in White Families.* London: Batsford Academic and Educational.

Goldsmith, Susan. 2004. "Transracial Adoptions Can Be Beneficial." In *Issues in Adoption,* William Dudley, ed. Farmington Hills, MI: Greenhaven Press, 37–41.

Gritter, James L. 1997. *The Spirit of Open Adoption.* Washington, DC: Child Welfare League of America Press.

Groze, Vic. 1995. "Single Adults Should Be Encouraged to Adopt Children." In *Adoption: Opposing Viewpoints,* Andrew Harnack, ed. San Diego: Greenhaven Press, 126–134.

Hall, Beth, and Gail Steinberg. 2005. "PACT Editor's Commentary." *Adoption Today.* June/July: 23.

Harnack, Andrew, ed. 1995. *Adoption: Opposing Viewpoints.* San Diego: Greenhaven Press.

Hogan, Maureen. 2004. "The Federal Government Must Regulate Adoption." In *Issues in Adoption,* William Dudley, ed. Farmington Hills, MI: Greenhaven Press, 88–92.

Jenny, Carole, Thomas A. Roesler, and Kimberly Poyer. 1994. "Are Children at Risk for Sexual Abuse by Homosexuals?" *Pediatrics* 94, no. 1 (July): 41–44.

Jervey, Gay. 2003. "Pricele$$." *Money* 32, no. 4 (April).

Johnston, Philip. 2005. "Gay and Lesbian Couples Given Adoption Rights." *News Telegraph.* December 31.

Jordan, Jinny, ed. 2005. "Our Reflections: What Type of Racial Prejudice Have You Experienced?" *Adoption Today.* June/July: 45–49.

Kirk, H. David. 1984. *Shared Fate: A Theory and Method of Adoptive Relationships,* rev. ed. Brentwood Bay, BC: Ben-Simon Publications.

Lowe, Heather. "What You Should Know if You're Considering Adoption for Your Baby." Encinitas, CA: Concerned United Birthparents. Accessed at http://cubirthparents.org.

Means, Marianne. 2000. "Whose Rights Rule in Adoption?" *Liberal Opinion Week.* June 19.

Melina, Lois R., and Sharon K. Roszia. 1993. *The Open Adoption Experience: A Complete Guide for Adoptive and Birth Families—from Making the Decision through the Child's Growing Years.* New York: HarperCollins.

Milbrand, Lisa. 2006. "Heritage Starts at Home." *Adoptive Families.* April, 36–37.

Miller, Naomi. 1992. *Single Parents by Choice: A Growing Trend in Family Life.* New York: Plenum Press.

Mitchell, Melisha, with Jane Nast, Barbara Busharis, and Pam Hasigawa. 1999. "Voluntary Registries Are an Inadequate Substitute for Open Records Laws." *Adoptive Families.* January/February. Reprinted in *Issues in Adoption,* William Dudley, ed. (2004) Farmington Hills, MI: Greenhaven Press, 132–138.

Montgomery, Michael. 2006. "New Law Offers Hope in Fighting Adoption Fraud." January 8. American RadioWorks and National Public Radio. Accessed at http://americanradioworks.publicradio.org/features/adoption/j1.html.

National Council for Adoption. "New Hampshire Eliminates Confidentiality in Adoption: Records Law a Harmful Aberration." Accessed at http://www.adoptioncouncil.org/media_news_04_0513.

News and Notes. 2006. "Domestic Transracial Adoptions Increase." *Adoptive Families.* March/April, 11.

News and Notes. 2005. "Positive Outcomes in Birth Family Reunions." *Adoptive Families.* September/October: 13.

Paton, Jean. 1954. *The Adopted Break Silence: Forty Men and Women Describe Their Search for Their Natural Parents.* Philadelphia: Life History Study Center.

Pertman, Adam. 2000. *Adoption Nation: How the Adoption Revolution Is Transforming America.* New York: Basic Books.

Prowler, Mady. "Single Parent Adoption: What You Need to Know." National Adoption Center. Accessed through the National Adoption Information Clearinghouse, http://naic.acf.hhs.gov.

Rappaport, Bruce M. 1998. *The Open Adoption Book: A Guide for Adoption without Tears.* New York: Hungry Minds.

Rappaport, Bruce M. 2005. "Not Open Adoption, Just Adoption." *Adoptive Families.* September/October: 17.

Robinson-English, Tracey. 2005. "The Joy of Adoption." *Ebony.* November: 182–186.

Romanchik, Brenda. 1999. *What Is Open Adoption?* Royal Oak, MI: R-Squared Press. Shorter version available at http://www.openadoptioninsight.org/what_is_open_adoption.htm.

Shawyer, Joss. 1979. *Death by Adoption.* Auckland, New Zealand: Cicada Press.

Silverman, Arnold R., and William Feigelman. 1990. "Adjustment in Interracial Adoptees: An Overview." In *The Psychology of Adoption,* David Brodzinsky and Marshall D. Schechter, eds. New York: Oxford University Press, 199-200.

Simon, Rita J., and Howard Alstein. 2000. *Adoption Across Borders: Serving the Children of Transracial and Intercountry Adoptions.* Lanham, MD: Rowman and Littlefield.

Smith, Jerome. 1997. *The Realities of Adoption.* Lanham, MD: Madison Books.

Smith, Jerome, and Franklin Miroff. 1987. *You're Our Child: The Adoption Experience.* Lanham, MD: Madison Books.

Solinger, Rickie. 2001. *Beggars and Choosers: How the Politics of Choice Shapes Adoption, Abortion, and Welfare in the United States.* New York: Hill and Wang.

Sorosky, Arthur D., Annette Baran, and Reuben Pannor. 1978. *The Adoption Triangle: The Effects of the Sealed Record on Adoptees, Birth Parents, and Adoptive Parents.* Garden City, NY: Anchor Press/Doubleday.

Sullum, Jacob. 2004. "Government Regulations and Procedures for Adoption Are Too Cumbersome." In *Issues in Adoption,* William Dudley, ed. Farmington Hills, MI: Greenhaven Press, 97–108.

U.S. Department of State. "Immigration Visas Issued to Orphans Coming to the U.S." Accessed at http://travel.state.gov/family/adoption/stats/stats_451.html.

Wardle, Lynn. 2004. "Restrictions on Gay and Lesbian Adoption Are Not Unconstitutional." In *Issues in Adoption,* William Dudley, ed. Farmington Hills, MI: Greenhaven Press, 181–187.

3

Adoption around the World

A doption practices vary across the globe; in much of the world, adoptions are informal and unofficial. Whatever the mechanism, however, most cultures agree on one principle—that adoption should meet the needs of society, the family, and the adopted children.

Although some Islamic societies interpret the Koran as banning adoption, in many cases families and friends still care for orphaned or abandoned children. According to *The Encyclopedia of Adoption* (2000), adoption is practiced in Iran (at least by Shiite Muslims) and in Tunisia and Indonesia. Christians in Egypt and Syria may also adopt children.

In the middle of the nineteenth century in the United States, Charles Loring Brace, a social reformer and founder of the New York Children's Aid Society, believed he had found an answer for the more than 10,000 homeless children in New York City. Brace started the Orphan Train movement, which moved approximately 150,000 children from the northeast United States on trains to foster and adoptive homes in the West and Midwest. Brace received both praise and criticism for his efforts, which ended in 1929.

Even though the preceding numbers are huge, they pale in comparison to today's orphan situation in Africa and Asia. "Children on the Brink" is a major international report released on July 10, 2004, at the fourteenth International AIDS Conference in Barcelona, Spain. It provides statistics on orphans from eighty-eight countries.

Millions of children in sub-Saharan Africa are orphans, one-third because of AIDS, according to some reports. And although a 2004 report from the United Nations Children's Fund (UNICEF) estimated a total of 43 million orphans in the region, intercountry adoption is rarely an option. Of 40,000 intercountry adoptions around the world each year, less than a thousand children come from Africa. According to a report from National Public Radio on February 15, 2006, a valid fear of child trafficking accounts for some of the reluctance. But suspicions and fears of cultural imperialism are even more prominent, as are disputes over the meaning of family and kinship. Nigeria, for example, has recently tightened its laws against intercountry adoption because of stories of children being "trafficked" as sex slaves or laborers.

In Rwanda, according to UNICEF, one million children are orphans. How to care for them is one of Rwanda's greatest challenges. The genocide of 1994 had an enormous role in creating the problem; HIV/AIDS adds to it. In Rwanda, the oldest child in the family is often the head of the household because both parents have died. Along with hunger, the children suffer from emotional scars. In 2001 UNICEF introduced a mentoring program in which volunteer "mothers" and "fathers" receive training in children's issues and rights. The volunteers, who are the children's neighbors, visit the children in the mornings and evenings to give them advice about everyday problems. Agricultural skills are also needed, and teaching the children these skills is another way UNICEF and Rwanda's Ministry of Social Affairs help the orphans build a better future.

In a three-part series on AIDS in the *Denver Post*, reporter Bruce Finley tells the heart-breaking stories of some of these orphans. One is thirteen-year-old Veneranda in Tanzania, who lost both parents to AIDS. Veneranda, who is now HIV-positive herself, has been caring for her brother and the two young children of her aunt. The estimated prevalence of HIV in Tanzania is 7 percent, or approximately two million people.

Africa has the greatest *proportion* of children who are orphans; Asia has the largest *number* of orphans, 65 million in 2001. Who will take care of these children?

Dr. Jane Aronson is one example of an individual trying to do what she can to help with an overwhelming problem. The clinical assistant professor at the Weill Medical College of Cornell University has evaluated more than 4,000 children adopted internationally. According to an article in *People* magazine, she has traveled to orphanages in Russia, Romania, Bulgaria, China, Vietnam,

Ethiopia, and Latin America. In 1997 she founded the Worldwide Orphans Foundation (WWO). The organization documents the medical and developmental conditions of children in orphanages around the world to identify health-care needs (Erwin, 2005). The Orphan Ranger program (something like a medical Peace Corps) uses university students and health-care professionals who live and work in the orphanages. They are fluent in the native language and work in conjunction with orphanage staff members to improve the physical, nutritional, and emotional health of the children. Since 1997, Orphan Rangers have worked in Russia, Ukraine, Kazakhstan, Bulgaria, India, Ecuador, Vietnam, China, Serbia, Montenegro, and Ethiopia. The program treats orphans with HIV/AIDS in Vietnam and Ethiopia and has started training programs for physicians in these countries to care for HIV-infected orphans.

On a larger scale, UNICEF with UNAIDS launched a campaign in late 2005 called the Global Campaign on Children and AIDS: Unite for Children, Unite against AIDS. The goal of the campaign is to bring attention and resources to address the impact of AIDS on children.

Although some countries have no formal adoption programs at this time, policies and practices concerning adoption continue to evolve. Countries that previously had few adoption laws are formulating them. New laws supplant older ones.

The following countries represent a cross-section of people and places: governments with differing structures, different religions, rich and poor, large and small, developed and not-as-developed.

Canada

Adoption policies and practices in Canada are similar in many ways to those of the United States. For example, the home study is a common requirement for all adoptions in Canada. But, just as regulations vary from state to state in the United States, rules and regulations vary in Canada from province to province and territory to territory. The mechanisms of a private adoption in Quebec will be different from one in Ontario. Same-sex couples can adopt as a unit in some provinces but not in others. Some provinces prohibit prospective adoptive parents from paying expenses of the birth mother.

As in the United States and the United Kingdom, the number of prospective adoptive parents for infants far exceeds the number of babies available for adoption within the country. This situation often leads prospective adoptive parents to pursue intercountry adoption.

Specialized rules and regulations apply to intercountry adoptions, including the need for a home study specifically geared to the country from which the child comes. In recent years, China has provided Canadians with the largest number of internationally adopted children. In 2003, Canadians adopted 1,108 children from China. According to *The Complete Adoption Book* (Beauvais-Godwin and Godwin, 2005), the number of intercountry adoptions in Canada has remained relatively stable for several years. One difference between Canadian and U.S. law has to do with the definition of the word *orphan*. Because U.S. law is more restrictive, a child from another country who cannot legally enter the United States may find a home in Canada. A website that explains each province's regulations regarding intercountry adoption can be found at www.interlog.com/~ladybug/canagen.htm.

If prospective adoptive parents choose domestic adoption, they can proceed through the public sector or the private sector. If they choose the private route to adoption, they will work with a social worker who will do the home study (involving at least three meetings, including a home visit), the submission of medical records, the securing of background checks, and letters of reference.

A similar process applies to those who adopt through Children's Aid Societies (CAS), but there will be no fees for the study. Pre-adoptive parents will likely be required to take eight to ten weeks of adoption preparation classes. Although a family might receive an infant through this route, they are more likely to do an adoption involving an older, hard-to-place child or a sibling group.

The North American Council on Adoptable Children (NACAC) promotes and supports permanent families for children and youth in the United States and Canada who have been in care, especially those in foster care and with special needs. The website is http://www.nacac.org.

The United Kingdom

The United Kingdom is sometimes mistakenly called Great Britain or Britain. The UK, however, consists of four countries—England, Scotland, Wales, and Northern Ireland. Specific adoption laws may apply to only certain countries in the UK, but in general the laws are similar.

According to the Department for Education and Skills, the Adoption Act of 1976 governed England and Wales until recently. In 2002 the Adoption and Children Act received royal assent and overhauled the older act. Goals of the new act were to modernize the legal framework for both domestic and intercountry adoptions.

On December 20, 2005, the British Association for Adoption and Fostering (BAAF) issued a press release about the new act, which became law on December 30, 2005. The act has several new provisions, including the following three: (1) unmarried couples in England and Wales, including gay and lesbian couples, can adopt jointly (previously only one member of the couple could be the legal parent); (2) special guardianship orders now give foster-care givers, relatives, and others who care for a child the opportunity to apply for a guardianship order lasting until the child turns eighteen (according to BAAF, which campaigned for some of these changes, special guardianship will give more security to children who cannot live with their birth parents for one reason or another, but for whom birth parent ties still exist); and (3) birth mothers and other birth relatives have the legal right to request that an intermediary trace an adopted person (who is now an adult) to find out if the adoptee would welcome contact. The latter provision will allow (for the first time) birth mothers to learn how their child is doing and possibly make contact. The adopted adult must give consent and may decline contact. Framers of the act say it puts children at the center of the adoption process where they belong, allows more people to adopt "looked after" (foster) children, provides an independent review mechanism for prospective adopters who believe they have been turned down unfairly, and helps cut harmful delays in the adoption process.

Adoption policies in the United Kingdom are similar in many respects to those in the United States. Randy Comfort, founder of Our Place, a center for families who foster and adopt, points out that the greatest similarity within both countries (and perhaps in most countries that do adoptions) is that there are exceptions to every rule, and that by its very nature, adoption is rarely a "straightforward" process. Other noteworthy similarities to U.S. practices are active recruitment of parents for older children, including the use of websites featuring children who are waiting for families; training for those preparing to adopt, including information about the process on several websites; the home-study process (or adoption assessment) as the cornerstone of the approval process; a "staged" (that is, in stages) visitation program for the to-be-adopted child entering a new family; and the child taking the last name of the adoptive family and having the right to inherit from them.

Requirements for adoptive parents in the UK also are similar to those in the United States. Requirements are not usually rigid, except for those having to do with a person's criminal record or age (over twenty-one). Religious beliefs, marital status, economic status, employment status, and home ownership *usually* will not affect the ability to adopt, although reality can differ from practice. (In the United States, similar requirements may depend on the agency or the state.) "Causes for delay" may include recent fertility treatments, a child in the home who is less than two years older or younger than the child to be adopted, very limited housing/bedroom space, a recent criminal conviction or a pending criminal charge, a new relationship, and having lost a child recently. "Causes for concern and further study" may be mental health problems or other health problems, depending on the severity. A criminal conviction for an offense against a child or other serious offenses to a child in the adoptive family who was "taken into care" are examples of situations that will derail the process. Details on this subject in the United Kingdom are available at http://www.adoption.org.uk/information/page1.htm.

Countries can and do share ideas as to new and better ways of helping children. The concept of *concurrent planning* is one such idea. According to the information website http://www.adoption-net.co.uk, Lutheran Family Services in Seattle, Washington, pioneered the concept of concurrent planning, which is widely used in the United States today. The approach is to ask the adults (prospective adoptive parents) to take the "risk" (of losing the child who has been placed with them for adoption—if a child is returned to birth parents) in order to spare the child a move (or many moves). Children who have had to leave their birth homes because of neglect or abuse are already feeling vulnerable. With concurrent planning, a family is not only approved for adoption but also for foster care. If the birth parents fulfill their requirements, the child may go back to the birth home, and the adoptive parents will have to go along with and help facilitate this move. But if the birth parents cannot fulfill their obligations under the court order in a reasonable time, the court may terminate their parental rights and the child may be able to stay in the pre-adoptive home (and be adopted).

In the "Director's Report" (*Adoption UK*, 2006, 7), Jonathan Pearce refers to ongoing problems that the Adoption and Children Act of 2002 should eventually help rectify. One has to do with discrepancies between funding available to children in foster care and that available to them in adoptive homes. Other problems concern support services to adoptive families, which even now sometimes seem inadequate, often because of lack of funding; and services to families dealing with children who have serious problems, for example, attachment-related behavior difficulties. Pearce observes that if services are not made available to families who adopt traumatized children, the whole adoptive family is traumatized. Then when a disruption occurs, professionals blame the family. All of these problems are similar to those encountered in the United States.

There are, however, important differences between the two countries. In the UK, the new Adoption Act allows same-sex couples to adopt as a unit, lets parents request paid parental leave for twenty-six weeks plus an additional twenty-six weeks, if needed; and minimizes costs and allows for a standard national child benefit allowance. In addition, intercountry adoptions are relatively small in number and are somewhat discouraged. According to the website http://www.adoption.org.uk.information/page1.htm, approximately 300 children are adopted from overseas each year in the United Kingdom. The website gives this cautionary advice: "Such adoptions can be plagued by legal and administrative complexities, and many believe that the needs of these children would be better served if they were able to secure a place within a family in their country of origin. For some the idea of allowing children to be adopted by a foreign person or family, who are almost always from a very different culture, and are often of different racial origin, is a very questionable practice."

Minor differences in terminology include the common description of children in foster care as "looked after" children and the description of foster parents as "foster carers."

Russia

A special *Adoptive Families* (September/October 2005) update on Russian adoption reports that new incentives are encouraging Russians to adopt more children in their country. (In 1996, for example, Russians adopted 9,000 children, but approximately 30,000 become available for adoption every year.)

As in China, Russia began to view intercountry adoption as a way of alleviating the problem of overcrowded orphanages, and in 1991 Russia began allowing intercountry adoptions. In 2004, U.S. citizens adopted 5,865 children from Russia. According to the U.S. State Department (http://travel.state.gov), that number dropped to 4,639 the following year. That year, the office responsible for adoptions, the Russian Ministry of Education and Science, started scrutinizing the adoption process more carefully than before and began to change some adoption procedures. As a result, U.S. families adopting from Russia now may experience a longer wait for a child.

One reason for the increased scrutiny had to do with reports that as many as thirteen Russian children had died over the years as a result of mistreatment by their American adoptive parents. In a recent case, police arrested the adoptive parents of an eight-year-old boy who had died of malnutrition. (The parents claimed malnutrition was the result of cystic fibrosis.)

Because of highly publicized cases such as this one, 62 percent of Russians responding to questions in a public-opinion poll said they wanted tighter restrictions on intercountry adoption; 39 percent wanted an end to intercountry adoptions.

The Ministry of Education and Science began officially reaccrediting agencies in the spring of 2005, although the process had actually started earlier. If one or more post-placement reports were missing, the foreign agency could lose accreditation.

The estimated number of orphans or abandoned children in Russian orphanages ranges from 170,000 to two million. In *Child Welfare* (March/April 1989), Valeria Sergeevna Mukhina, a psychologist, unsparingly describes what may happen to children without parents in residential institutions such as orphanages:

"Deviations in physical and mental development can be observed in many of them" (235).

One of the reasons for difficulty is that children in large residential facilities must adapt to great numbers of peers, which creates "emotional tension and anxiety, and boosts aggressiveness" (236). The children lack "a private place" where they can go when they want to get away from other children and adults.

Because of competition with peers, along with an unrealized need for attention and love, they may treat peers and younger children with cruelty. In addition, a "we-ness" may develop, in which the attitude toward the institution may be "you owe us" or "give it to us." According to the author, children in large institutions simultaneously seek attention and reject it. They need and crave love, but their behavior may push it away.

Mukhina describes how the government under Mikhail Gorbachev began meeting to try to give "real care and psychology-based assistance" to these children in order "to eliminate their posture of parasitism, negativism, and alienation" (237). A new children's fund resolved to reduce the number of children in each facility and to staff these homes with "conscientious persons who love children" (238). Even if a residential facility has the best equipment, furniture, clothes, and toys, says the author, children still need an adult in whom to put their trust. Teachers must be trained in caring for children deprived of parents. This care must teach children to be responsible for themselves and others.

In 1998, the Publishing House of Lenin State Pedagogical Institute in Moscow published a textbook entitled *Deprived of Parents' Care*. Later, a series of articles, "Development of Individuality in a Child Deprived of Parents' Care," contained the results of work with children brought up in homes for small children, older children's homes, and boarding schools. Children who grow up in residential care, says Mukhina, must each have a "mediator," someone who will introduce them to "real life" (240).

Since the time of Mukhina's writings, new evidence has surfaced to support her views. For example, Carol Weitzman and Lisa Albers in *Pediatric Clinics of North America* (2005) report that, based on longitudinal studies of Romanian children, "a substantial number of post-institutionalized children demonstrate significant cognitive difficulties" (1400). Weitzman and Albers cite a landmark longitudinal study of institutionalized children in Britain that followed these children for sixteen years. The children who had previously showed "indiscriminate sociability and attention seeking in their earlier years had problems with peers by age sixteen" (1409).

Some observers say that the concept of adoption in general does not seem as accepted in Russia as it is in some other countries. In the past ten years, domestic adoptions in Russia have dropped by 50 percent. For the first time (in 2004), the number of intercountry adoptions exceeded the number of domestic adoptions.

To encourage more people to adopt within the country, Russia has now passed legislation requiring orphans to stay for at least six months on a list of children available for adoption in the country before becoming eligible for adoption by foreigners. Also, there are no longer stringent requirements for a certain income level and type of housing for prospective Russian adoptive parents.

Some Russian authorities have called for a moratorium on all U.S. adoptions of Russian children. Others have demanded psychological testing of prospective adoptive parents; judges in at least one region have implemented this requirement. Some have called for an end to independent adoptions, as well as stricter control over accredited agencies.

At this time the Russian Ministry of Education and Science still supports intercountry adoptions. Those most involved are hopeful that important reforms will prevent a moratorium.

China

China is another country that has attempted to deal with the problem of overcrowded orphanages through intercountry adoption. As a result of overpopulation, China instituted the One-Child Policy in 1979. (Mao Tse-tung had earlier encouraged families to have as many children as possible as a way of showing that the country was strong and wealthy.) In a 2003 article in the *Arizona Journal of International and Comparative Law,* Sara R. Wallace writes that the One-Child Policy produced 100,000 parentless babies, 95 percent of which were girls.

China has a short history of both domestic and international adoption. Chinese law first recognized the practice of domestic adoption in 1981. Ten years later, the government enacted the Adoption Law of China, which allowed people outside the country to adopt Chinese children. The following year, the country enacted the 1992 Adoption Law of China, which treated foreigners, regardless of their heritage or Chinese connections, the same as its own citizens. The purpose of the 1992 Adoption Law was to protect lawful adoptions and eliminate black market adoptions. Nevertheless, illegal adoptions continued, which caused the Chinese government in 1993 to suspend all adoptions for ten months. During this time the government ratified procedures for international adoptions and established the China Adoption Organization (CAO) as a central administrative entity to coordinate intercountry adoptions of Chinese children. Applications must now include a police report and proof of age, marital status, occupation, finances, and health conditions. If and when the CAO approves the application, it helps find a child for the potential adoptive parents.

In 1999 the government made changes to allow more individuals and families (both domestic and foreign) to adopt. These changes included: (1) a lowering of the minimum age of applicants from thirty-five to thirty years; (2) permission for those adopting orphans, handicapped, and abandoned children to adopt more than one child; and (3) a relaxation of procedural requirements for domestic as compared to intercountry adoptions.

In 1998, Kay Johnson, Huang Banghan, and Wang Liyao published a behind-the-scenes study of domestic Chinese adoptions titled *Population and Development Review.* The authors wanted to know why orphanages, especially in southern and central China, had significant increases in their populations in the late 1980s and early 1990s. They pointed out that the timing of the increases coincided with the government's efforts to strictly implement birth-control policies.

Beginning in 1991, the State Council had restricted the adoption of healthy "foundlings" to those who had no other children *and* were over thirty-five years of age. (This law codified previous local regulations from the 1980s used to support the one-child norm for population control.) Also beginning in 1991, the new law permitted international adoptions by childless couples who were more than thirty-five years of age, therefore enlarging the pool of potential adopters to include those who lived outside of China.

The authors report that until the time of their study, no one since 1949 had done much systematic study of Chinese adoption practices. (Before that time, the studies were mainly historical and anthropological.) In the 1980s, however, some demographers began to wonder about the fate of the so-called missing girls. This term referred to a shortfall in recorded female births compared to the biologically normal ratios of female-to-male births. Questions arose, such as: What was happening to the infant girls? Were they not being recorded, or were they being aborted or killed? Some studies indicated that perhaps people were informally *adopting* the missing girls.

Questions led to more questions. Were people "hiding" the girls from authorities? Were these arrangements permanent or temporary? How did abandonment fit into the picture? (The authors say that Chinese demographers argued that abandoned girls would ultimately end up in government-run welfare centers, which would then record them.)

No one knows how many children are abandoned in China each year. Estimates range from 100,000 to 160,000, but the authors speculate that the actual number is higher. If the estimate that 20 percent of abandoned children end up in the care of the government is correct, what happens to the rest of the children?

The authors report that a "continuum" of care and planning seems to be involved. On one end of the continuum are parents who leave their children in a place that allows the parents not to get caught. (Abandonment *is* a crime in China, but few of these crimes have been prosecuted.) On the other end are parents whose abandonment appears to involve the making of an "adoption plan." About 20 percent of the parents who abandoned a child said they had placed a child on someone's doorstep, possibly because they knew those people would make good parents. Favored couples were those with no other children or with a son but no daughters. About half of the birth parents claimed to know what had happened to their child. The authors concluded that because of the care with which many parents try to find a new home for their child, abandonment becomes more like arranging an adoption.

At the beginning of the study, the authors noted three phenomena affecting young girls: (1) female child abandonment, (2) skewed sex ratios, and (3) some kind of informal adoption involving girl children. They hoped the study would discover the answers to these questions: Was there a "culture" that allowed for the adoption of foundling girls? Were prospective adoptive parents deterred by the 1991 law?

The authors observed that several scholars have written that the adoption of foundlings is uncommon today because of cultural and societal attitudes. Were people willing to adopt unrelated children of unknown parentage? Or was it the law that kept them from adopting?

Before setting out to answer their questions, the authors noted that abandonment of girl children has a long history in China. (Infanticide and abandonment of children also occurred in many other countries and cultures, including Europe, worsening in times of famine and stress.) After 1949, abandonment and infanticide declined in China (except during the famine of 1959–1961) with the rise of political stability and improved economic conditions.

But, beginning in the 1980s, the government began campaigns to implement a one-child policy, even in rural areas. Because of resistance to this policy, the provincial governments in the late 1980s allowed a second birth child if the first was a girl. In fewer areas, policies allowed two children—if they were several years apart in age.

In late 1995 and 1996, the authors used questionnaires to gather information from 629 families. Of these families, 237 had abandoned a child, and 392 had adopted a child. More than 95 percent of those who had abandoned a child or children lived in rural villages or towns; approximately 85 percent of the adoptive families also lived in rural villages or towns. The adoptions spanned the period between the 1950s to the study's publication (1998), with more than 90 percent occurring in the 1980s and 1990s. All but ten of the 237 abandonments occurred in that same time period.

The authors also interviewed forty of the adoptive families. They collected more data from welfare centers and from interviews with local officials, articles in government publications, newspapers, magazines, and journals.

The report gives many details. Highlights include the following: (1) except for three unmarried birth mothers of the 237 sampled, the birth parents were married; (2) most of the abandoning parents (88 percent) were engaged in "agriculture" as their occupation and lived in rural villages; and (3) the typical profile of an abandoned child is a healthy newborn girl with one or more older sisters and no brothers. Her parents do not make the decision lightly. They do so because they want a son. Family planning policies gave them "no choice." In 50 percent of cases, the birth father made the decision.

In addition to caring about what happened to the abandoned infants, the authors were interested in changes in *adoption customs* in decades of political change, rapid economic development, and severe legal restrictions in family size. The authors wondered if Chinese society resembled Korean society, in which bloodlines are of prime importance.

As mentioned earlier, in December 1991 when the government passed the first adoption law of the People's Republic, only childless couples over thirty-five years of age could adopt. Earlier, the government had made similar prohibitions to keep people from adopting girls as servants or as wives for other children in the family.

The authors report that partly as a result of legal restrictions, the number of officially recorded adoptions in China is low. Civil affairs officials say that as of 1996, they recorded approximately 8,000–10,000 *legal* adoptions per year. Other sources say the number is higher, perhaps 20,000 per year. As in the United States, statistics vary and may be incomplete. But the United States (with one-quarter as many citizens) has approximately 100,000 legally processed adoptions a year. As per longstanding custom, Chinese families may arrange many adoptions through private contracts that are not technically legal. These unofficial adoptions are thought to be one of the places where the missing girls can be found.

The majority of the adoptions studied were of children *not related* to the birth parents; less than 10 percent involved relatives. Most (307 of 392) adopted children were girls, and 60 percent had been abandoned. The authors point out that because of custom (for old-age security and continuation of the family line), boys still seem more valued than girls in China.

Except for two single women and seven single men, all of those adopting children were married couples. Approximately half (195) of the adoptive parents had no children at the time of the adoption. Only thirty-five involved people over age thirty-five as required by law for the adoption of healthy nonorphaned children. Most people in China consider age thirty-five too long to wait to become parents, and most Chinese people want to have children.

The other half of those adopting already had children. This contradicts the opinion of many Chinese scholars and officials who claim that only those unable to have children by birth would want to adopt.

The reason for adopting was most often to get a child of the other gender. Most of the families adopted girls because girls were most available. In some cases the families said that the gender of the child did not matter. The reasons people wanted girls tended to be emotional, such as the belief that girls are closer to their parents and tend to be more obedient than boys; they are usually caring and thoughtful. Some people wanted boys for the previously mentioned financial and functional reasons, such as someone to care for them in their old age, or a male to carry on the family line. For many people the ideal family is one boy and one girl.

The authors admit that some of their conclusions about children were "anecdotal" because they obviously spoke with those who were open (rather than secretive) about their adoptions. But these researchers found no situations in which a family had adopted a "daughter-in-law" or had adopted for the purpose of acquiring a family servant. Contemporary adoption in China for the child is similar to that in western countries: in general, parents adopt children for the joy the parents hope the children will bring to the family.

More than half (55 percent) of the adoptions in this study were "open" in the sense that the children knew of their adoptive status from the beginning (even though the government may not have known). Twenty percent of the parents in the sample planned to wait to tell the child the truth until the child was older. Approximately 25 percent of the parents hoped to be able to keep the secret of the adoption from the child forever—even if others in the community knew of the adoption.

In the case of infertile couples, the desire for secrecy had more to do with the "shame" of infertility than a reflection on the status of the child. For example, parents might consider secrecy more important with a boy who is expected to carry on the parents' bloodline.

In interviews, almost all of the parents in the study expressed as much affection for their adopted children as for birth children. Some claimed they loved the adopted child *more* than their birth children. In three cases the adoptive parents returned children to the birth family. But these situations did not have permanency as their goal; the aim was to hide the children from birth-planning authorities. In general, adoptive parents expected their "rights and duties" to be "complete and permanent" even when the children knew their birth parents.

Certain negative consequences did result from the 1991 Adoption Law. (One factor that did not turn out to be a problem for families in this study was adopting under age thirty-five.) Childless couples adopted approximately half of the healthy abandoned children, and most were below the required age. None received a fine. But a third of the adoptive parents who broke the law by adopting when they already had a child or children received fines, sometimes quite large. The remaining two-thirds of the families who broke the "childless" law did *not* receive a fine, either because the authorities did not know or because they "looked the other way." The authors concluded that if the children were not registered as adopted, they might be some of the "missing girls."

Another negative consequence (of requiring the adoptive parents to be over thirty-five and childless) was the narrowing of the adoptive-parent pool. Although many of the foundlings eventually found homes, the children lacked full legal status, a second problem. In some cases, the inability to obtain proper legal status for the child made school enrollment more difficult; the child would likely be ineligible for benefits such as land allotments, and the child might not be able to get health benefits such as routine immunizations. In the early 1990s, by allowing intercountry adoptions, the government expanded the pool of childless potential adoptive parents over the age of thirty-five.

By mid-1998, more than 15,000 foundlings had found homes overseas, mostly in the United States and Canada. Although accused by some people of "baby selling," the program seems to have been relatively free from corruption, according to the authors. Funds from the program have been used to improve conditions for children in the orphanages.

In summary, the authors saw *government policy* as the biggest obstacle to finding homes for abandoned children. One Chinese writer estimated that only 20 percent of abandoned children made it into the child welfare system. Critics of government policies have implied that there are few adoptions of foundlings within China and that most of the abandoned children die. But the authors of this study believe that a large numbers of people within the country have come forward to adopt these children, in many cases defying government policy to do so.

The majority of adopted children have done very well in their new homes; most of them are treated like birth children. The authors observe a "popular culture" that supports the adoption of girls and children who are not related to the birth parents. Punishments, such as fines, have not deterred the adoptive parents, which seems to make China different from countries such as Korea and India, where efforts by the government have not produced a great number of internal adoptive families.

Families in general do not adopt disabled children. If the family chooses to abandon a disabled child, it is usually because the family finds the financial burden unbearable. The authors suggest that if the state gave more help to the families, fewer disabled infants would be abandoned.

In the past decade, say the authors, conditions in the orphanages have improved due in part to fees from intercountry adoption, as well as from donations from Chinese citizens and charitable foundations at home and abroad.

The authors recommended changes in adoption law that took place soon after the study was completed (e.g., lowering of the age requirement for adoptive couples). The researchers took comfort in the knowledge that Chinese families had come forward to adopt orphaned and abandoned children.

Romania

Romania is another country in which population policies contributed to child abandonment and created a link with intercountry adoption. During the tenure of dictator Nicholae Ceausescu from 1967 to 1989, the government banned contraception and abortion, and mandated every Romanian couple to have at least five children (and in some cases ten children) for the nation. The government also gave mandatory pregnancy tests and punished women who did not have children. As a result of these policies, coupled with difficult economic conditions, many of the children ended up in orphanages. The state-run orphanages for healthy children became grossly overcrowded. State-run asylums housed physically and mentally ill children. After the overthrow of Ceausescu in 1989, media coverage revealed the plight of these children (which numbered between 100,000 and 300,000), and families from various parts of the world rushed to Romania to adopt them.

Romania put a moratorium on intercountry adoptions in 1991 because child traffickers were selling orphaned and abandoned Romanian children to anyone willing to pay high prices. Allegations surfaced of bribery, forged documents, and the bullying of birth mothers to give up their children.

That year the Romanian government changed its adoption laws regarding intercountry adoption. The first change was to eliminate all *private* international adoptions. Intercountry adoptions would have to be accomplished through an approved agency in the country of the prospective adoptive parents. Second, the amendments encouraged domestic adoptions by making available for intercountry adoption only those children who had been waiting for a family in Romania for at least six months. During that time, those who worked with children were to try to find a Romanian family for the child, who were required to be registered with the Romanian Adoption Committee. After these changes, the Romanian government reopened its intercountry adoption program but announced another moratorium on the practice beginning in 2001.

Several articles in professional journals at the time described the efforts of the Romanian government to press for preventive services, family preservation (when possible), foster care, and in-country adoptions. In June 2000, the government of Romania doubled budget allocations for child protection to the equivalent of $209 million annually to finance 440 orphanages that sheltered 100,000 abandoned or sick children.

On September 14, 2005, Thomas Atwood, president and CEO of the National Council for Adoption, testified before the Commission on Security and Cooperation in Europe to protest the Romanian ban on intercountry adoptions. According to the transcript of his testimony, Americans adopted more than 8,200 Romanian orphans between 1990 and 2004. In the year 2000, Atwood says, U.S. citizens adopted more than 1,100 Romanian orphans. In 2004, only 57 orphans found homes in the United States; in 2005, none did. Atwood observed that at the time of his presentation, Romanian law restricted intercountry adoptions to biological family members. Although Atwood described the ban on intercountry adoption as "cruel and arbitrary," he admitted that domestic adoption is preferable to intercountry adoption.

Atwood further argued that Romania's own adoption authority, the Child Protection and Adoption Authority, had estimated that 37,000 children (or more) filled state institutions in Romania, and that the government should allow these children to be placed with nonrelatives outside the country. Although Atwood believed that Romania could be in violation of the Hague Adoption Convention, the U.S. State Department admitted that parties to the convention can put further conditions and restrictions on the process. The ban on intercountry adoption was one of a number of measures designed by the European Union (EU) to decrease the number of children in state institutions by the time Romania joins the EU.

As pointed out by Sara Wallace in a 2003 article, the Hague Adoption Convention expands on the general principles put forth in earlier declarations and conventions, the goals of which were to set specific standards and procedures for intercountry adoption. Unlike an earlier declaration that says international adoption is *less* desirable than foster care in the child's country of origin, the Hague Convention modifies the hierarchy of preferred situations for orphaned and abandoned children.

Unfortunately, according to a 2005 report in the British medical journal *Lancet*, "Romania's abandoned children are still suffering." Author Carmiola Ionescu says that authorities frequently tout improved conditions for orphans. (Authorities have stated that in 2004 only 1,483 children under two years of age were in state institutions, compared with 7,483 in 1997.)

But, writes Ionescu, official figures do not include the number of children abandoned in hospitals. The mothers of these healthy children are too poor to take care of them, but under the new laws, abandoned children cannot go into orphanages until they are two years of age.

Overworked doctors and nurses have time only to feed and change the children's diapers, little more. The only "out" for the children whose parents do not come back for them is foster care, and there are too few foster parents. (If birth parents do come for a child, they will be eligible for some benefits.)

But statistics released at the beginning of 2005 from UNICEF show that birth parents abandon approximately 4,000 newborns each year in maternity wards; approximately 5,000 are left in pediatric hospitals. Also according to UNICEF, these figures are close in number to those of twenty-five years ago when Ceausescu was in power. According to Ionescu's sources, most abandoned children stay in the hospital for at least six months. Not only do these babies get little attention, but sick children also get suboptimal care.

According to Ionescu, the Romanian government is aware of the problem of babies being abandoned in hospitals, and officials are trying to find solutions. A spokesperson for the National Authority for the Protection of Children's Rights said that the child protection system was unprepared for the legislation forbidding the transfer of children under the age of two to state orphanages. At the same time, the government is also aware that children need to start their lives in a family.

South Korea

One of Korea's greatest challenges, writes Byung Hoon Chun (1989), has been the historic belief in adoption as a way of continuing the family line or family property. In the patriarchal agricultural society, families consider boy children an asset. The idea of adoption as a way of giving a child a permanent home because the child is in need of one has been a concept slow to catch on in South Korea.

The Korean War began in 1950, lasted for 3 1/2 years, and left the Korean peninsula devastated. The war also left many orphans in its wake—including many fathered by U.S. soldiers. Ten years later, industrialization had taken hold, and South Korea witnessed great economic growth. Population shifted to cities, and sexual taboos fell along with the traditional family system. Results included unmarried mothers, out-of-wedlock births, and abandoned children. Because a large part of the country's budget went to defense spending, protecting South Korea from its hostile neighbor North Korea, South Korea had difficulty taking care of its homeless children, leaving a smaller portion of the budget for child welfare services.

To its credit, the South Korean government gave priority to the idea of home placement over orphanage placement. The government also took several steps to popularize the concept of *domestic* (in-country) adoption. For example, it authorized child guidance clinics and orphanages to provide adoption services and spent money on recruiting Korean families to adopt Korean orphans. The government also limited the number of agencies working with intercountry adoptions and urged them to concentrate instead on domestic adoptions.

In spite of these efforts, the surge in domestic adoption lasted only about a decade (1970–1980). The importance of the family line continues as the main motivator for adoption within the country. Korean families seem to prefer healthy male infants. Girls and older or handicapped children have an uphill battle in finding homes. This is not unlike the difficulty older, handicapped children have in finding homes in other countries, including the United States.

Two main differences exist. One is that unlike the move toward openness in many other countries such as the United States, adoptions in Korea are mostly kept confidential, with families trying to act as if the children were born to them. Another difference has been that biological families have had the right to cancel the adoption for up to a year after the child is placed with an adoptive family.

The government of South Korea is very active in the entire intercountry adoption process, including setting standards for adoptive parents, assuming (along with the foreign country) responsibility for the home study, and requiring post-placement reports. The government limits both the number of agencies within the country that can arrange intercountry adoptions and the countries to which orphaned or abandoned children can be sent. Thus, the Korean government can focus on post-placement and other services to children to lessen their cultural adjustment issues.

The Social Welfare Society, now a private organization, received its name in 1971 and oversees many programs besides interlocutory adoptions. These include domestic adoption programs, foster care, counseling of birth mothers, and other programs of general social welfare. The society also publishes guides such as "Korea Guide" and "Guidelines for Adoptive Parents." Although escorts may take Korean children to their new homes in other countries, the government encourages adoptive parents to pick up their children and also to return later for visits.

Finland

In an article in *Child Welfare*, Sirpa Utriainen (1989b) provides a glimpse into child welfare and adoption programs in Finland and how they have evolved over the years. Much of Finland's history is tied to Russia, which seized Finland in 1809. Nicholas II of Russia ruled Finland between 1894 and 1917, at which time Finland declared its independence; civil war broke out the following January. In 1939 Russian forces attacked Finland; the Finns under General Carl G. Mannerheim fought two wars with Russia—in 1939 and 1944.

Urbanization and industrialization in the late nineteenth century gave rise to the Finnish child welfare system. Parents had to work long hours in the mills and factories, leaving many children without anyone to care for them. In the late 1860s, the Great Famine left 26,000 orphans in need of care. On the initiative of the Russian general governor, the country set up an association to help orphans and "troublesome children."

Private child welfare associations organized street kitchens, schools for girls of working parents, and orphanages. Beginning in the 1870s, various statesmen embraced the idea of elementary schools. Most people still considered social problems as moral problems.

In 1918 the civil war left more orphans, especially on the losing side. According to Utriainen, the editor-in-chief of the *Poor Relief Journal* wrote that it would be cheaper and safer for society to educate orphans than to put them in prison.

The first plans called for placing orphans (or "half orphans") in foster homes in the country, but some mothers of half-orphans objected. The government then created a state subsidy system to allow many of the children to stay in their own homes. According to the author, 6,000 children received assistance to allow them to stay at home, 2,500 children entered children's homes, and 1,700 went into family foster care. Some mothers did not apply for "poor relief" because they would have lost their right to vote. Soon the labor movement created its own programs, and between 1919 and 1922 assisted more than 30,000 children.

In the 1920s, services expanded even more, and two large private child welfare organizations came into being. One was the Mannerheim League for Child Welfare, which had as its goal the improvement of the health of Finnish children through children's clinics. The other was the Finnish Child Welfare Association, which began to work in foster care and adoption.

After years of preparation, the Finnish parliament approved a new child welfare act in 1936 that formalized the conditions under which a child could be taken into care. If parents could not adequately provide for their children, the social welfare board would intervene.

The Child Welfare Act of 1984 put into effect stricter rules, all of which are geared toward "the best interests of the child." Not only do professionals have the duty to notify authorities of any child in need of protection, but every citizen has this right.

In practice, public authorities on various levels, such as local, provincial, and national, do the work of child welfare. For example, the Provincial Administrative Court must confirm the order if a child is taken into care against the parents' wishes. In actuality, private child welfare organizations assist the government and abide by the same rules.

The list of areas in which the government helps families is long. Child welfare services include health care, daytime care, education, social security, and other forms of financial help related to those with low incomes or special needs.

The Child Welfare Act provides a framework for situations in which the government must intervene and provide substitute care for children. These situations include cases in which remaining in the birth home would endanger the child's health and development, and cases in which children endanger their own health and development by using dangerous substances or committing serious illegal acts.

As in the United States and other countries with similar laws, there are always those who find it hard to accept the fact that some people cannot take proper care of their own children. Utriainen (1989b) points out that everyone should remember the overarching principle of the best interests of the children; the goal is not to punish parents. Many times, writes Utriainen, social service agencies try supportive measures aimed at keeping the child at home, sometimes for too long; taking a child into care is always the last step. These principles are similar to child protection principles in the United States.

The reasons why children in Finland have ended up in care have changed over the years. In the 1930s and 1940s, many parents died; in the 1950s and 1960s, parents may have been sick or they may have lacked housing. From the 1970s until the present, parents tend to have abused alcohol or drugs.

More than half of the children are placed in foster homes, and almost all of these (90 percent) are long-term foster-care placements. Introduced in the relatively recent past, legislation has made it possible for children to keep in touch with (sometimes even visiting) biological parents, except in cases in which such contact would endanger the child or anyone else involved. This tendency toward contact is in keeping with U.S. trends, especially in the cases of older children. Residential care may include children's homes, nursery homes, reception homes, mother and child homes, family group homes, youth homes, and community homes.

The Adoption Act (amended in 1985) covers all Finnish adoptions. Before a birth mother consents to a relinquishment, she must have had counseling, which is focused on the best interests of the child. One section of the act states that the birth mother must have recovered from the delivery (no earlier than eight weeks after the child's birth) before she gives consent to adoption (Utriainen 1989a).

The only private agency licensed to provide counseling is the Finnish Child Welfare Association; the local social welfare board also may do the counseling. As with birth mothers in the United States, if a client has already decided on an adoption plan, the number of counseling sessions may be limited to two or three. Sometimes, however, many more sessions may be necessary. The birth mother has many opportunities to reflect on her decision. For example, she may come to the children's home to nurse and take care of her child as a way of helping her decide if she can or cannot parent the child. Newer legislation in Finland also takes into consideration the rights of birth fathers, and establishing paternity is a goal for all children.

Whereas in many countries it seems that the welfare of children takes a back seat to such concerns as the defense budget, in Finland, state and municipal taxes finance services, along with social security fees from employers and employees. Clients pay minimal fees for services such as adoption counseling.

The Planning and State Subsidies for Welfare and Health Act of 1982 made subsidies to private agencies possible as part of long-term national planning. Two "unusual" means of helping to finance private agencies are the Slot-Machine Association, a state-controlled monopoly whose profits are used to finance the work of social welfare and health-care organizations; and the Children's Day Foundation, which has six child welfare organizations as shareholders.

As is the case with most private nonprofit adoption agencies in the United States, private agencies also must work to finance their own activities. "They collect membership fees, receive donations, and carry out fund-raising campaigns [and] sell their own products, such as bags, towels, scarfs, candles, post-cards, posters, and all types of publications" (Utriainen, 1989b, 140). In addition, clients pay a small user's fee, and municipalities may purchase places for their children in a children's home run by the agency.

Sweden

In a related story, Anitha Ronstrom points out that social workers in Sweden and in other countries who have responsibility for making decisions about the welfare of children work under difficult circumstances. "They are either accused of not intervening in time to protect children in harmful situations, or they are accused of taking children into care without reason" (Ronstrom, 126).

She goes on to point out that the debate has raged for many years. One group points out how damaging it is for children to be separated from biological parents. Another group points out the damage done to children who remain in an unsafe home.

Usually, says Ronstrom, people tend to emphasize the parents' rights (to an intact family) at the expense of the children's rights. How long, she asks, can children be neglected? Although the scars of physical abuse and neglect may heal with time, emotional scars often last a lifetime.

In Sweden, Ronstrom says, children are usually taken into care for one of four reasons: drug addiction of parents, parents' alcoholism, mentally ill parents, and developmentally delayed parents. (Most often parents in the last category get support from the community and keep their children, but she says many of these children have delayed development too, or severe behavior problems.)

Finally, Ronstrom wonders if the people who think it is always best for children to stay with biological parents have ever talked to a child who has grown up in an abusive or neglectful home. She asks if they have ever "seen a baby who after a few months has already lost its zest for life and has ended up in a hospital because of failure-to-thrive or depression; or a ten-year-old who has attempted suicide several times because life is unbearable . . .if they have ever wondered why an eight-year-old starts to sniff or use drugs or play 'suicide-games' . . .why 12-year-old girls are prostitutes" (Ronstrom, 128). She goes on to say that children who grow up in destructive homes often become self-destructive. We know this, Ronstrom says, but we don't "act" on this knowledge because of the conflict it creates between the best interests of children and the interests of adults. The conflicts Ronstrom describes are similar to conflicts in the United States.

The Philippines

In the early days of the Philippines, religious organizations provided care for poor and abandoned children. The Hospicio de San Jose began taking care of abandoned babies in 1810; in 1885, Asilo de St. Vincent De Paul began caring for destitute and orphaned girls. In 1917, under U.S. auspices, the country established its first governmental orphanage (Balanon, 1989).

Greek and Roman law provided the core of adoption law for the Philippines. For example, in 1923 the legislature authorized public institutions or duly incorporated charitable agencies chosen by the Public Welfare Commissioner to place children under the age of eighteen for adoption and give consent for their adoption. Later that year, the attorney general wrote an opinion that allowed a foreigner who permanently resided in the Philippines to adopt.

In the 1950s, the New Civil Code of the Philippines provided for childless couples, including resident aliens, to adopt. At that time the courts handled most adoptions. On January 1, 1964, the Rules of Court took effect; these rules laid out new procedures for adoption.

The Child and Youth Welfare Code of December 10, 1974, which went into effect the following year, eased the limitation that only childless couples could adopt: "any person in full possession of his or her civil rights, including nonresident aliens," could be considered as an adoptive parent (Balanon, 244). A social worker from the Department of Social Welfare and Development (DSWD) conducts case studies of the child to be adopted, the adopting parents, and the birth parents. As in many other countries, including various states in the United States, a period of six months is required before finalization of the adoption unless a judge waives this waiting period.

Moving on to February 23, 1976, the Council for the Welfare of Children promulgated a series of rules and regulations on foreign adoption. The adoption of a Filipino child by someone from another country would be allowed only when professionals could not find a suitable home in the Philippines. The secretary of the DSWD has the authority to approve placements and the travel of children to the other country.

The laws have since changed many times. As is the case in the United States, there are those who question whether or not an

American, Scandinavian, or Australian couple can fully meet the cultural needs of a Filipino child. There is the question of "imperialism," and an observation that some foreign parents have a feeling of "privilege" and that at times have been given "immediate attention or preference over their Filipino counterparts" (Balanon, 245). Foreign couples sometimes try to get requirements lifted and may have politicians intervene on their behalf. They forget "that the Philippines is an independent nation and no longer a colony of the United States" (Belanon, 245). However, according to the U.S. State Department, which issues immigrant visas to orphans coming to the United States, from 1995 to 2005 the number of adoptions of Filipino children to the United States remained steady, at under 300 children per year.

Poverty continues to be a serious problem in the Philippines. Add to that high population growth, disruptions in family life, unstable political situations, and inadequate social services, which must cope with working children, street children, exploited and migrant children, and children who are "disabled, abused, abandoned, and neglected" (Belanon, 241). Some scholars estimate that approximately 8,000 children are in institutions in the Philippines; they may be without parents or have parents who cannot cope with their needs.

Extended families have tended to take care of orphaned children, many of whom are never legally adopted. The concept of adopting an unrelated child is somewhat new to Filipinos and is evolving.

In the past, the concept of placing the child's best interests at the forefront may have been secondary to other concerns; for example, prospective parents may have taken in a child who will care for them in their old age or as a domestic helper. In recent years, however, the government has shown a growing concern for the best interests of the child. Even so, adoptions continue to take place primarily within the extended family (i.e., relative adoptions). For example, between 1986 and 1987, the government recorded 2,500 adoptions. Of these, 82 percent were in-country (or domestic) adoptions, and 18 percent were international (or intercountry) adoptions. Of the domestic group, 75 percent involved relatives. Likewise, 30 percent of the international adoptions were by relatives. Of the domestic adoptions only 5 percent involved licensed child-placement agencies and were children not related to the adopting family. The other 20 percent were private adoptions.

According to Lourdes Balanon, adopting families tend to prefer a healthy female infant with fair skin, a high-bridged nose, and a "fairly good" family background. (This preference, at least for the sex of the child, is not very different from the preference of adoptive families in the United States.) According to Lisa Milbrand, most adoption agencies and adoption attorneys in the Philippines will not allow parents who want domestic infants to choose the sex of the child. But she quotes Susan Myers of the Lutheran Adoption Network as saying that 80 percent of families, if given a choice, would choose to adopt a girl. (Intercountry adoption is another matter, especially for those adopting from China, where 95 percent of the available children *are* girls.)

As in most countries with adoption programs, families in the Philippines complete the application process, matching, placement, and post-placement supervision (or support) before filing a Petition to Adopt in court. The DSWD has local offices spread throughout the country, and the Kaishang Buhay Foundation is a licensed child-placement agency.

When adoption professionals in the Philippines cannot find a family to meet a child's needs, only then does the country turn to intercountry adoption to keep a child from growing up in an institution. More male children than female children are available because of the preference of Filipino families for girls. Approximately 75 percent of the children available in this category go to American families, including relative adoptions with Filipino Americans. Most of the remaining children go to Norway, France, Germany, and the Netherlands.

The government carefully regulates the process of international adoption. The DSWD is the only agency authorized to place Filipino children in other countries. This agency screens and accepts applicants, endorses home studies, selects the best placement for a child, approves the placement, prepares the child for travel, processes travel documents, and monitors the placement until finalization.

The whole process usually takes a year, not including the waiting period. The DSWD requires regular reports on the children in placement as the basis for consenting to the final adoption. Even after finalization, the DSWD keeps in touch with the children and their adoptive families through follow-up visits from escort social workers, visits of the children and families to the Philippines, and by an entity called the Motherland Tour.

The first Motherland Tour (July 1987) involved five young adults who had left the Philippines for adoptive homes in the United States when they were between the ages of nine and sixteen years. The tour, as part of the postadoption services of Holt International Children's Services, brought the young people back to their homeland to explore their roots and their cultural heritage. Feedback from their adoptive parents after the tour showed the experience to have been a great success. The adoptees "experienced greater self-esteem and security; they have continued to have contact with one another" (Balanon, 251). (Homeland tours are available through many countries. The Ties Program provides a travel experience for adoptive families who want to visit the child's country of origin with their child. More information on this program is available through *Adoptive Families* magazine or http://www.adoptivefamilytravel.com.)

India

In spite of progressive legislation in child welfare through its Juvenile Justice Act, India still has had difficulty implementing some of its laws for the benefit of children. Part of the problem, according to Deenaz Damania, of Bangalore, India, is poverty. If 40 percent of India's population lives below the minimum subsistence level, then approximately 108 million children are victims of poverty, she observes. The population of India is approximately 42 percent children; about 22 million Indian children are born each year.

Damania cites statistics from 1980 that estimate the number of orphaned children under the age of fourteen at around 38 million; by 1991 the total number of orphans was projected to be about 30 million. Damania points out that not all orphans are destitute and not all destitute children are orphans. Nevertheless, probably 12 million at the time of her writing *were* orphans.

So, she asks, what happens to an abandoned child found by the wayside? Probably the child will appear before a juvenile court magistrate, who will order the child placed in an institution until he or she reaches the age of eighteen.

Generally in India, the government formulates policies but leaves the implementation of these policies up to voluntary organizations. If the child is lucky, he will end up in an institution with progressive policies and practices. If the child is unlucky, he may end up in an institution in which caretakers are unresponsive to the child's needs.

In one study, Damania reports, researchers found that children who lived in poverty *before* their entrance into institutions had physical and nutritional health that actually *got worse* in institutional care. The researchers discovered that 85 percent of the children suffered from malnutrition.

These statistics go along with the findings of Jennifer Chambers, who reported in *Pediatric Clinics of North America* (1252) that "there is a degree of neglect in all orphanages because it is impossible to provide one-on-one care for each child." She goes on to write that "neglect alone, even in the presence of adequate calories, can cause global growth failure, but it affects height most drastically" (1252). The longer a child suffers from nutritional as well as emotional deprivation, the less likely the child will ever be able to catch up to the normal range.

Damania believes that giving voluntary agencies decision-making powers regarding the fate of orphaned and destitute children may not be a good idea. In some cases, an institution had made the decision that a particular child should stay in the institution even though alternatives for family placement in the community were available. Another scenario found institutions combining the care of the very young with the care of the very old. She calls for more governmental control, not only of policy formulation but also of program implementation. As things stand, duplication of services and waste exist. If government policy gives preference to families as the best place for a growing child, then the government must provide more funds for promoting noninstitutional programs, such as in-country adoption, family foster care, and sponsorship.

Mexico

If, over the years, citizens of the United States have had one major misconception about adopting from Mexico, it is that the adoption of a child from that country would be a simple process. Perhaps someday it will be easy (or easier). Currently it is difficult. According to the U.S. Department of State, of the 22,728 children adopted internationally in 2005 by U.S. families, only 98 came from Mexico.

An estimated 350,000 abandoned or orphaned children live

in public or private institutions in Mexico. Many are crowded, and funding is in short supply. With such a need for families, with Mexico so close, and with so many Spanish speakers in the United States, why is adoption from Mexico so hard?

Bureaucratic "layers" and legal differences, such as what constitutes the definition of an orphan, are parts of the problem. Until recently, Mexican officials pointed out that the United States had *signed* the Hague Convention but had not *implemented* it. In an article in the *Denver Post* (July 22, 2001), reporter Bruce Finley quotes Cesar Sotomayer Sanchez, director of the System for Full Development of the Family, Mexico's federal office dealing with family matters, as saying that for U.S. families interested in adopting children from Mexico, "the only problem is that agreement" (18A). However, another problem has been that Mexican authorities want to retain the right to bring a child back to Mexico if the adoption fails.

Some might say that Jim Polsfut was one of the lucky ones. But luck was only part of the process. Polsfut, a financial manager in Denver, had worked in Mexico and had supported a home for street children there for ten years. Polsfut, who is single, had visited an orphanage, Casa del Sol, a relatively well-funded private orphanage in Puebla, Mexico. One day, Polsfut saw a six-year-old boy, Javier, who had reached the upper limit for living in the orphanage. When Polsfut mentioned that he had an interest in adopting the boy, authorities were skeptical. Polsfut agreed to provide Mexican authorities with a video of Javier, a report from a social worker, and a school evaluation every six months for three years. In addition to the paperwork involved with any intercountry adoption, Polsfut had two long psychological interviews but appreciated the thoroughness of the Mexican professionals, who said they ultimately made an exception for Polsfut because he agreed to raise Javier under Mexican supervision, and they knew him. The U.S. consulate handled visa paperwork. Javier eventually walked with Polsfut across the border to El Paso, Texas.

Javier's adoption raised the hopes of many of the other children at Casa del Sol. One of these children was Juan Carlos, another six-year-old, who said, "Yes, I'd like to have parents." "But," wrote Finley in the *Denver Post* report, "his hopes almost certainly will be crushed."

Not if one person could help it. Valerie Moore, another Denverite, saw a picture of the smiling brown-eyed boy in the *Denver*

Post. Valerie, too, had worked in Mexico and spoke fluent Spanish. She had a teenage daughter from a previous marriage and wanted another child. She and her husband, Jeff, married for ten years, had been unsuccessful in having a birth child. Moore, who says she has "always had an infatuation with the Latin culture," went with her mother to Mexico to see Juan Carlos in person and "fell in love with him" (discussion with the author, March 18, 2006). But the adoption was a "bureaucratic challenge. We didn't tell him about the possibility of adoption," says Moore. "We just visited him as often as possible for three or four days at a time and shared his life—back and forth to Mexico about twenty times over a 2 1/2 year period." Although Juan Carlos had lived in the orphanage for three years, the parental rights of his birth parents had not yet been terminated. (Eventually this did happen, making Juan Carlos free for adoption.)

Moore explains that the Departmento Integral Familiar tries to do everything possible to find relatives or family friends who would be able to adopt a particular child before turning to outsiders. Even so, Europeans find adoption of children from Mexico less of a challenge than do individuals from the United States.

Finally, everything came together and the Moores were able to bring Juan Carlos "home." When he arrived at age eight, says Moore, he didn't know English or how to write in Spanish. But with three years of supplemental education in the Denver public schools, Juan Carlos is now almost up to grade level. Although he prefers to speak English, his mom speaks Spanish to him at home. "He's a very determined guy," says his mother. "We've been lucky with him; his teachers love him. He works very hard."

Yes, the family has gone back to the orphanage. "We have good friends there," says Valerie Moore. Now at age eleven, Juan Carlos has a mother, a father, and a big sister. He also has a godfather, Jim Polsfut. "Jim's son Javier," says Moore, "is like a brother."

References and Further Reading

Adamec, Christine, and William Pierce. 2000. *The Encyclopedia of Adoption*, 2nd ed. New York: Facts on File.

Albers, L. H., E. D. Barnett, J. A. Jenista, and D. E. Johnson. 2005. "International Adoption: Medical and Developmental Issues." *Pediatric Clinics of North America* 52, no. 5 (October).

Atwood, Thomas C. 2005. "Testimony of National Council for Adoption:

In the Best Interest of Children?" Security and Cooperation in Europe Public Hearing: September 14. Available from National Council for Adoption, http://www.adoptioncouncil.org.

Balanon, Lourdes G. 1989. "Foreign Adoption in the Philippines: Issues and Opportunities." Special issue. *Child Welfare* 68, no. 2 (March/April): 241–253.

Beauvais-Godwin, Laura, and Raymond Godwin. 2005. *The Complete Adoption Book: Everything You Need to Know to Adopt a Child,* 3rd ed. Holbrook, MA: Adams Media.

Byung, Hoon Chun. 1989. "Adoption in Korea." Special issue. *Child Welfare* 68, no. 2 (March/April): 255–260.

Chambers, Jennifer. 2005. "Preadoption Opportunities for Pediatric Providers." *Pediatric Clinics of North America* 52, no. 5 (October): 1247–1269.

Commission on Security and Cooperation in Europe. *In the Best Interest of Children? Romania's Ban on Intercountry Adoption.* Testimony of National Council for Adoption. September 14, 2005.

Crowe, Sarah, with assistance of Sabine Dolan. "Helping Orphans in Rwanda Build a Better Future." Accessed at http://www.unicef.org/infobycountry/rwanda_31013.html.

Damania, Deenaz. 1989. "Observations on the Child Welfare Scene in India." Special issue. *Child Welfare* 68, no. 2 (March/April): 141–144.

Dickens, J. 2002. "The Paradox of Inter-Country Adoption: Analysing Romania's Experience as a Sending Country." *International Journal of Social Welfare* 11, no. 1 (January): 76–83.

Erwin, Steve. 2005. "Helping Ethiopia's Lost Children." *People Weekly.* May 2: 89.

Finley, Bruce. 2001. "Adoption Gulf Strands Kids: Legal, Political Issues Leave Mexico Orphans Homeless But Hoping." *Denver Post.* July 22: 18A.

Finley, Bruce. 2005. "Orphaned by AIDS . . .Embraced by Strangers." *Denver Post.* November 13: 1A, 12A, 13A.

Ionescu, Carmiola. 2005. "Romania's Abandoned Children Are Still Suffering. *Lancet* 366, no. 9497 (November 5): 1595.

Johnson, Kay, Huang Banghan, and Wang Liyao. 1998. "Infant Abandonment and Adoption in China." *Population and Development Review* 24, no. 3 (September): 469.

Milbrand, Lisa. 2006. "Daughters in Demand." *Adoptive Families.* April: 42–45.

Mukhina, Valeria Sergeevna. 1989. "Care of Children Brought up at Boarding-Type Institutions in the USSR." Special issue. *Child Welfare* 68, no. 2 (March/April): 233–240.

News Focus. 2005. "Special Adoptive Families Update: Adoption from Russia." *Adoptive Families.* September/October: 11.

Ronstrom, Anitha. 1989. "Sweden's Children's Ombudsman: A Spokesperson for Children." Special issue. *Child Welfare* 68, no. 2 (March/April): 123–128.

USAID, UNAIDS, and UNICEF joint press release. 2002. "Number of Children Orphaned by AIDS Will Rise Dramatically." June 10. Accessed at http://gbgm-umc.org/health/aids/childrenonthebrink.cfm.

Utriainen, Sirpa. 1989a. "Adolescent Pregnancy: Standards and Services in Finland." Special issue. *Child Welfare* 68, no. 2 (March/April): 167–182.

Utriainen, Sirpa. 1989b. "Child Welfare Services in Finland." Special issue. *Child Welfare* 68, no. 2 (March/April): 129–140.

Wallace, Sara R. 2003. "International Adoption: The Most Logical Solution to the Disparity between the Numbers of Orphaned and Abandoned Children in Some Countries and Families and Individuals Wishing to Adopt in Others?" *Arizona Journal of International and Comparative Law* 20, no. 3: 684–724.

Weitzman, Carol, and Lisa Albers. 2005. "Long-Term Developmental, Behavioral, and Attachment Outcomes after International Adoption." *Pediatric Clinics of North America* 52, no. 5 (October): 1395–1419.

Wilson, Brenda. 2006. "A Painful Struggle over Nigeria's Abandoned Children." National Public Radio. February 18.

Zurbrig-Tull, Sandy. "Adoption Information for Canadians." Accessed at http://www.canadianadoption.org.

4

Chronology

This chapter gives a time line of important conferences; initiation of child welfare policies, practices, and minimum standards; federal laws; ground-breaking books; and the founding dates of organizations important in adoption history. The list is necessarily selective, and students of adoption may know more events to add to the list.

ca. 1780 BC   King Hammurabi of Babylonia puts forth the Code of Hammurabi, which includes the oldest written adoption law.

ca. 600 BC   The Athenian laws of Solon require the commander of an army to protect and raise, at government expense, children of citizens killed in battle.

ca. 200 BC   The Hindu laws of Manu mention the concept of adoption.

AD 291   Under Roman law, women are allowed to adopt—under special circumstances.

335   Emperor Constantine orders children born to unmarried parents who later marry to be considered "legitimate."

787   Datheu, archpriest of Milan, establishes the first foundling hospital.

123

1597 England passes the first Poor Law, providing for abandoned, orphaned, and poor children in that country.

1648 The Massachusetts Bay Colony legislates that children can be taken from their birth parents and put with new families if the children are "rude, stubborn, and unruly."

1691 Boston becomes the first U.S. city to offer incentives for the poor to remain in their own homes rather than to live in an institution.

Poorhouses, or almshouses, are the forerunners of orphanages.

1693 Sir William Phips, governor of Massachusetts, mentions his adopted son (actually his nephew) in his will and is allegedly the first recorded adoptive father in the original thirteen colonies.

1729 Ursuline nuns found the first orphanage in North America after a massacre of adult settlers in Natchez, Mississippi.

1783 In the state of Virginia, Thomas Jefferson eliminates primogeniture, the practice in which the oldest son inherits the family property.

1850 Alabama law specifies the right of an adopted child to inherit from his adoptive parents.

1851 Massachusetts passes an adoption law with focus on the best interests of the child.

1853 Charles Loring Brace founds the Children's Aid Society of New York, the oldest formal child placement agency in the United States.

1854 Brace begins the Orphan Train Movement, in which thousands of homeless children between the ages of two and fourteen are sent west from New York City to adoptive homes.

1868   The Massachusetts Board of State Charities begins to pay for foster children to board in private homes, the beginning of "placing out," caring for children in family homes rather than in institutions.

1869   The Massachusetts Board of State Charities begins sending agents to visit the children in their placements.

1872   The New York State Charities Aid Association, one of the first organizations in the United States to have a specialized child-placement program, begins its work.

1883   The Reverend Martin Van Buren Van Arsdale founds the National Children's Home Society (originally the American Education Aid Society), a nonprofit organization for the placement of children.

1886   With high standards for that time, Van Arsdale founds his state's organization, the Illinois Children's Home and Aid Society, to ensure proper homes for children.

1891   Michigan's law is the first to order an investigation of prospective adoptive parents. Thus, the first official "home study" is born.

1898   The St. Vincent De Paul Society organizes the Catholic Home Bureau, the first Catholic agency to place children in private homes rather than in orphanages.

1904   The first school of social work, the New York School of Applied Philanthropy, opens.

1909   The first White House Conference on the Care of Dependent Children recommends the establishment of the U.S. Children's Bureau; it also suggests that poverty alone should not be the sole grounds for removing children from families.

1909 (cont.)	President Theodore Roosevelt appeals for governmental financial assistance to allow widowed mothers to keep their homes and children.
1910	From approximately this date until 1925, the concept of *eugenics* is popular. Eugenics is the belief (later discredited) that some children are "defective" and therefore unsuitable for adoption.
1911	Dr. Arnold Gesell sets up a psychological clinic at the New Haven Dispensary in Connecticut. He directs this clinic, later known as the Clinic of Child Development at Yale University, until 1948.
	Alice Chapin, wife of prominent pediatrician Dr. Henry Dwight Chapin, founds the Alice Chapin Adoption Nursery, one of New York City's first private adoption agencies.
	Illinois passes the first statewide mothers' pension law. Other states follow the lead of Illinois and pass similar laws.
1912	Congress creates the Children's Bureau in the Department of Commerce and Labor to investigate and report on "the welfare of children and child life." Julia Lathrop is appointed chief of the Children's Bureau, the first woman in history to head a federal agency.
1915	The Bureau for Exchange of Information among Child-Helping Organizations is founded. It is later renamed the Child Welfare League of America.
	Norway's Castberg Law decrees that "legitimate" and "illegitimate" children have equal rights before the law.
1916	Louise Wise, wife of Reform rabbi Stephen Wise, founds the Child Adoption Committee, which becomes Louise Wise Services, the largest Jewish adoption agency in New York City.

1917   The Children's Code of Minnesota becomes the model for state laws during the next twenty years. In addition to requiring a "home study" of the prospective adoptive family, it also requires the state to check the adoption petition and to give recommendations to the court on each adoption matter. The statute requires a six-month postplacement probationary period before finalization of the adoption. It further orders that adoption records be *closed.*

Sweden enacts its first adoption laws.

1919   The U.S. Children's Bureau sets minimum standards for child placing.

The Russell Sage Foundation publishes the first child-placing manual.

1920   The Child Welfare League of America is formally renamed; it is a national, nonsectarian, professional child-advocacy organization composed of more than 600 private and public children's agencies. The organization publishes standards of practice for child welfare services.

The American Association of Social Workers is founded.

1921   The Sheppard-Towner Infancy and Maternity Protection Act provides for federal appropriations to promote maternal and infant health.

1924   Sophie Van Senden Theis publishes the first major outcome study, "How Foster Children Turn Out," based on her work with 910 children and the New York State Charities Aid Association.

1926   The Adoption of Children Act, the first adoption legislation in the United Kingdom, becomes law.

1929   In their legal statutes, all forty-eight states provide for adoption.

1930   The American Public Welfare Association (APWA) is founded as a nonprofit professional organization representing the interests of human services departments across the United States.

1933   Social reformer Edna Gladney leads the fight to have references to illegitimacy removed from birth certificates in Texas.

1935   On August 14, President Franklin D. Roosevelt signs into law the Social Security Act, which, in addition to helping the elderly, forms the basis for subsequent legislation benefiting children.

Justine Wise Polier, a later critic of matching in adoption, is appointed to head the Domestic Relations Court of Manhattan.

1937   The first Child Welfare League of America initiative sets up separate standards for adoptive (permanent) and foster (temporary) placements.

1938   The Child Welfare League of America endorses secrecy in adoption.

1939   A picture book and also an adoption "classic," *The Chosen Baby* by Valentina P. Wasson, seeks to tell a child his or her adoption story. It attempts to fulfill a need for a "universal" adoption story but becomes controversial because it tends to simplify and "mythologize" adoption. For example, the child may believe that the chosen child was selected at a baby store or was "made to order" for the adoptive parents.

1944   The U.S. Supreme Court hears a case involving Jehovah's Witnesses. In *Prince v. Massachusetts*, the Court upholds the principle of *parens patriae*, in which the state has the power to restrict parental control in order to guard the general interest in the child's well-being.

1948   The U.S. Congress passes the Displaced Persons Act, which allows 3,000 orphans and more than 200,000 adult European refugees to emigrate to the United States.

Jim Casey and his siblings establish the Annie E. Casey Foundation in honor of their mother. The foundation is the nation's largest philanthropy dedicated exclusively to improving the lives of disadvantaged children and families.

Minnesota records the first transracial adoption of an African American child by Caucasian parents.

1949   Author Pearl Buck opens Welcome House, a nonprofit organization for the care and adoption of Asian American children.

New York is the first state to pass a law (which proves unenforceable) to prohibit black-market adoptions.

1953   The U.S. Congress grants 500 "special visas" for Korean orphans to be adopted by Americans; the Refugee Relief Act of 1953 allows for 4,000 more orphan visas over the next three years.

The first version of a Uniform Adoption Act (UAA) is drafted. The proposed act is an effort to achieve uniformity in adoption laws.

Jean Paton, an adoptee and social worker, founds the Life History Center, as well as Orphan Voyage, the first search-and-support network for adopted persons.

1954   Paton publishes *The Adopted Break Silence,* a book that records the thoughts and feelings of a varied group of adopted persons and promotes the idea that they have a distinct identity.

1955   The Child Welfare League of America sponsors the first professional conference on adoption, leading to reforms in adoption and foster care. Special-needs adoption becomes a recognized entity.

1955
(cont.)   Senator Estes Kefauver (D-TN) heads a U.S. Senate inquiry into black-market and interstate adoption practices. Kefauver and Senator Edward Thye (R-MN) propose a federal law on black-market adoptions, which does not pass.

Pearl S. Buck accuses religious institutions and some social workers of maintaining the black market in adoptions and holding back the adoption of children in order to save their jobs.

The National Association of Social Workers is founded.

The National Urban League along with fourteen New York agencies found Adopt-A-Child to promote the adoption of African American children.

Bertha and Harry Holt, a farm couple from Oregon, receive a special act of Congress to allow them to adopt eight Korean War orphans.

1956   The Holts found Holt International Children's Services, a nonprofit organization devoted to finding homes for children worldwide.

1957   The International Conference on Intercountry Adoptions issues a report on problems with international adoptions.

Sweden recognizes child abuse as a pediatric problem. The Swedish National Board of Health issues regulations, offers counseling services, and sets up a research institute to study child abuse

1958   The Child Welfare League of America publishes *Standards of Adoption Service.* (These standards are revised in 1968, 1973, 1978, 1988, and 2000.) At this time, unmarried mothers, with some exceptions, are considered unable to care for their infants. Adoptive parents are generally only given background information that will not be too upsetting for them to know about their child or his history.

The Indian Adoption Project begins and continues through 1967. The project, administered by the Child Welfare League of America, is funded by a federal contract from the Bureau of Indian Affairs and the U.S. Children's Bureau. It places Native American children in non-Indian families.

1959   The United Nations General Assembly adopts the Declaration of the Rights of the Child, a nonbinding resolution that delineates ten principles or rights for every child, including a name and a nationality; health and social security; love and understanding from parents; free and compulsory education (at least at the elementary level); protection from neglect, cruelty, and exploitation; freedom from employment before a certain age; and a life lived with understanding, tolerance, friendship among peoples, and universal brotherhood. A child who is handicapped in any way is expected to be given special education and treatment.

1960   The Golden Anniversary White House Conference on Children and Youth endorses the above Declaration.

Marshall Schechter, a psychiatrist in Beverly Hills, California, reports that adopted persons are a hundred times more likely than nonadopted persons to have or develop serious emotional problems. Schechter's research is based on a small number of patients in his practice, and his conclusions generate much controversy.

1961   The Immigration and Nationality Act includes a permanent reference to the immigration of orphans from other countries to be adopted by citizens of the United States.

1962   A special conference of the U.S. Children's Bureau on child abuse generates proposals for new laws requiring doctors to notify law enforcement agencies in cases of suspected child abuse. In the coming years, most states adopt such legislation.

1962
(cont.)

Dr. C. Henry Kempe and his associates publish a paper in the *Journal of the American Medical Association* on the physical abuse of children and introduce the term *battered child syndrome* to describe injuries resulting from repetitive nonaccidental trauma. (Battered child syndrome later becomes a reason for terminating a parent's rights.)

1963

The National Institute of Child Health and Human Development is established as part of the National Institutes of Health.

1964

H. David Kirk publishes *Shared Fate,* an examination of adoptive family relationships from a sociological/psychological viewpoint. Before Kirk's book, people tended to ignore the differences between birth and adoptive families. Kirk points out that families who acknowledge the differences make a better adjustment as families than those who don't. *Shared Fate* paves the way for more openness in adoption.

1965

The Los Angeles County Bureau of Adoptions launches the first organized program for prospective single parents with the goal of locating more homes for hard-to-place (so-called special needs) children.

1966

The Indian Adoption Project becomes the National Adoption Resource Exchange and is later renamed the Adoption Resource Exchange of North America (ARENA). It is the first national "adoption exchange" with a mission of finding homes for special needs or hard-to-place children. Researcher David Fanshel studies the outcomes of one-fourth of the children adopted as a result of the program and their adoptive families, and discovers that most have made a good adjustment. However, Fanshel is able to look ahead and anticipate objections from Native American tribes, which are ultimately successful in passing the Indian Child Welfare Act.

1967

Adoptive Families of America, Inc. is reestablished as

the Organization for a United Response (OURS, Inc.). The national nonprofit organization is the largest adoptive parent group in the nation.

1968   The Children's Home Society in St. Paul, Minnesota, begins providing postplacement services for children being adopted.

The Child Welfare League's revised *Standards* come out in favor of transracial adoption and continue to recommend the confidentiality of adoption records.

Five hundred African American social workers found the National Association of Black Social Workers (NABSW) at the National Conference of Social Workers in San Francisco.

1969   President Nixon creates the Office of Child Development in the Department of Health, Education, and Welfare (HEW) to coordinate functions of the U.S. Children's Bureau and Head Start.

1970   Adoptions peak at 175,000 per year, 80 percent of which are arranged by adoption agencies.

1971   Florence Fisher, an adopted person, founds the Adoptees' Liberty Movement Association (ALMA), a national search and support organization in favor of open records.

1972   The National Association of Black Social Workers takes a position against the adoption of black children by white parents.

The Council of Adoptive Parents (CAP), an adoptive parent support group, initiates the *CAP Book*, a photo listing of waiting children.

The National Adoption Center in Philadelphia, Pennsylvania, is founded to promote the adoption of children with special needs throughout the United States.

1972 (cont.)	A court case, *Stanley v. Illinois,* increases the rights of unwed fathers in adoption; it requires informed consent and proof that the parent is "unfit" before termination of parental rights.

1973   *Roe v. Wade,* the U.S. Supreme Court decision legalizing abortion, is implemented.

Joseph Goldstein, Anna Freud, and Albert Solnit publish *Beyond the Best Interests of the Child,* which validates the "psychological parent" and focuses attention on the needs of children as the primary concern in the adoption process.

Marian Wright Edelman founds the Children's Defense Fund, an organization with the goals of educating the nation about the needs of children and encouraging preventive investment in children.

Barbara Eck Menning founds RESOLVE, Inc., for those experiencing infertility.

Hope Marindin founds the Committee for Single Adoptive Parents, a national organization for singles involved in adoption.

1974   The North American Council on Adoptable Children (NACAC) is formed to advocate for the placement of waiting children.

Single Parents Adopting Children Everywhere (SPACE) is formed to support single parents before, during, and after an adoption.

Congress passes the Child Abuse and Prevention and Treatment Act (CAPTA), P.L. 93–247, the key federal legislation concerning the prevention of child abuse and neglect. The act is subsequently amended in 1978, 1984, 1988, 1992, 1996, and 2003.

1975   Emma May Vilardi founds the International Soundex

Reunion Registry (ISRR), a nonprofit organization for the reunion of members of the adoption triad.

After the fall of Saigon, the Vietnam "Baby Lift" begins bringing to the United States thousands of Vietnamese orphans to be adopted by Americans.

The U.S. federal government stops keeping adoption statistics.

Betty Jean Lifton's book, *Twice Born: Memoirs of an Adopted Daughter*, is published. Lifton, adopted at age 2½, tells the story of her search for her birth parents. Although Lifton's reunion with her biological mother does not have the hoped-for happy result, Liftons continues to believe strongly in open adoption records.

Great Britain passes the Children Act, which, among other provisions, gives adult adopted persons the right to obtain copies of their original birth certificates.

1976   Lee H. Campbell, a Massachusetts woman, founds Concerned United Birthparents (CUB) to provide support for birth parents who have placed a child for adoption.

Social workers Annette Baran and Reuben Pannor, in conjunction with psychiatrist Arthur Sorosky, propose the concept of "open adoption," generally defined as a process in which birth parents and prospective adoptive parents meet, share identifying information, and often keep in contact.

The Joint Council on International Children's Services is formed. Members include adoption agencies, child welfare organizations, parent support groups, and medical specialists with an interest in intercountry adoption.

1977   West Germany enacts its first adoption laws.

1977
(cont.)

A revised edition of Valentina P. Wasson's book, *The Chosen Baby*, omits references to the "choosing" of babies, except in the title.

1978

P.L. 95–608, The Indian Child Welfare Act (ICWA), is enacted to protect the best interests of Indian children and families. It mandates special provisions for Native American children who are placed in foster and adoptive homes. Under the act, preference must be given first to persons from the child's tribe and last to those of another culture.

The American Adoption Congress (AAC) is formed as a national umbrella organization of search groups dedicated to achieving more openness with respect to adoption records.

Louise Brown, the world's first "test-tube baby," is born in England.

The Child Welfare League of America's revised *Standards* recommends that adoption social workers provide nonidentifying information such as medical history and backgrounds of birth family members to the prospective adoptive family.

1979

Betty Lanning, AnnaMarie Merrill, and Patricia Sexton found International Concerns for Children (ICC), a nonprofit organization with emphasis on support for those involved in intercountry adoptions.

The Gay and Lesbian Parents Coalition International (GLPCI) forms as a support group for gay fathers and lesbian mothers.

Journalist Lorraine Dusky publishes *Birthmark*, an autobiography, the first to give a birth mother's perspective on the relinquishment of a child for adoption.

1980

The Adoption Assistance and Child Welfare Act (P.L. 96–272) is enacted to promote permanency for children, including reasonable efforts to keep children with their birth parents or, when that fails, to provide for out-of-home care in the least restrictive and most permanent setting. The act also establishes the Adoption Assistance Program, which partially subsidizes special needs adoptions.

The U.S. Department of Health, Education, and Welfare (HEW) proposes the Model State Adoption Act and Model State Adoption Procedures. (The National Conference of Commissioners on Uniform State Laws, a group of varied law professionals, usually is the group that proposes model statutes. States may then decide whether to adopt all, part, or none of the model.) The act originates in the mandate of P.L. 95–266, an amendment to the Child Abuse Prevention and Treatment and Adoption Opportunities Act of 1978. An advisory panel of representatives from various public and private adoption organizations are interested in getting more openness in adoption. However, procedures require that HEW solicit commentary from the general public. Of more than 3,000 comments received, 82 percent oppose the Model State Adoption Act. Not only that, but a committee of the Child Welfare League of America reviews the report and rejects it. The proposed statute goes too far, too fast in the opinion of the committee. One suggestion is that the Minnesota procedure, which requires both parties involved in a search to agree to sharing identifying information, be substituted. The proposal is renamed the Model Act for Adoption of Children with Special Needs, and the original suggestions for openness are rewritten in order to protect the privacy of birth parents.

The National Council for Adoption (NCFA) is formed as a nonprofit organization to improve adoption standards and practices. It lobbies on behalf of adoption and provides information and assistance in all areas of adoption. The organization has historically favored closed (confidential) records.

1981   Reverend George H. Clements initiates the One Church, One Child project at the Holy Angels Church,

1981
(cont.)
a predominantly black Catholic Church in Chicago. The project encourages black churches to recruit members to adopt a waiting child.

1982
Minnesota's legislature revises the state's adoption law to shift to the birth parent(s) responsibility for keeping adoption records sealed. In other words, the biological parents would now have to file an affidavit denying consent to the release of information. In the absence of this affidavit, the birth parents are assumed to have consented to the release of information in the adoption record.

1984
Carol Cocoa and seven other foster parents found the National Coalition to End Racism in America's Child Care System. The nonprofit organization aims to change policies at all levels of government and supports transracial foster parenting and adoption.

Rabbi Susan Abramson and Phyllis Nissen begin Stars of David, a national support group for Jewish adoptive families.

1986
Congress establishes the National Adoption Information Clearinghouse (NAIC) under the Omnibus Budget Reconciliation Act (P.L. 99–509). This government-funded organization provides professionals and the general public with information on all aspects of adoption, including infant and intercountry adoption and the adoption of children with special needs.

1987
The Orphan Train Heritage Society of America (OTHSA) is formed as a clearinghouse for information regarding the approximately 150,000 children who were sent west to new homes between the years 1854 and 1929.

The Reagan administration forms the Interagency Task Force on Adoptions to "identify barriers to adoption, propose appropriate solutions, and suggest methods to promote adoption."

1989   The UN Convention on the Rights of the Child is adopted by the United Nations on the thirtieth anniversary of the Declaration of the Rights of the Child. The 1989 convention spells out the basic human rights to which children everywhere are entitled.

1990   The American Academy of Adoption Attorneys (AAAA) is formed.

1991   The W. K. Kellogg Foundation launches Families for Kids (FFK) to bring about fundamental reforms in the U.S. adoption system.

1992   Dave Thomas, an adopted person and founder of the Wendy's International food chain, establishes the Dave Thomas Foundation for Adoption, a not-for-profit organization that gives grants to national and regional adoption organizations and does other charitable activities for the benefit of "waiting" children.

1993   After a four-year drafting period, sixty-six nations approve the final text of the Convention on Protection of Children and Co-operation in Respect of Intercountry Adoption (the Hague Adoption Convention), a multilateral treaty with the goal of protecting children, birth parents, and adoptive parents involved in intercountry adoptions.

1994   Congress passes the Multiethnic Placement Act (MEPA), P.L. 103–382, which prohibits agencies receiving federal funds from denying transracial placements solely on the basis of race. It permits the use of race as one of the factors to be considered in adoptive and foster placements.

        The United States signs the Hague Adoption Convention on March 31, showing its intent to proceed with efforts to ratify the convention.

        Administered by the Children's Bureau of the U.S. Department of Health and Human Services, the

1994
(cont.)   Court Improvement Program is established as a response to dramatic increases in child abuse and neglect cases and acknowledgment of the expanded role of courts in achieving stable, permanent homes for children in foster care. All fifty states, as well as the District of Columbia and Puerto Rico, participate in this program.

Norman and Judy Goldberg, with the help of a philanthropist friend, establish the National Adoption Foundation, a nonprofit organization to provide financial support, information, products, and services for adoptive and prospective adoptive parents.

1995   On May 1, the Hague Adoption Convention enters into force among the first three countries to ratify it—Mexico, Romania, and Sri Lanka.

1996   Congress revisits the Multiethnic Placement Act in the form of a revision, the Interethnic Provisions of the Small Business Job Protection Act, P.L. 104–188, Removal of Barriers to Interethnic Adoption, which makes the consideration of race impermissible in foster and adoptive placements. Any entity that receives funds from the federal government and is involved in foster care or adoptive placements may not delay or deny a child's foster care or adoptive placement based on race, color, or national origin of the parent or the child.

President Bill Clinton signs the Personal Responsibility and Work Opportunity Reconciliation Act (PRWORA), the so-called welfare reform act, which among other things states a preference for permanent kinship care when children cannot live with their birth parents.

President Clinton launches his Adoption Initiative, which has as one of its goals the doubling (to 54,000) of the number of children adopted domestically or placed in permanent homes by the year 2002.

The Evan B. Donaldson Adoption Institute is established through the initiative of the board of Spence-Chapin Services to Families and Children. The board sees a need for an independent and unbiased adoption research and policy organization. It is named in honor of Evan B. Donaldson, a long-term advocate for children and member of the board of directors of Spence-Chapin from 1977 until her death in 1994.

Bastard Nation is founded to advocate for the rights of adult citizens, adopted as children, to their own birth records.

1997   The U.S. Congress approves the Adoption and Safe Families Act (ASFA), P.L. 105–89. It amends Title IV-E of the Social Security Act and aims to increase adoptions of waiting children by moving them more quickly from foster care to permanent homes while also keeping children safe.

1998   Oregon voters pass Ballot Measure 58, allowing adult adopted persons to have access to their original birth certificates.

1999   The Convention on the Rights of the Child is ratified by 191 parties, including almost all of the nations of the world except Somalia and the United States. The prevailing view in the United States is that children "belong" to their birth parents, and the notion that the "entire community" must take care of its children is not widely accepted.

The Foster Care Independence Act, P.L. 106–169, indirectly affects adoption in that it increases funding of adoption incentive payments, emphasizes permanent placements, and mandates that state plans prepare prospective parents for foster care and adoption.

2000   The Intercountry Adoption Act, P.L. 106–279, is designed to provide implementation by the United States of the Hague Adoption Convention.

2000
(cont.)

The Child Citizenship Act of 2000 allows internationally adopted children to automatically become citizens when they enter the United States.

The Child Abuse Prevention and Enforcement Act, P.L. 106–177, is passed by Congress to address concerns regarding the level and quality of responses to reports of child maltreatment.

The Children's Health Act, P.L. 106–310, authorizes funding for adoption awareness activities and public awareness campaigns for adoption of infants and children with special needs.

The Child Welfare League's *Standards for Excellence for Adoption Services,* revised for 2000, states that although the current trend in adoption is for openness, a spectrum of options exists, from closed placement to open adoption. If possible, all members of the triad, including the child if old enough, should be consulted as to the amount of openness desired.

The Census of 2000 includes the category "adopted son/daughter" for the first time in U.S. history.

2001

At a meeting of the National Indian Child Welfare Association, the executive director of the Child Welfare League of America, Shay Bilchik, officially apologizes for the Indian Adoption Project, which placed many Native American children in non-Indian homes. Bilchik also goes on record as supporting the Indian Child Welfare Act.

The Promoting Safe and Stable Families Amendments, P.L. 107–133, extend and amend the Promoting Safe and Stable Families Program and the Foster Care Independent Living Program.

The Economic Growth and Tax Relief Reconciliation Act, P.L. 107–16, includes provisions to permanently extend the adoption tax credit.

2003   The Adoption Promotion Act, P.L. 108–145, reautho-
            rizes the adoption incentive program under Title IV-E
            and provides additional incentives for the adoption of
            older children (ages nine and up) from foster care.

            The Keeping Children and Families Safe Act, P.L.
            108–36, extends and amends the Child Abuse Preven-
            tion and Treatment Act, the Adoption Opportunities
            Act, the Abandoned Infants Assistance Act, and the
            Family Violence Prevention and Services Act.

            The Prosecutorial Remedies and Other Tools to End
            the Exploitation of Children Today Act (PROTECT),
            P.L. 108–21, creates a national Amber Alert System
            and provides for stronger penalties for child sexual
            abuse, sexual exploitation, and child pornography.

            On March 1, the service and benefit functions of the Im-
            migration and Naturalization Service (INS) transition
            into the U.S. Citizenship and Immigrations Services
            (USCIS) in the Department of Homeland Security.

            Ellen Herman, faculty member in the Department of
            History at the University of Oregon, creates the Adop-
            tion History Project. The website introduces the his-
            tory of child adoption in the United States by profiling
            individuals, organizations, topics, and studies that
            have shaped adoption in the twentieth century.

            The Dave Thomas Foundation for Adoption incorpo-
            rates in Canada.

2005   The Adoption and Children Act of 2002 is imple-
            mented in England and Wales. The law allows unmar-
            ried couples, including gay couples, to adopt jointly
            (as long as the two people are living in a secure and
            stable relationship). Other provisions are special
            guardianship orders and changes that include giving
            birth mothers and other birth relatives the legal right
            to ask for an intermediary service to trace an adoptive
            adult to find out if contact is welcome.

2006   On February 15, the U.S. Department of State issues
             the final rule on the Accreditation and Approval of
             Agencies and Persons to implement the Hague Adop-
             tion Convention.

5

Biographical Sketches

Individuals in social work, psychology, sociology, medicine, law, and theology have contributed to adoption as we know it today. Some have made an impact without intending to or without even knowing that they changed adoption. Not all who have influenced adoption are professionals. Adoptive parents, birth parents, and adopted persons have helped move adoption in new directions. They have shared their ideas and experiences in books, articles, tapes, movies, and videos. The sharing continues on the Internet.

This chapter presents sketches of thirty men and women. Some are living; some have died. The goal is to present a cross-section of "adoption pioneers" from the beginnings of the field to the present. The alphabetical list is not all-inclusive but a sampling of some of those who have influenced adoption philosophy and practice.

Viola Wertheim Bernard (1907–1998)

The scope of the work of this pioneering psychiatrist/psychoanalyst is difficult to capture in a short summary. Born into a well-to-do family in New York City, she was one of only four women in her medical school class at Cornell University. She received her medical degree in 1936. After her marriage to Theos Casimir Bernard, an anthropologist and explorer, she traveled with her husband. In 1946 she received her certification in psychiatry, having already completed several psychiatric residencies.

Bernard used her intelligence, knowledge, and vision for the good of all. She was a champion of civil rights, civil liberties, and peace. During World War II she made her mother's country home at Nyack, New York, available to European refugees fleeing Nazi persecution. As a social activist, she joined the battle against nuclear war. She was the founder and director of Columbia University's Division of Community and Social Psychiatry, which trained psychiatrists and public health specialists. She worked to make psychiatric help available to the underprivileged and minorities. Throughout her long career, she encouraged medical professionals and organizations to open up to African American participation.

At the same time she pursued an academic career and did clinical work with patients; she won many professional awards. Bernard's work on behalf of children extended to those who were already adopted or were to be adopted. Not only did she serve for forty years as chief psychiatric consultant to the adoption agency Louise Wise Services, she was also on its board of directors for fifty years.

In an effort to understand the conflict over "nature versus nurture," she did studies of adopted twins separated at birth. While championing the idea that children with disabilities, older children, and children of all races were "adoptable," she knew that adoption had no guarantees. However, she opposed the idea that adopted children were at greater risk than others for maladjustment.

Bernard was a believer in telling children as soon as possible in age-appropriate terms that they were adopted. She also rejected the "chosen baby" story, saying that parents did not choose a baby; they chose an agency.

According to the Adoption History Project, Viola Bernard's ideas helped shape policy in psychiatry and adoption in the final third of the twentieth century.

John Bowlby (1907–1990)

Dr. John Bowlby (Edward John Mostyn Bowlby), a British psychiatrist, was a pioneer in "attachment theory" and the emotional trauma that a disruption in a child's bonding with his mother can cause. Bowlby believed, however, that a warm, nurturing constant presence could substitute for the mother figure. Without such an adequate substitute, Bowlby believed that depression, pathological mourning, anxious attachment, delinquency, and the inability to love could result. Bowlby's theories have remained generally intact and have formed the basis for today's attachment theories.

Bowlby attended Dartmouth Royal Naval College and Trinity College, Cambridge, where he majored in psychology and the natural sciences. He took his medical training at the University College Medical School in London. During World War II he served as a psychiatrist in the British army. From 1946 to 1972 Bowlby served as a consulting psychiatrist at the Tavistock Clinic and Tavistock Institute of Human Relations in London.

While in medical school, Bowlby entered the field of psychoanalysis; later, after observing animal behavior and the behavior of children with their mothers, he "re-thought" some of the prevailing psychoanalytic theories of the time. Bowlby's most influential work was the three-volume series that included *Attachment* (1969), *Separation* (1973), and *Loss* (1980). After serving as a consultant to the World Health Organization in 1950 and studying institutionalized children, Bowlby wrote a best-seller, *Child Care and the Growth of Love* (1953), which condemned institutions that deprived a child of a consistent mother figure. His last book, published in the year he died, was *Charles Darwin: A New Biography*, which proposed that childhood losses caused some of Darwin's many illnesses.

Charles Loring Brace (1826–1890)

Charles Loring Brace is best known as the man who initiated "orphan trains." Brace began the program called "placing out" in response to overcrowded orphanages and almshouses in New York City. Beginning in 1854, Brace's agency, the Children's Aid Society, sent more than 100,000 homeless children to the West to be fostered or adopted by farm families.

The program proved to be controversial for several reasons. First, many of the children still had one or both parents. But Brace believed that the urban environment harmed them, especially if they lived on the streets or in orphanages. Not only would the rural life be more healthy for them, Brace believed, but farm families would take better care of them than their birth families had. However, reports surfaced that some farmers treated their new children like slaves. Some of the rural residents complained about the numbers of children being "dumped" into their communities. Also, in many cases, children lost all communication with their birth families, and their parents never learned what had happened to them. Sometimes, though, when parents were living, the agency or the parents (either of which may have retained custody) could have the children moved if they were mistreated. If the children were orphans and met the legal requirements, their foster parents could adopt them; many did. Although the new families had little investigation before, or supervision during, the placement, many of the children adapted well to their new families.

Brace received his undergraduate degree from Yale University and his postgraduate education from Yale Divinity School. As a minister, he preached to the prisoners of Blackwell's Island, New York. Following a trip to Europe, he returned to New York City and was moved by the numbers of homeless children he saw on the streets. After helping to organize the Children's Aid Society of New York City, Brace served as its director for forty years. The organization developed innovative programs for homeless and needy children, including shelters, lodging houses for newsboys, industrial schools, reading rooms, night schools, summer camps, dental clinics, and special classes for disabled children. Brace's most famous book, *The Dangerous Classes of New York and Twenty Years' Work among Them* (1872), brought about positive public sentiment on behalf of the needs of children. Reaction to some of his methods led to reforms of the system.

Pearl S. Buck (1892–1973)

Pearl Buck was the first American woman to win a Nobel Prize in Literature (1938). Earlier (in 1931) she had won a Pulitzer Prize for her novel *The Good Earth.* Buck wrote at least eighty works of literature for children, as well as books for adults. In addition to her writing, Pearl Buck was active in child welfare work and in work with developmentally disabled children.

Although born in West Virginia, Buck spent many of her first forty years in China, where her parents were missionaries. As a young child she received lessons from her American mother in the morning and lessons from a Chinese tutor in the afternoon; she spoke Chinese before she spoke English. In 1914 she graduated from Randolph Macon College in Virginia, and in 1926 she received a master's degree from Cornell University. Later in life she became a crusader for improved relations between the East and the West.

Pearl Buck was married twice, first to John Lossing Buck, an agricultural economist. Their birth daughter Carol had developmental disabilities because of phenylkentonuria, a metabolic disease. The couple also adopted an infant, but the marriage ended in divorce.

In 1935 Pearl Buck married Richard J. Walsh, president of the Day Publishing Company. Together they adopted two infant boys and, later, four mixed-race children.

In 1949 Buck started her own adoption agency, Welcome House, because, as she said, other agencies had been unwilling to place mixed-race children in her family. In 1991 Welcome House merged with the Pearl S. Buck Foundation to form Pearl S. Buck International. The latter organization has three distinct parts— Welcome House, which carries on Buck's mission of adoption services, advocacy, and support; Opportunity House, which expands opportunities for health care, education, jobs, and psychological support to those who would otherwise be denied these services; and Pearl S. Buck House, a National Historic Landmark residence.

Reverend George Clements (1932–)

The Rev. George Clements began the One Church, One Child project, a multidenominational organization, in 1981 at the Holy Angels Church, a predominantly black Catholic church in Chicago, Illinois. One Church, One Child urges every black church to recruit from its members at least one family who will adopt a waiting child.

Father Clements's efforts led to a national recruiting campaign in 1988. Currently more than half of the fifty states use all or parts of the concept, and the organization has facilitated more than 100,000 adoptions across the United States. As a single man, Clements has adopted four children with special needs. *The Father Clements Story*, a 1993 movie starring Louis Gossett Jr., Malcolm-Jamal Warner, and Carroll O'Connor, tells the story of the organization's start and the beginnings of the adoption of Clements's first son.

Clements was born in Chicago, the fourth of six children. He received his BA and MA degrees from St. Mary of the Lake

Seminary. Ordained in 1957, he was the first black graduate of Quigley Seminary. The National Committee for Adoption inducted Clements into its Hall of Fame in 1989 for his efforts on behalf of the adoption of black children.

Dorothy DeBolt and Robert DeBolt

In 1973, Dorothy and Robert (Bob) DeBolt founded the organization now called Adopt a Special Kid (AASK), one of the first national referral programs for children with special needs. AASK has since placed more than 3,000 children in California alone. Requests to replicate its program elsewhere led AASK to operate independently in other states, such as Arizona, Ohio, and New Mexico.

Widowed in 1963, Dorothy was left with seven children between the ages of three and fifteen, including two children adopted from Korea. She then added two boys from Vietnam to the family. Soon thereafter, she met Bob DeBolt, who had one child. Together, the couple parented twenty children, fourteen of them through adoption. The children had multiple challenges, including developmental and physical disabilities. The children are now adults with families of their own. The DeBolts are also great-grandparents.

Dorothy and Bob are the subjects of a 1978 Academy Award–winning documentary, *Who Are the DeBolts?* In 1996 they received the Child Advocates of the Year Award from the North American Council on Adoptable Children (NACAC).

Michael Dorris (1945–1997)

The author Michael Dorris made a large contribution to adoption literature with the 1989 publication of *The Broken Cord.* The book tells how he adopted as a single man Adam, a Sioux child with fetal alcohol syndrome. The book focused public attention on the effects a woman's drinking during pregnancy can have on her unborn child.

Since 1990 the federal government has required alcoholic beverages sold in the United States to carry the following warning: "According to the surgeon general, women should not drink alcoholic beverages during pregnancy because of the risk of birth defects." Dorris's book also provides information on the less severe possible effects of a mother's drinking, currently called fetal alcohol spectrum disorder. Dorris tells of his struggles in raising his son, as well as the role played by his wife (whom he married after adopting Adam), the writer Louise Erdrich, during Adam's adolescent years.

Marian Wright Edelman (1939–)

Attorney, educator, activist, reformer, and children's advocate Marian Wright Edelman is best known for establishing (in 1968) the Washington Research Project, which in 1973 became the Children's Defense Fund (CDF). The CDF aims to create a support network so tightly woven that no child can slip through. The organization is a voice for poor and minority race children, as well as for those with handicapping conditions. The agency not only advocates for these children but also acts as a research center, documenting the problems as well as possible solutions for children in need. It has advocated pregnancy prevention, childcare funding, health care funding, prenatal care, parental responsibility for education in values, the reduction of violent images presented to children, and selective gun control. Edelman has served as president and administrative head of the organization; she has also served as a public speaker and lobbyist in Congress.

Edelman was born in Bennettsville, South Carolina, and grew up there as one of five children. Her father, a Baptist minister, taught his children about service in the world. Edelman attended Spellman College, studied abroad on a Merrill scholarship, and traveled to the Soviet Union on a Lisle fellowship. After returning to the United States and becoming involved in the civil rights movement, she studied law at Yale University. She married Peter Edelman, an assistant to Robert Kennedy; the couple has three sons. She has published several books, including *The Measure of Our Success: A Letter to My Children and Yours*. In 1998 she was honored with a Hannah Neil World of Children award.

Vera Fahlberg (1934–)

Born in Madison, Wisconsin, Vera Fahlberg, MD, is editor of the book *Residential Treatment: A Tapestry of Many Therapies* (1990) and author of *A Child's Journey through Placement* (1991), two influential books in adoption. She and her husband had two birth daughters and many foster children.

Beginning in 1964, Dr. Fahlberg began to specialize in working with disturbed children, including some adopted children and some in foster care. For thirteen years she was the medical director of Forest Heights Lodge, a psychiatric facility for children and adolescents in Evergreen, Colorado. In 1974 she began focusing her attention on treating children with separation issues and attachment difficulties, giving extra attention to children in out-of-home placement. She contributed to child welfare training materials, served as a psychological consultant, and conducted workshops in most of the states, as well as in Canada, England, Scotland, Ireland, Norway, Sweden, Australia, Greece, and Israel. Her workshops addressed such topics as grief and loss, the identity issues of adopted persons, the social and emotional needs of children after adoption, the effects of early trauma and/or frequent moves in foster care, self-esteem issues, and many other topics. Vera Fahlberg retired in 1998.

Florence Anna Fisher (ca. 1929–)

Florence Fisher was born in Brooklyn, New York, and adopted as an infant. Fisher did not know she was adopted until she became a young adult. The search for her birth mother took twenty years.

As the result of her search, Fisher founded the Adoptees' Liberty Movement Association (ALMA) to aid and support adopted persons in their searches. Fisher admitted to being "militant" and uncompromising. She would not stop short of getting free access for adopted persons to their original birth certificates and their adoption records. Fisher organized local ALMA branches in New York, Florida, and California. In 1973 she published *The Search for Anna Fisher,* the story of her search and reunion with her birth family. Fisher's efforts led eventually to the creation (in 1978) of the American Adoption Congress (AAC), an umbrella group with the goal of changing the public's attitudes toward sealed records and lobbying legislators to repeal sealed records laws.

Anna Freud (1895–1982)

Anna Freud was the youngest child of the famous Sigmund Freud, father of psychoanalysis, as well as his companion and colleague through much of his life. Although the older Freud's theories influenced adoption, the work of his daughter and her colleagues had a more direct impact on adoption.

Born and educated in Austria, Anna Freud entered psychoanalysis with her father (not an unusual arrangement at the time) in 1918. In 1922 she joined the Vienna Psychoanalytic Society. Although she followed in her father's footsteps professionally, she chose to specialize in child psychoanalysis.

Living in England during World War II, Freud and her friend Dorothy Burlingham observed babies and preschoolers in three nurseries in Hampstead. The Hampstead Child Therapy Training Course and Clinic later became the Anna Freud Centre. The two researchers discovered that children who were separated from their parents as a result of the war rocked themselves obsessively, banged their heads, and sucked their thumbs constantly. In their book, *Infants without Families,* Freud and Burlingham pointed out that attachment to the mother (or other constant parental figure) was imperative for healthy development. They further concluded that residential facilities could not offer this arrangement. Although their attachment theories and observations were not new, Freud and Burlingham gave psychoanalytic reasons for their conclusions.

Later, Freud's travels to the United States took her to Yale Law School. In the 1970s and 1980s she collaborated with Joseph Goldstein and Albert Solnit. Their books include *Beyond the Best Interests of the Child* (1973), *Before the Best Interests of the Child* (1979), and *In the Best Interests of the Child* (with Sonja Goldstein, 1986). These professionals argued for permanent adoptive homes in which a child, who could not grow up with an involved birth parent, could attach to a "psychological parent." But, according to some experts, the authors still believed strongly in birth family autonomy and family preservation. They believed that the state should intervene only in cases of the most severe abuse. Even then, they thought, every effort should be made to keep a child with birth parents.

Sigmund Freud (1856–1939)

Although Anna Freud's theories and practice had more of a *direct* influence on adoption than those of her father Sigmund Freud, one has to admit there would have been no Anna without Sigmund.

Sigmund Freud was born in what is now the Czech Republic, but the family moved when he was of preschool age to Vienna, Austria, where he lived for most of his life. Freud's father was already a grandfather when he married his second wife, Amalie Nathanson. The couple had eight children; Sigmund was the oldest and his mother's favorite. By the time Sigmund was eight years old, he was reading Shakespeare and could speak several languages.

Freud studied medicine at the University of Vienna, graduated in 1881, and became a neuropathologist. In 1885 a grant enabled him to study in France with the famous neurologist Jean Martin Charcot. The next year he started his own practice and married his long-time fiancée, Martha. The couple had six children; the youngest was Anna. In 1938 Freud, who was Jewish, fled to London to escape the Nazis. He died there the next year.

Freud believed that memories from the subconscious influence a person's behavior and that psychoanalysis could cure certain mental disturbances. He also believed that dreams were important in revealing the unconscious. Among other works, Freud wrote *The Interpretation of Dreams* (1900), *General Introduction to Psychoanalysis* (1920), *Autobiography* (1927), and *Civilization and Its Discontents* (1930). Carl Jung, Alfred Adler, and Freud's daughter carried on his work (in modified ways) after his death.

Freud's theories had many connections to adoption. For one thing, Freud believed that children in general needed to mentally "escape" from parental control, which they often did by having an active fantasy life. In "family romance" images, children might imagine an adoption scenario in which their imaginary parents were kinder and more gentle than their real parents. But with children who were adopted, the "story" was reality. Adopted children's questions such as "Who were my original parents?" "What was *wrong* with me?" and "Why did they give me away?" took on new meaning and often led to confusion, sadness, and feelings of abandonment. No wonder, some thought, that given these challenging questions, adopted persons faced special risks of psychological problems.

Arnold Gesell (1880–1961)

The "normal" child's development (which turned out to have implications for adoption) was Arnold Gesell's main interest. Aspects of his theories are still accepted today. For example, Gesell believed that a child's maturation follows regular developmental pathways.

Born in Alma, Wisconsin, Gesell received his bachelor's degree from the University of Wisconsin. In 1906 he earned his PhD at Clark University in Worchester, Massachusetts. He taught elementary school in New York City before moving on to Yale University, from which he received his MD in 1915. Earlier (in 1911) he had set up a psychological clinic at the New Haven Dispensary. He directed this clinic, which later became known as the Clinic of Child Development, until 1948. In his "laboratory," Gesell did studies on hundreds of New Haven children, testing them with specific developmental tasks, such as catching a ball or climbing stairs. He was one of the first human behaviorists to use photography and one-way mirrors in his observations.

Gesell had opinions on adoption and worked with influential organizations such as the United States Children's Bureau and the Child Welfare League of America. He believed in minimum standards for adoption and thought that trained adoption experts associated with reputable agencies should facilitate adoptions. Professionals used his norms to help them decide which children they considered suitable for placement with which prospective parents. Although Gesell espoused "matching," which was popular at the time, he did not agree with some other experts about eugenics, the so-called science of superior bloodlines, or as some have called it, "weeding out the weak."

Some experts criticized Gesell for basing his work on the observations of middle-class Caucasian children from a single city in New England and for not considering individual and cultural differences. However, Gesell believed that clinical testing would reveal a child's native intelligence that might be hidden because of poverty and/or neglect.

Clara McBride Hale (1905–1992)

Clara McBride Hale was the first director of Hale House, a nonprofit childcare agency that she set up to serve children born addicted to drugs and alcohol. She was born in Philadelphia and moved to New York City after her marriage to Thomas Hale. Her husband died at a young age, leaving her with three children to support. Over the years, she did foster care for more than forty children.

After her "retirement" in 1969, she founded Hale House, located on 122nd Street in Harlem. Hale's goal was to take in children born addicted to drugs at birth, care for them until their mothers graduated from a drug-treatment program, and then reunite them when their mothers were drug-free.

In 1985, Hale's work attracted the attention of President Ronald Reagan, who appointed her (at age eighty) to his American Commission on Drug-Free Schools. The same year, she was awarded an honorary doctorate of humane letters by John Jay College of Criminal Justice in New York City. She received the Booth Community Service award from the Salvation Army in 1990.

Joan Heifetz Hollinger (1940–)

Joan Heifetz Hollinger is a prominent scholar and teacher on adoption law and practice and on the psychosocial aspects of adoptive family relationships. She has been active in efforts to streamline laws governing intercountry adoptions, as well as domestic adoptions, and has worked with legal issues related to open adoption. She was a research consultant for the proposed Uniform Adoption Act, which the National Conference on Uniform State Laws approved in 1994 and the American Bar Association approved in 1995. Hollinger has served as a member of the Children's Bureau task force on Achieving Permanency for Dependent and Foster Children. She has also served on the U.S. State Department's advisory group on intercountry adoption, and is the author of the American Bar Association's guide to the Multiethnic Placement Act. More recently she has worked on drafting model parentage laws for the needs of children conceived by assisted reproductive technology.

Hollinger was born in New York City. She earned a BA degree with high honors from Swarthmore College in 1961, an MA degree in history from the University of California at Berkeley in 1963, and a JD degree cum laude from SUNY Buffalo Law School in 1973. After practicing law in New York State, she taught at the law schools of SUNY Buffalo, Michigan, Stanford, UC Hastings, and the University of Detroit. Since 1993 she has been a faculty member at the Boalt Hall School of Law at the University of California at Berkeley.

Hollinger is the editor and principal author of the three-volume work *Adoption Law and Practice*. Her book *Families by Law: An Adoption Reader* was published in 2004. She and her students at Boalt Hall School of Law have worked on behalf of children and have written *amicus* briefs on behalf of children in contested adoption and custody cases.

Harry Holt (1905–1964) and Bertha Holt (1904–2000)

In 1954, soon after the end of the Korean War, Harry and Bertha Holt saw a documentary film about Amerasian children in Korean orphanages. At the time, they were raising six birth children on a farm near the Willamette Valley town of Creswell, Oregon. In addition to farming, Harry ran a lumber company; Bertha, trained as a nurse, took care of the children and the home. In spite of their busy lives, they decided they would like to adopt some of the orphaned children. But as Harry made plans to go to Korea, the Holts discovered that nothing short of an act of both houses of Congress would allow them to adopt children from Korea. Two months later, the Holts had succeeded in conquering that challenge, and the "Holt Bill" had passed. In October 1955, Harry arrived at the Portland airport with eight Korean orphans in tow.

In 1956 Harry and Bertha founded Holt International Children's Services, which some say was the beginning of intercountry adoption. That same year, Bertha Holt wrote *The Seed from the East,* an account of their adoptions. Her 1972 book, *Outstretched Arms,* tells of the beginnings of the Holt organization. *Bring My Sons from Afar* includes Bertha Holt's observations (through journal excerpts) of the early days of Holt International's work in Korea. In *Created for God's Glory,* she describes the lives of disabled children at the Il San Center in South Korea.

Since then, Holt International Children's Services has cast a wide net in setting standards for excellence in adoption practice, as well as fulfilling its mission to find families for children while keeping in mind the question, "What is best for the child?"

After Harry died in 1964, Bertha—or "Grandma Holt," as many called her—carried on the mission of the organization until her death from a stroke on July 31, 2000. Throughout her long life she received nearly fifty awards, including the National Mother of the Year Award in 1965, the Korean Order of Merit Award

(1995), and the Hannah Neil World of Children Award (2000). Harry and Bertha Holt chose to be buried together in Korea.

Patricia Irwin Johnston (1945–)

Patricia Irwin Johnston is an infertility and adoption educator and publisher of Perspectives Press, which publishes books about infertility and adoption. She was born in Indianapolis, Indiana, and received her BA (1968) and BS (1973) degrees from Butler University in Indianapolis.

Since the mid-1970s, she has written, spoken, volunteered, and advocated for those interested in infertility and adoption. She helped organize a local chapter of RESOLVE, Inc., in Indiana and chaired the organization's national board of directors for three years. She also served on the national board of Adoptive Families of America.

Her books include *Understanding Infertility: Insights for Family and Friends; Taking Charge of Infertility; Adopting after Infertility; Launching a Baby's Adoption;* and *Adoption Is a Family Affair! What Relatives and Friends Must Know.* She edited *Perspectives on a Grafted Tree: Thoughts for Those Touched by Adoption,* a poetry anthology, and for five years wrote a column for *Adoptive Families* magazine. She gives workshops on a variety of infertility, adoption, and parenting issues for consumers and professionals.

Her awards include a 1989 Adoption Activist Award from the North American Council on Adoptable Children, the 1992 Friend of Adoption Award from the Adoptive Parents Committee of New York and New Jersey, a "110 percent" award from the Joint Council on International Children's Services (2005), and the 2006 Robert Todd Duncan Award from her alma mater in recognition of personal and professional achievement that brings honor and distinction to the University.

Patricia Johnston's husband, Dave, was adopted, and they are parents to three young adults (one son and two daughters) who joined the family by adoption.

C. Henry Kempe (1922–1984)

Born in Breslau, Germany, C. Henry Kempe, MD, came to the United States in the 1930s to escape Nazi oppression. He graduated from the University of California School of Medicine in San Francisco and, as a pediatrician, was famous for his interest in protecting children. When he joined the University of Colorado to chair the Department of Pediatrics, he introduced many pioneering practices for the good of children, including unlimited visiting hours for hospitalized children and allowing parents to spend the night in their children's rooms.

In 1958 he created the Child Protection Team (along with Elizabeth Boardman and Betty Elmer) at Colorado General Hospital in Denver. He and pediatrician Ray E. Helfer published the first edition of their book *The Battered Child* in 1968; by that year every state had passed a law mandating the reporting of child abuse. In 1972 he was instrumental in founding the National Center for the Prevention and Treatment of Child Abuse and Neglect at the University of Colorado Health Sciences Center as a national resource on issues of child abuse and neglect. He founded the International Society for the Prevention of Child Abuse and Neglect and edited *The International Journal of Child Abuse and Neglect,* which the society publishes.

Kempe was the author or editor of many books and journal articles on child abuse and neglect. Books include *Helping the Battered Child and His Family,* with Ray Helfer (1972); *Child Abuse* (1978); *Sexually Abused Children and Their Families,* with Patricia Beezley Mrazek (1981); and *The Common Secret: Sexual Abuse of Children and Adolescents,* with wife and child psychiatrist Ruth Kempe (1984). The International Society for the Prevention of Child Abuse and Neglect (ISPCAN) established the C. Henry Kempe Award in 1984; it gives the award every two years to an outstanding young professional or organization that works in preventing child abuse and neglect. That same year, Kempe was nominated for a Nobel Peace Prize for his work on behalf of children.

H. David Kirk (1918–)

H. (Henry) David Kirk, adoptive parent and sociologist, is the author of *Shared Fate: A Theory and Method of Adoptive Relations* (published in 1964 and revised in 1984) and *Adoptive Kinship—An Institution in Need of Reform* (published in 1981 and revised in 1984). Another book, *Exploring Family Life* (1988), is a collection of Kirk's papers, published in honor of his seventieth birthday. Topics include adoption of children, the preference for girls, adoption and child development, adopted children and stress, and the legal application of the best interests of the child. The book also includes Kirk's original instruments for the *Shared Fate* studies.

In *Shared Fate,* Kirk used his studies of 2,000 adoptive families in Canada and the United States to show that adoptive families (usually those who could not have children by birth) are different from families created by birth. At the time, this concept of "differentness" was a new idea.

Kirk points out that if adoptive parents ignored or tried to conceal the differences in their way of family making, as many had in the past, they may have escaped the "stigma" of not having had children by birth. But if they joined with their adopted children in acknowledgment of differences, they could "share" their fate. Kirk's research and observations based on his research laid the foundation for the rejection of "matching" as a policy in the placement of children and pointed toward policies of more openness in adoption. While embracing adoption as a valuable way of family-making, Kirk did not deny its "specialness" and challenges.

Kirk was born into a Jewish family, the Kirchheimer family, in Düsseldorf, Germany. When he was twenty years old, his family escaped Nazi Germany and anglicized their name. Kirk completed his undergraduate studies at the City College of New York and received his PhD from Cornell University. His own experience with "forced migration" and his experiences as a foster parent and adoptive parent of four children led to his subsequent research. From 1954 to 1964, Kirk was an associate professor of sociology at McGill University in Montreal, Canada. In 1964, the year that his classic work *Shared Fate* was published, Kirk moved his employment to the University of Waterloo in Ontario, where as a professor of sociology he taught for twenty-two years.

According to Kirk himself (*Contemporary Authors Online*), he became a sociologist with historical interests because of his curiosity about social change. The study of adoptive kinship, he believed, illustrated some of these patterns in microcosm.

Janusz Korczak (1878–1942)

Thanks to Betty Jean Lifton (profiled next) people in the United

States and elsewhere can now join those in Europe who are more likely to know the story of this hero of orphans. Lifton wrote *The King of Children: The Life and Death of Janusz Korczak,* which was published in 1988 and reprinted in 1997 with an introduction by Elie Wiesel.

Even before World War II, Korczak was known as the "Pied Piper" of poor and orphaned children. He was not only a pediatrician but also a writer and educator who fought for the rights of children. As a Jewish person, he ran orphanages in Poland. But his were not ordinary orphanages; they were progressive institutions for both Jewish and Catholic children in Warsaw. Among other innovative practices designed to protect and educate children, he gave the residents a voice in decision making. He made the orphanages into "just" communities with children's courts and legislative bodies.

Although Korczak could have escaped from the Nazis, he chose to stay with "his" children. When the Nazis took two hundred children under his care in the Warsaw Ghetto to die at the Treblinka concentration camp, Korczak died with them in the gas chambers.

According to the jacket of Lifton's book, "Korczak founded the first national children's newspaper, testified in juvenile courts on behalf of children, and trained teachers and parents in 'moral education' with his books, *How to Love a Child* and *How to Respect a Child.*"

Betty Jean Lifton (1926–)

Betty Jean Lifton was born in New York City and adopted by Oscar and Hilda Kirschner. Lifton did not learn that she had been adopted until she was seven years old. Although her mother told her the truth at that time, she asked her daughter to keep her adoption a secret. According to E. Wayne Carp in *Family Matters: Secrecy and Disclosure in the History of Adoption* (1998, 162), these circumstances became an "obsession" for Lifton, motivated her search, and affected all of her relationships and activities. Lifton graduated from Barnard College in 1948. In 1952 she married Robert Jay Lifton, a psychiatrist who later was awarded a Pulitzer Prize. The couple has four children.

Betty Jean Lifton is well-known for her books about adoption written for adults and young people. She has also written a biography about another adoption pioneer (Janusz Korczak) and several plays. From 1952 to 1954 Lifton and her husband lived in Tokyo, Japan. From 1954 to 1956 they lived in Hong Kong, and in 1960 they returned for another two-year stay in Japan. These years and these experiences provided the setting for many of Lifton's children's books.

But it was Lifton herself and her own experiences with adoption that provided the impetus for her books about adoption for adults and young people. *Twice Born: Memoirs of an Adopted Daughter* was published in 1975. According to one critic, the book was a "parable about a search for identity." *Lost and Found: the Adoption Experience* (1979) tells of Lifton's search for her birth mother and speaks to the need (in Lifton's view) for open adoption records. Lifton's book *Journey of the Adopted Self: A Quest for Wholeness* (1994) includes interviews with other adoptees interwoven with her own experiences. Again Lifton argues for open adoption records.

For younger readers, Lifton wrote *I'm Still Me* (1986), which tells the story of a junior in high school who explores her roots for a history project. The project, which turns into a search for her birth parents, includes the main character's feelings of abandonment and also her guilt at keeping the search secret from her adoptive parents.

A picture book entitled *Tell Me a Real Adoption Story* was published in 1994. In this tale, a little girl feels relieved when her mother tells her the facts of her adoption rather than telling her a made-up story. In dialogue, the book answers some of the questions young children frequently ask about adoption.

Lois Ruskai Melina (1952–)

Lois Melina, formerly editor and publisher of *Adopted Child*, a monthly newsletter for adoptive parents, now writes a regular column on "The Adopted Child" for *Adoptive Families* magazine. She was born in 1952 in Cleveland, Ohio, and received her BA in journalism in 1973 from the University of Toledo (Ohio) and her MA in journalism from Ohio State University in 1976.

Melina is the author of several books about adoption, including *Raising Adopted Children: Practical Reassuring Advice for Every Adoptive Parent* (revised edition, 1998); *The Open Adoption Experience: A Complete Guide for Adoptive and Birth Families—From*

Making the Decision through the Child's Growing Years, with Sharon Kaplan Roszia (1993); and *Making Sense of Adoption* (1989). She has produced several audiotapes on various aspects of adoption, which include *Rituals in Adoption, Raising a Child of a Different Race or Ethnic Background*, and *While You Wait to Adopt*.

In addition, she serves on the board of directors of the Evan B. Donaldson Institute, which is dedicated to improving the quality of information about adoption and providing guidance for practice and policy change in adoption. She speaks frequently about adoption to professionals and adoptive parents in the United States, Canada, and Australia.

Melina and her husband, who live in northern Idaho, are the parents of two children by adoption.

Jean Paton (1908–2002)

Jean Paton, one of the first persons in the United States to question the effects of sealed records on adoptees, was born in Detroit, Michigan. As a social worker and adopted person, she devoted much of her life to helping those who had been adopted.

She received her BA degree from the University of Wisconsin in 1932 and her MA in 1933. In 1942 she was able to look up her adoption records at the probate court in Detroit and found there the full name of her birth mother. (At that time, nearly half the states did not provide for confidentiality of birth records.) In 1945 she received her MSW from the Pennsylvania School of Social Work in Philadelphia. In her early career, Paton was a researcher in labor relations in Washington, DC. She worked for ten years in child placement (social work) and after two years at the Philadelphia Child Guidance Clinic became qualified as a psychiatric social worker.

In 1953 Paton began her emphasis on adoption with a program she initially called the Life History Study Center. In 1954 she privately issued *The Adopted Break Silence*, a book reviewing the results of forty questionnaires from adopted adults about their own feelings regarding adoption. According to E. Wayne Carp in *Family Matters: Secrecy and Disclosure in the History of Adoption* (1998, 140), "Paton's legacy was to give adoptees a voice, by collecting and publishing their life histories." Her book *Orphan Voyage*, published in 1968 under the pseudonym Ruthena Hill Kitson, is a sequel to the first and contains reports of interviews with adopted persons in various parts of Lower Michigan. In subsequent publications, Paton gave her views on such topics as intercountry adoption, why adopted persons are "different," the destructiveness of sealed records, and a memorial statement about her birth mother.

In her later years, Paton moved to Arizona, where she renamed her program Orphan Voyage. She was involved in several adoption-related programs, including Kinship, an alternative-to-adoption program.

Justine Wise Polier (1903–1987)

Justine Wise Polier, a New York Family Court judge and adoption advocate, was born in Portland, Oregon, to well-known parents. Her father, Rabbi Stephen Wise, was one of the founders of the National Association for the Advancement of Colored People (NAACP). Her mother, Louise Waterman Wise, was an artist, humanitarian, and community leader who started an adoption agency for Jewish orphans in 1916. The Free Synagogue Child Adoption Committee was one of the first specialized adoption agencies in the United States at a time when Jewish adoption was uncommon.

After Justine Wise's first husband, a professor of criminal law, died in 1932, she married Shad Polier, an attorney who shared his wife's passion for child welfare. In the 1930s and 1940s she criticized racial and religious "matching," the prevailing practice at the time. She equated matching with discrimination and believed in pluralism, as well as the separation of church and state. Polier believed that children should not be considered "property" of their birth parents or of any organized religion.

Beginning in 1946 Polier served as president of the board of the agency her mother had founded and renamed it Louise Wise Services in honor of her mother. In the 1950s and 1960s Polier helped revise the focus of the organization, changing from sectarian practices to innovative practices in providing services for children of color and in placing children transracially. In addition to its value on a personal level, Polier believed in adoption for its "civic value." In other words, permanent, loving homes would produce happier and more productive citizens.

Jessie Taft (1882–1960)

In many ways, Jessie Taft was a woman ahead of her time. Born in rural Iowa, she graduated from the University of Chicago in 1913 with a PhD in philosophy. In those days, few women pursued such a high level of education. Although she might have preferred teaching or research at a university, not many doors of academia opened to women in the early 1900s.

Instead, Taft carved out a career in social work that lasted twenty years. In 1934 she joined the faculty of the University of Pennsylvania School of Social Work. She also worked for the Children's Aid Society of Pennsylvania, where she pioneered modernizing adoption practices. For example, she led a movement to adopt minimum standards in adoption and to use empirical research to evaluate outcomes for adopted children.

Taft, who had studied with Viennese psychoanalyst Otto Rank, knew adoption from a personal perspective. She and her life-partner, Virginia Robinson (also a child welfare professional), adopted two children. Taft led the way in espousing her belief that the adoption of children, though not second best, is *different* from raising children a person has given birth to. She believed that everyone involved in the adoption, including the birth parents, the adoptive parents, and the children themselves, could and should play an active role in making the adoption a success.

Jessie Taft believed in the concept of therapeutic adoption, which included psychological therapy. In other words, love may not be enough. Taft also believed that adoption could give children love, belonging, and a sense of security.

Sophie van Senden Theis (1885–1957)

An acquaintance of Jessie Taft (above), Sophie van Senden Theis graduated from Vassar College in 1907. At the time, little formal training in social work existed. Theis worked for the New York State Charities Aid Association for forty-five years. Some call her "the first *adoption* social worker in the United States."

In 1921, with her colleague Constance Goodrich, Theis published one of the first training manuals for adoption professionals. The manual offered step-by-step advice to those who placed children in adoptive homes. *The Child in the Foster Home* helped workers decide who would make adequate parents for foster children and who might not, and why and how to reject inappropriate candidates. It also gave advice on placing siblings and suggested when and how to talk to the child about adoption.

In 1924, after documenting what had happened to children placed by her association, she published a study called *How Foster Children Turn Out*. (In general, they "turned out" very well.) Although the first of its kind, Theis's study became a prototype for later outcome studies.

A single woman herself, Theis encouraged single women and female couples to adopt. In fact, she personally facilitated the placement of Jessie Taft and Virginia Robinson's children. According to the Adoption History Project, in some ways attitudes about those who might make acceptable parents may have been more flexible in the early twentieth century than they are today.

Dave Thomas (1932–2002)

The founder of Wendy's International food chain, Dave Thomas was born in Atlantic City, New Jersey, in July 1932. Six weeks later a Michigan couple, Rex and Auleva Thomas, adopted him. When Dave was five years old, his adoptive mother died. His father, not an affectionate man, was a laborer who traveled widely and married three more times. Dave Thomas's grandmother, Minnie Sinclair of Michigan, influenced her grandson's early life, teaching him to do the right thing, to treat people well, and to serve others. His grandmother was the person who decided, when Dave was thirteen, to tell him of his adoption. Thomas believed in open records for adoptees when they turned twenty-one and he thought they should be able to initiate a search for their birth parents.

As an adoptee, Thomas was not bitter about his history. In fact, the opposite was true. He realized many goals in support of adoption, especially for older "waiting" children. He focused his efforts on two main objectives: increasing adoptions from the public system and persuading businesses to make adoption easier for their employees.

In 1990 President George H. W. Bush tapped Thomas to head a White House Initiative on adoption. Through this experience, Thomas discovered obstacles to the process that included overwhelming amounts of paperwork, much "red tape," and high expenses. As a result, he began to try to entice companies and states to offer adoption assistance to those interested in adopting. For example, he started a letter-writing campaign to Fortune 1000 CEOs, asking them to make adoption benefits available to their employees. At the time of his death, approximately 75 percent offered some kind of assistance to employees wanting to adopt.

In 1992 he established the Dave Thomas Foundation for Adoption, a not-for-profit organization that gives grants to national and regional adoption organizations and also does outreach on behalf of waiting children. (In 2003 the foundation incorporated in Canada.)

In 1996 President Bill Clinton signed the Small Business and Job Protection Act of 1996, which gave many adoptive parents of hard-to-place children a one-time tax credit of $6,000 for their adoption and $5,000 for all other types of adoptions. In signing the bill, President Clinton recognized the contributions of Dave Thomas.

In 1997 Clinton signed the Adoption and Safe Families Act, which reduced the time children in foster care had to wait for adoption and provides state incentives and accountability. To call attention to adoption and to these laws, Thomas and his foundation partnered with the U.S. Postal Service in making a first-class stamp (available in 2000) featuring adoption.

Thomas and his wife, Lorraine, were married for forty-seven years and had five children and sixteen grandchildren. Thomas named Wendy's after his second-youngest daughter.

Barbara Tremetiere (1939–)

Barbara Tremitiere, formerly an adoption specialist for Tressler Lutheran Services in York, Pennsylvania, was born in Oak Park, Illinois. (Tressler Lutheran is now part of Diakon Lutheran Social Ministries.) Tremitiere received her BA in 1961 from Miami University in Oxford, Ohio; her MSW from the Graduate School of Social Work at the University of Pittsburgh; and a PhD in social work in 1991 from Union Institute, Cincinnati, Ohio. She served as an adjunct faculty member at three Pennsylvania colleges: York College, Lebanon Valley College, and Pennsylvania State University.

As the parent of fifteen children (including twelve adopted as special needs children), Tremetiere gave practical, anecdotal, and humor-filled trainings and workshops for adoptive parents, social workers, and others interested in the placement of "waiting children." She is the author or coauthor of a number of publications and training materials, including *Kids in Batches* (with Margaret Ward, 1990) and *The Large Adoptive Family: A Special Kind of "Normal"* (1994).

6

Facts and Data

T his chapter provides statistics and methods of data collection on adoption, and discusses how federal laws and Supreme Court verdicts have affected adoption. In several cases, excerpts of testimony from Senate hearings have been included.

The Children's Bureau

President William Howard Taft created the Children's Bureau in 1912 to investigate and report on important social issues of his time, such as infant mortality, birth rates, orphanages, and juvenile courts. The Children's Bureau is one of several bureaus in the Administration on Children, Youth and Families, in the U.S. Department of Health and Human Services. The primary responsibility of the Children's Bureau is the administration of federal child welfare programs. Its mission is to provide for safety (preventing child abuse), permanency (finding "forever" homes for children who cannot return to their birth parents), and for the well-being of children through partnerships with states, tribes, and communities. More information on policies of the Children's Bureau is available at http://www.acf.hhs.gov/programs/cb and in chapter 7.

The Child Welfare Information Gateway

Under the auspices of the Children's Bureau, two separate but related information clearinghouses were available to students of adoption. These two repositories of information were the National Clearinghouse on Child Abuse and Neglect Information (NCCANCH) and the National Adoption Information Clearinghouse (NAIC). Congress established the NCCANCH in 1974 with the Child Abuse Prevention and Treatment Act to collect, organize, and disseminate information on child mistreatment. Congress later (1987) established the National Adoption Information Clearinghouse to provide information on all aspects of adoption, including domestic and intercountry adoption. On June 21, 2006, the Child Welfare Information Gateway (CWIG) combined, consolidated, and expanded the resources of the NCCANCH and the NAIC. It now offers a website, http://www.childwelfare.gov. The following are three questions that reports from CWIG have been able to answer.

How Many Children Were Adopted in 2000 and 2001?

In order to estimate trends in adoption, it is helpful to know how many children are adopted in the United States in any given year. This information is not easy to collect and takes years to assemble. The Child Welfare Information Gateway has made available an estimate of the number of children adopted in 2000 and 2001. These figures are presented in Figure 6.1.

The number of adoptions, ranging from 118,000 to 127,000, has remained relatively constant since 1987. The numbers in 2000 and 2001 were approximately 127,000.

- Public agency adoptions and intercountry adoptions together now account for more than half of all adoptions. (Formerly, kinship adoptions and private-agency adoptions dominated.)
- Adoptions through publicly funded child welfare agencies increased, accounting for two-fifths of all adoptions. The more than 50,000 (40 percent of the total) of these adoptions in each of the years (2000 and 2001) was up from 18 percent in 1992 for the thirty-six states reporting at that time.
- Intercountry adoptions made up 15 percent of the total. This represented an increase from 5 percent to 15 percent of adoptions in the United States between 1992 and 2001.

- The final two-fifths of the adoptions were private agency, kinship, or tribal. (It was not possible to separate the percentages within this group, although the numbers have decreased.) For example, in 1992 stepparent adoptions (a form of kinship adoption) accounted for 42 percent of all adoptions.

FIGURE 6.1
How Many Children Were Adopted in 2000 and 2001?

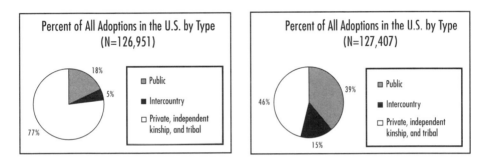

Source: Child Welfare Information Gateway. Accessed at
http://www.childwelfare.gov/pubs/s_adoptedhighlights.cfm. Reprinted with permission.

How Many People Are Seeking to Adopt?

In a report entitled "Persons Seeking to Adopt: Numbers and Trends," CWIG (2005) reports that although most people in the United States have favorable ideas about adoption, few have taken steps to adopt a child and even fewer have adopted.

According to polls, more than a third of Americans have considered adopting. However, no more than 2 percent have actually adopted. Figure 6.2 presents data from the 1995 National Survey of Family Growth (NSFG).

- In 1995, almost 10 million "ever-married" American women between the ages of eighteen and forty-four had considered adoption, which was more than one-fourth (26.4 percent) of all ever-married women.

- Approximately 16 percent of those who had considered adoption (4 percent of the total of ever-married women) had taken concrete steps to adopt.
- Only 31 percent of those who had taken concrete steps to adopt (1.3 percent of all ever-married women) had completed an adoption.

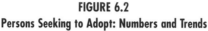

FIGURE 6.2
Persons Seeking to Adopt: Numbers and Trends

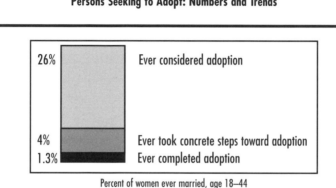

26%	Ever considered adoption
4%	Ever took concrete steps toward adoption
1.3%	Ever completed adoption

Percent of women ever married, age 18–44

Source: Child Welfare Information Gateway, reprinted from Chandra et al., 1999. Accessed at http://www.childwelfare.gov/pubs/s_seek.cfm.

The report goes on to say that the characteristics of those who had adopted varied according to whether they adopted a related or nonrelated child. Women who had problems with fertility and/or had no other children, were Caucasian, and had higher income and education levels were more likely to adopt an unrelated child. Black families and families with lower levels of income and education were more likely to adopt a child related to them.

Another survey (Harris Interactive, 2002) in a study of 1,400 Americans found that the highest percentages of Americans who had considered adopting were between the ages of thirty-five and fifty-five, married, and female. In contrast to the findings of the National Survey of Family Growth, the Harris poll found that income and education were not factors. The greatest differences were that Hispanic populations had a higher likelihood of consideration of adoption than African American or white populations.

All of the studies found discrepancies between those who considered adoption and those who actually adopted. Authorities guessed (and also found some evidence) that the reason some people do not continue with an adoption plan is that they are concerned about the health or behavioral problems of children adopted from the foster-care system. (The Harris poll found that race and the age of the child did not play as big a part as might have been expected.)

Trends include fewer ever-married women adopting in the mid-1990s than in the mid-1970s, but an increasing proportion of women adopting stepchildren and children of relatives. Also, the interest in adoption seems to have remained relatively stable over time.

The report suggests that future research might include studies to find out how many men seek to adopt, more information on what keeps those who consider adoption from actually following through, and an exploration of differences in reasons why people of different ethnic/racial/socioeconomic groups adopt.

How Many Women Place Their Children for Adoption, and Who Are the Women Who Place Their Children?

"Voluntary Relinquishment for Adoption: Numbers and Trends" (2005) is another report available from the Child Welfare Information Gateway. The NSFG collected statistics that show that the number of voluntary relinquishments of infants for adoption in the United States is very small and getting smaller.

According to the 1995 survey, less than 1 percent of children born to never-married women were placed for adoption from 1989 to 1995. According to the CWIG report, since the mid-1970s relinquishments declined from nearly 9 percent to less than 1 percent. Estimates from researchers at the Centers for Disease Control and Prevention in 2004 show that birth mothers relinquished fewer than 14,000 children in 2003. (The percentage of children relinquished by white never-married women—1.7 percent—is higher than for black never-married women—close to zero percent. Relinquishment by married and formerly married women is even rarer, and percentages are not available.)

Figure 6.3 shows how rare voluntary relinquishment is for both black and white women.

FIGURE 6.3
Percent of Infants Relinquished for Adoption by
Never-Married Women Under 45 Years

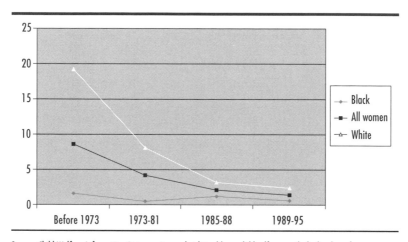

Source: Child Welfare Information Gateway. Accessed at http://www.childwelfare.gov/pubs/s_place.cfm.

Very little additional data is available on which women voluntarily relinquish their children, except that unmarried teens who do relinquish are usually Caucasian and have higher educational levels and perhaps stronger career aspirations than those who do not relinquish. Another factor in a teen's decision to voluntarily relinquish is a strong preference expressed by the teen's mother or by the birth father.

Researchers and professionals in adoption offer several possible reasons for the recent decline in relinquishments. One is that social acceptance of single parents has increased, leading more unmarried women to parent their children. Another is that informal adoptions have become more common than they were in the past. Also, unmarried mothers are increasingly older (in their twenties rather than in their teens), so they may have more financial security.

More research will probably be done in the future on the role of birth fathers. However, the low numbers of infants being placed for adoption make research (and generalizations based on the research) difficult. Currently the courts have not given birth fathers much power to veto a relinquishment if they have not taken an active role before or immediately after the birth of the child. The report "Voluntary Relinquishment or Adoption: Numbers and Trends" is available from CWIG at http://www.child-welfare.gov/ppubs/s_place.cfm.

Data Collection History and Sources

Since the 1940s, a number of sources have collected adoption data. Through the Children's Bureau (CB) and the National Center for Social Statistics (NCSS), the federal government collected data sporadically during the years from 1944 to 1957. From 1957 to 1975 the government compiled annual statistics on adoption. In 1975, however, the NCSS dissolved, and data collection stopped. Congress tried to address the problem of lack of data with the enactment of the Adoption Assistance and Child Welfare Act of 1980 (P.L. 96–272).

In 1982 the U.S. Department of Health and Human Services (HHS) funded the American Public Welfare Association to conduct a voluntary annual survey of the states. This survey was called the Voluntary Cooperative Information System (VCIS) and collected data only on children from the public child welfare system. Beginning in 1995, federal statutes and regulations mandated the states to report adoptions through the public child welfare system to the Children's Bureau. These data are entered into the Federal Adoption and Foster Care Analysis and Reporting System (AFCARS), which replaced VCIS. AFCARS data, along with other measures, monitor the states' progress in achieving the goals of the Adoption and Safe Families Act of 1997.

Adoption and Foster Care Analysis and Reporting Systems (AFCARS)

If state child welfare agencies have responsibility for placement, care, or supervision of certain children, AFCARS collects case-level information on these children. AFCARS also collects information on children who are adopted under the auspices of a state's public child welfare agency. This data, available through the Child Welfare Information Gateway, goes back to the first report in 1999 and at press time was available through June 2006. (A "trends" document, which gives a summary of several years of

AFCARS information, is available at http://www.acf.hhs.gov/programs/cb/stats_research/afcars/trends.htm.) The states are required to submit AFCARS data semi-annually to the Administration for Children and Families.

Some of the reports are *preliminary,* some are *interim,* and others are *final.* Preliminary reports include data received by September 30 for the period ending March 31, and by March 31 for the period ending September 30. Interim reports include subsequent data used to calculate awards for the Adoption Incentive Program or the Children's Bureau's Annual Report to Congress. Final reports are issued when it is likely that outcomes can no longer be improved. Later AFCARS information as it becomes available in the future will be found at http://www.acf.hhs.gov/programs/cb/stats_research/index.htm#afcars.

Statewide Automated Child Welfare Information System (SACWIS)

The Statewide Automated Child Welfare Information System (SACWIS) is a comprehensive case management tool that supports and assists case management practices of social workers in adoption and foster care. The Children's Bureau funded the states to develop their individual SACWIS systems. Some states, however, did not choose to access that funding. With or without SACWIS, states must submit certain data to the Children's Bureau on a mandated schedule.

What Is the Difference between AFCARS and SACWIS?

SACWIS is a "case management" system that serves as an electronic case file for children and families involved with the child welfare programs of the states. One of the reports that these data generate is the AFCARS information, which is then sent to the Administration for Children and Families on a semi-annual basis. Of all of the potential data sources, AFCARS is the only one that contains information about the characteristics of children being adopted as well as information on the birth families and adoptive families.

AFCARS Data

Tables 6.1 through 6.26 show results from the eleventh AFCARS report. All of these tables are available from the Children's Bureau website at http://www.acf.hhs.gov/programs/cb/stats_research/afcars/tar/report11.htm.

TABLE 6.1
What were the ages of the children in foster care?

Mean Years	10.1	
Median Years	10.9	
Less than 1 Year	5%	26,642
1 Year	6%	30,749
2 Years	6%	28,446
3 Years	5%	26,263
4 Years	5%	23,638
5 Years	4%	22,338
6 Years	4%	21,382
7 Years	4%	20,495
8 Years	4%	20,242
9 Years	4%	20,292
10 Years	4%	21,151
11 Years	4%	23,051
12 Years	5%	25,194
13 Years	6%	29,406
14 Years	7%	33,929
15 Years	8%	39,041
16 Years	8%	41,872
17 Years	7%	38,379
18 Years	3%	14,706
19 Years	1%	6,185
20 Years	1%	3,601

Source: Adoption and Foster Care Analysis and Reporting System (AFCARS) data submitted for the FY 2004, October 1, 2003, through September 30, 2004.

Note: Data from both the regular and revised submissions received by June 2006 are included in the data. Missing data are not used in the calculation of percentages.

TABLE 6.2
What were the lengths of stay in foster care?

Mean Months	30.0	
Median Months	16.5	
Less than 1 Month	5%	25,136
1 to 5 Months	18%	94,559
6 to 11 Months	17%	88,610
12 to 17 Months	18%	64,394
18 to 23 Months	9%	44,543
24 to 29 Months	7%	35,534
30 to 35 Months	5%	26,081
3 to 4 Years	12%	61,206
5 Years or More	15%	76,938

Source: Adoption and Foster Care Analysis and Reporting System (AFCARS) data submitted for the FY 2004, October 1, 2003, through September 30, 2004.

TABLE 6.3
What were the placement settings of children in foster care?

Pre-Adoptive Home	4%	21,483
Foster Family Home (Relative)	24%	122,528
Foster Family Home (Nonrelative)	46%	238,084
Group Home	9%	45,609
Institution	10%	51,585
Supervised Independent Living	1%	5,858
Runaway	2%	10,931
Trial Home Visit	4%	20,923

Source: Adoption and Foster Care Analysis and Reporting System (AFCARS) data submitted for the FY 2004, October 1, 2003, through September 30, 2004.

TABLE 6.4
What were the case goals of the children in foster care?

Reunify with Parent(s) or Principal Caretaker(s)	49%	255,280
Live with Other Relative(s)	4%	22,785
Adoption	20%	102,777
Long-Term Foster Care	8%	40,832
Emancipation	6%	32,370
Guardianship	3%	16,277
Case Plan Goal Not Yet Established	9%	46,679

Source: Adoption and Foster Care Analysis and Reporting System (AFCARS) data submitted for the FY 2004, October 1, 2003, through September 30, 2004.

TABLE 6.5
What was the race/ethnicity of the children in foster care?

American Indian/Alaska Native — Non-Hispanic	2%	10,323
Asian—Non-Hispanic	1%	3,099
Black — Non-Hispanic	34%	175,089
Hawaiian/Pacific Islander — Non-Hispanic	0%	1,474
Hispanic	18%	93,759
White—Non-Hispanic	40%	205,561
Unknown/Unable to Determine	2%	12,050
Two or More Races—Non-Hispanic	3%	15,645

Source: Adoption and Foster Care Analysis and Reporting System (AFCARS) data submitted for the FY 2004, October 1, 2003, through September 30, 2004.

Note: Using U.S. Bureau of the Census standards, children of Hispanic origin may be of any race. Beginning in FY 2000, children could be identified with more than one race designation.

TABLE 6.6
What was the gender of the children in foster care?

Male	53%	271,780
Female	47%	245,220

Source: Adoption and Foster Care Analysis and Reporting System (AFCARS) data submitted for the FY 2004, October 1, 2003, through September 30, 2004.

TABLE 6.7
What were the ages of the children who entered care during FY 2004?

Mean Years	8.3	
Median Years	8.1	
Less than 1 Year	14%	43,721
1 Year	6%	19,667
2 Years	6%	17,614
3 Years	5%	16,246
4 Years	5%	14,631
5 Years	5%	13,803
6 Years	4%	12,957
7 Years	4%	12,069
8 Years	4%	11,473
9 Years	4%	11,129
10 Years	4%	11,366
11 Years	4%	11,897
12 Years	5%	13,943
13 Years	6%	16,993
14 Years	7%	20,445
15 Years	8%	23,164
16 Years	7%	20,636
17 Years	4%	12,394
18 Years	0%	703
19 Years	0%	112
20 Years	0%	37

Source: Adoption and Foster Care Analysis and Reporting System (AFCARS) data submitted for the FY 2004, October 1, 2003, through September 30, 2004.

TABLE 6.8
What was the race/ethnicity of the children who entered care during FY 2004?

American Indian/Alaska Native—Non-Hispanic	2%	6,728
Asian—Non-Hispanic	1%	2,468
Black — Non-Hispanic	27%	81,253
Hawaiian/Pacific Islander—Non-Hispanic	0%	1,057
Hispanic	18%	54,433
White — Non-Hispanic	46%	141,506
Unknown/Unable to Determine	3%	7,830
Two or More Races—Non-Hispanic	3%	9,726

Source: Adoption and Foster Care Analysis and Reporting System (AFCARS) data submitted for the FY 2004, October 1, 2003, through September 30, 2004.

Note: Using U.S. Bureau of the Census standards, children of Hispanic origin may be of any race. Beginning in FY 2000, children could be identified with more than one race designation.

TABLE 6.9
What were the ages of the children who exited care during FY 2004?

Mean Years	9.9	
Median Years	9.8	
Less than 1 Year	5%	13,413
1 Year	6%	17,882
2 Years	7%	18,522
3 Years	6%	17,012
4 Years	5%	15,143
5 Years	5%	14,137
6 Years	4%	12,733
7 Years	4%	12,076
8 Years	4%	11,429
9 Years	4%	11,781
10 Years	4%	11,059
11 Years	4%	11,191
12 Years	4%	11,499
13 Years	4%	12,522
14 Years	5%	14,531
15 Years	6%	16,403
16 Years	6%	17,599
17 Years	7%	19,762
18 Years	7%	19,608
19 Years	1%	3,514
20 Years	1%	2,073

Source: Adoption and Foster Care Analysis and Reporting System (AFCARS) data submitted for the FY 2004, October 1, 2003, through September 30, 2004.

TABLE 6.10
What were the outcomes for the children exiting foster care during FY 2004?

Reunification with Parent(s) or Primary Caretaker(s)	54%	151,648
Living with Other Relative(s)	12%	33,397
Adoption	18%	51,413
Emancipation	8%	23,121
Guardianship	4%	12,519
Transfer to Another Agency	2%	6,126
Runaway	2%	4,261
Death of Child	0%	514

Source: Adoption and Foster Care Analysis and Reporting System (AFCARS) data submitted for the FY 2004, October 1, 2003, through September 30, 2004.

Note: Deaths are attributable to a variety of causes including medical conditions, accidents, and homicide.

TABLE 6.11
What were the lengths of stay of the children who exited foster care during FY 2004?

Mean Months	21.5	
Median Months	11.9	
Less than 1 Month	18%	50,565
1 to 5 Months	16%	46,183
6 to 11 Months	16%	45,802
12 to 17 Months	12%	34,751
18 to 23 Months	9%	24,316
24 to 29 Months	6%	17,756
30 to 35 Months	5%	13,142
3 to 4 Years	10%	27,137
5 Years or More	8%	23,347

Source: Adoption and Foster Care Analysis and Reporting System (AFCARS) data submitted for the FY 2004, October 1, 2003, through September 30, 2004.

TABLE 6.12
What was the race/ethnicity of the children who exited care during FY 2004?

American Indian/Alaska Native—Non-Hispanic	2%	5,846
Asian—Non-Hispanic	1%	2,400
Black—Non-Hispanic	29%	82,373
Hawaiian/Pacific Islander—Non-Hispanic	0%	1,043
Hispanic	17%	47,832
White — Non-Hispanic	45%	127,866
Unknown/Unable to Determine	3%	7,191
Two or More Races — Non-Hispanic	3%	8,449

Source: Adoption and Foster Care Analysis and Reporting System (AFCARS) data submitted for the FY 2004, October 1, 2003, through September 30, 2004.

Note: Using U.S. Bureau of the Census standards, children of Hispanic origin may be of any race. Beginning in FY 2000, children could be identified with more than one race designation.

TABLE 6.13
What is the gender distribution of the waiting children?

Male	53%	62,886
Female	47%	55,114

Source: Adoption and Foster Care Analysis and Reporting System (AFCARS) data submitted for the FY 2004, October 1, 2003, through September 30, 2004.

Note: Waiting children are identified as children who have a goal of adoption and/or whose parental rights have been terminated. Children sixteen years old or older whose parental rights have been terminated and who have a goal of emancipation have been excluded from the estimate.

TABLE 6.14
How many months have the waiting children been in continuous foster care?

Mean Months	43.8	
Median Months	32.5	
Less than 1 Month	1%	661
1–5 Months	4%	4,151
6–11 Months	8%	9,191
12–17 Months	11%	13,415
18–23 Months	11%	13,390
24–29 Months	11%	13,352
30–35 Months	9%	10,361
36–59 Months	21%	25,335
60 or More Months	24%	28,144

Source: Adoption and Foster Care Analysis and Reporting System (AFCARS) data submitted for the FY 2004, October 1, 2003, through September 30, 2004.

TABLE 6.15
What is the racial/ethnic distribution of the waiting children?

American Indian/Alaska Native–Non-Hispanic	2%	2,316
Asian–Non-Hispanic	0%	484
Black–Non-Hispanic	38%	45,025
Hawaiian/Pacific Islander — Non-Hispanic	0%	357
Hispanic	14%	16,997
White — Non-Hispanic	38%	44,991
Unknown/Unable to Determine	3%	3,644
Two or More Races — Non-Hispanic	4%	4,186

Source: Adoption and Foster Care Analysis and Reporting System (AFCARS) data submitted for the FY 2004, October 1, 2003, through September 30, 2004.

Note: Using U.S. Bureau of the Census standards, children of Hispanic origin may be of any race. Beginning in FY 2000, children could be identified with more than one race designation.

TABLE 6.16
**How old were the waiting children when they were removed
from their parents or caretakers?**

Mean Years	5.1	
Median Years	4.5	
Less than 1 Year	24%	27,732
1 Year	8%	9,730
2 Years	7%	8,808
3 Years	7%	8,211
4 Years	7%	8,031
5 Years	7%	7,815
6 Years	7%	7,902
7 Years	6%	7,399
8 Years	6%	6,849
9 Years	5%	6,353
10 Years	5%	5,534
11 Years	4%	4,444
12 Years	3%	3,538
13 Years	2%	2,635
14 Years	1%	1,663
15 Years	1%	878
16 Years	0%	386
17 Years	0%	80
18 Years	0%	8
19 Years	0%	3
20 Years	0%	2

Source: Adoption and Foster Care Analysis and Reporting System (AFCARS) data submitted for the FY 2004, October 1, 2003, through September 30, 2004.

TABLE 6.17
Where were the waiting children living on September 30, 2004?

Preadoptive Home	15%	17,165
Foster Family Home (Relative)	17%	20,510
Foster Family Home (Nonrelative)	55%	65,324
Group Home	4%	5,370
Institution	7%	8,282
Supervised Independent Living	0%	209
Runaway	1%	707
Trial Home Visit	0%	432

Source: Adoption and Foster Care Analysis and Reporting System (AFCARS) data submitted for the FY 2004, October 1, 2003, through September 30, 2004.

TABLE 6.18
How old were the children on September 30, 2004?

Mean Years	8.8	
Median Years	8.7	
Less than 1 Year	4%	4,207
1 Year	7%	8,079
2 Years	7%	8,358
3 Years	6%	7,870
4 Years	6%	7,011
5 Years	6%	6,672
6 Years	5%	6,403
7 Years	5%	6,148
8 Years	5%	5,950
9 Years	5%	6,145
10 Years	5%	6,397
11 Years	6%	6,800
12 Years	6%	6,956
13 Years	6%	7,062
14 Years	6%	6,931
15 Years	6%	6,553
16 Years	5%	5,976
17 Years	3%	3,252
18 Years	1%	899
19 Years	0%	237
20 Years	0%	90

Source: Adoption and Foster Care Analysis and Reporting System (AFCARS) data submitted for the FY 2004, October 1, 2003, through September 30, 2004.

TABLE 6.19
As of September 30, 2004, how many months had elapsed since the parental rights of these foster children were terminated?

Mean Months	28.3
Median Months	16.8

Adoptions can be reported to the AFCARS adoption database at any time after the adoption has been finalized. This report includes adoptions finalized in FY 2004 reported in regular and revised submissions by June 1, 2006.

Notes: The number of adoptions reported here do not equal the number of adoption discharges reported under foster care exits because the adoptions reported here include adoptions of some children who were not in foster care but received other support from the public agency. In addition, states have historically underreported adoption discharges. In contrast, states tend to more accurately report the adoptions to the AFCARS adoption database because those are the adoptions used to calculate adoption incentive awards. Missing data are not used in the calculation of the percentages.

TABLE 6.20
What is the gender distribution of the children adopted from the public foster care system?

Male	51%	26,324
Female	49%	25,676

Source: Adoption and Foster Care Analysis and Reporting System (AFCARS) data submitted for the FY 2004, October 1, 2003, through September 30, 2004.

TABLE 6.21
How old were the children when they were adopted from the public foster care system?

Mean Years	6.9	
Median Years	5.9	
Less than 1 Year	2%	957
1 Year	2%	4,482
2 Years	12%	6,141
3 Years	11%	5,557
4 Years	9%	4,742
5 Years	8%	4,092
6 Years	7%	3,536
7 Years	6%	3,241
8 Years	5%	2,848
9 Years	5%	2,708
10 Years	5%	2,572
11 Years	5%	2,477
12 Years	4%	2,227
13 Years	4%	1,891
14 Years	3%	1,474
15 Years	2%	1,109
16 Years	2%	834
17 Years	1%	587
18 Years	0%	149
19 Years	0%	28
20 Years	0%	7

Source: Adoption and Foster Care Analysis and Reporting System (AFCARS) data submitted for the FY 2004, October 1, 2003, through September 30, 2004.

TABLE 6.22
What percentage of the children adopted receive an adoption subsidy?

Yes	89%	46,561
No	11%	5,469

Source: Adoption and Foster Care Analysis and Reporting System (AFCARS) data submitted for the FY 2004, October 1, 2003, through September 30, 2004.

TABLE 6.23
What is the racial/ethnic distribution of the children adopted from the public foster care system?

American Indian/Alaska Native — Non-Hispanic	1%	630
Asian—Non-Hispanic	0%	258
Black—Non-Hispanic	32%	16,726
Hawaiian/Pacific Islander—Non-Hispanic	0%	128
Hispanic	17%	8,719
White—Non-Hispanic	42%	21,971
Unknown/Unable to Determine	2%	1,280
Two or More Races—Non-Hispanic	4%	2,288

Source: Adoption and Foster Care Analysis and Reporting System (AFCARS) data submitted for the FY 2004, October 1, 2003, through September 30, 2004.

Note: Using U.S. Bureau of the Census standards, children of Hispanic origin may be of any race. Beginning in FY 2000, children could be identified with more than one race designation.

TABLE 6.24
How many months did it take after termination of parental rights for the children to be adopted?

Mean Months	15.8	
Median Months	11.3	
Less than 1 Month	3%	1,511
1–5 Months	20%	10,642
6–11 Months	29%	15,257
12–17 Months	19%	9,673
18–23 Months	11%	5,512
24–29 Months	6%	3,203
30–35 Months	4%	1,901
3–4 Years	6%	2,998
5 Years or More	3%	1,304

Source: Adoption and Foster Care Analysis and Reporting System (AFCARS) data submitted for the FY 2004, October 1, 2003, through September 30, 2004.

TABLE 6.25
What is the family structure of the child's adoptive family?

Married Couple	68%	35,578
Unmarried Couple	2%	812
Single Female	27%	14,240
Single Male	3%	1,370

Source: Adoption and Foster Care Analysis and Reporting System (AFCARS) data submitted for the FY 2004, October 1, 2003, through September 30, 2004.

TABLE 6.26
What was the relationship of the adoptive parents to the child prior to the adoption?

Nonrelative	16%	8,435
Foster Parent	59%	30,884
Stepparent	1%	56
Other Relative	24%	12,624

Source: Adoption and Foster Care Analysis and Reporting System (AFCARS) data submitted for the FY 2004, October 1, 2003, through September 30, 2004.

Federal Laws and Policy

In the United States, the primary responsibility for child welfare services belongs to the individual states. Each state makes laws and sets up administrative structures to address the needs of children. In order to be eligible for federal funds for adoption, foster care, and other child welfare services, the states must comply with federal guidelines. In addition to state laws, the federal government also makes laws to try to improve the welfare of children, and these laws impact adoption services in many ways.

In the middle of the 1900s, Congress passed laws that affected intercountry adoption. For example, in 1948 Congress passed the Displaced Persons Act, which permitted more than 200,000 European refugees to enter the United States. This act also allowed 3,000 displaced orphans to emigrate from their countries to the United States. Congress periodically renewed the temporary provisions of the act for varying time periods—from one to three years. In 1953 Congress allowed up to 500 special visas for Korean orphans to be adopted by U.S. service personnel or civil servants. (This was the first instance of the immigration of orphans other than European children.) The Refugee Act of 1953 opened the way for 4,000 additional orphans to enter the country over the following three years. In 1957 Congress removed numerical quotas from orphan visas, and in 1961 the Immigration and Nationality Act included a permanent reference to orphans Americans planned to adopt.

This section presents examples of more recent federal legislation pertaining to adoption. The Child Welfare Information Gateway has prepared a summary of major federal legislation (beginning in 1974) that has had an impact on adoption in particular and child welfare in general. This information and a table ("Timeline of Major Federal Legislation Concerned with Child Protection, Child Welfare, and Adoption") are available at http://nccanch.acf.hhs.gov/pubs/otherpubs/fedlegis.pdf.

An index of federal child welfare laws is available at http://childwelfare.gov/systemwide/laws_policies/federal/federalchildlaws.cfm. The Public Law (P.L.) numbers link to summaries of the bills, which are provided by http://www.Thomas.gov, a service of the Library of Congress. The Children's Bureau has a website that covers all federal and tribal laws concerning child maltreatment, child welfare, and adoption at http://

www.acf.hhs.gov/programs/cb/laws_policies/index.htm#laws. The present summary will address provisions of the acts that specifically apply to adoption.

The Child Abuse Prevention and Treatment Act of 1974 (P.L. 93–274)

Congress enacted the original Child Abuse Prevention and Treatment Act (CAPTA) of 1974 in response to the findings of medical reports revealing large numbers of cases of child abuse, and the government's recognition of the problem of abused and neglected children. The original act has been amended several times (in 1978, 1984, 1988, 1992, and 1996) and most recently was amended and reauthorized on June 25, 2003, by the Keeping Children and Families Safe Act (P.L. 108–36).

With the passage of the original CAPTA, which dealt in many ways with the problem of child abuse, the U.S. Congress subsequently implemented amendments that have helped protect children and have impacted adoption. As a response to the lead of the federal government, the states have also enacted new adoption laws and programs for the benefit of children.

The Child Abuse Prevention and Treatment Act and Adoption Reform Act of 1978 (P.L. 95–266)

This first reauthorization of CAPTA established the Adoption Opportunities Program, which aimed to facilitate the placement of children with special needs in permanent adoptive homes, set "quality standards" for adoptive placements and the rights of adopted children, and provided for a national adoption information exchange system.

The Child Abuse Amendments of 1984 (P.L. 98–457)

One of the provisions of this amendment to CAPTA concerned the care of disabled infants with life-threatening conditions. It required state-level programs to facilitate adoption opportunities for these infants and also required the states to have protective systems in place for response to reports of medical neglect of children. Another feature was a provision for the establishment and operation of a federal adoption and foster care data-gathering and analysis system.

The Child Abuse Prevention, Adoption, and Family Services Act of 1988 (P.L. 100–294)

This reauthorization of CAPTA included amendments to expand the Adoption Opportunities Program. Included were requirements to increase the number of minority children placed in adoptive homes with an emphasis on recruitment of minority families, a provision for postlegal adoption services for families who had adopted children with special needs, and a requirement to increase the permanent placement of foster children who were legally free for adoption.

The Child Abuse, Domestic Violence, Adoption, and Family Services Act of 1992 (P.L. 102–295)

Provisions of this amendment to CAPTA required the Department of Health and Human Services to provide information and services related to adoption and foster care, including on-site technical assistance, awareness campaigns on a national level to place children in need of adoption with appropriate adoptive parents, and the operation of a National Resource Center for Special Needs Adoption.

The Child Abuse Prevention and Treatment Act Amendments of 1996 (P.L. 104–235)

This law again reauthorized CAPTA and addressed false reporting of child abuse and neglect. It also required states to institute an expedited "termination of parental rights" process for abandoned infants or for infants who had been subjected to serious injury by their parents. It also authorized the continuation of such programs as the Adoption Opportunities Act, the Abandoned Infants Assistance Act, the Victims of Child Abuse Act, and the Children's Justice Act Grants.

The Keeping Children and Families Safe Act of 2003 (P.L. 108–36)

This reauthorization of CAPTA keeps several of the provisions of previous acts but also implements programs aimed at increasing the number of older foster children placed in adoptive homes. Grants to programs that will eliminate barriers to placing children across jurisdictions are included. The act also amends the Abandoned Infants Assistance grants program to prohibit grants unless the applicant gives priority to infants and young children who have been exposed in utero to dangerous drugs or who have a life-threatening illness or exposure to HIV/AIDS.

The Indian Child Welfare Act of 1978 (P.L. 95–608)

The Indian Child Welfare Act (ICWA) was the first major national act legislating adoption in the United States. To some people it was—and still is—controversial (see Chapter 2).

According to the Child Welfare Information Gateway, there were two main reasons for the act. First, state courts at the time removed 25 to 35 percent of Native American children from their birth homes and put them in foster care; approximately 85 percent of these children went to non-Indian homes. Second, there was concern that these children would lose their Indian culture and heritage.

The Indian Child Welfare Act requires adoption agencies to make a concerted effort to find Native American families for Native American children. Under the provisions of the act, anyone involved in the placement of a Native American child must first notify the Bureau of Indian Affairs or the child's tribe, so that the tribe can make custody arrangements. Tribal courts have jurisdiction over children living on reservations and some rights over Native American children living off reservations. Even a Native American birth mother who wants to place her child for adoption must go through the process and receive the tribe's permission. Placement preference is given first to members of the child's tribe and last to those of another culture.

Both federal and state laws govern a child of Native American heritage. According to the ICWA, termination of parental rights or involuntary relinquishment may be held before a tribal court. If a state court hears the case, the child's tribe has the right to intervene and to object to the placement preferences of the child's parents or those of an adoption agency. A birth parent who initially agrees to the placement of a Native American child has a chance to withdraw consent until a decree of adoption is entered in court. If the consent to the adoption was obtained by fraud or duress, the birth parent has at least two years to get the adoption nullified. Prospective adoptive parents who have had a Native American child in their home for months, or in some cases for years, may have their adoption petitions denied. The Indian Child Welfare law trumps all other adoption laws.

The Adoption Assistance and Child Welfare Act of 1980 (P.L. 96–272)

The Adoption Assistance and Child Welfare Act has many goals, including the requirement that reasonable efforts be made to prevent the placement of a child in foster care and to reunite that child with birth parents. Another of its goals was to get children already in the foster-care system adopted as quickly as possible and off the foster-care rolls. The act requires a foster-care review every six months and a judicial review when the child has been in foster care for eighteen months. At that time, the judge must decide whether to return the child to his birth family, to make the child legally free for adoption, or to authorize some other permanent plan for the child.

Before 1980 many children were considered "unadoptable." They were children with special needs—older, part of a sibling group, of an ethnic minority, or with elaborate medical or emotional needs. In 1968, New York State started providing financial benefits to families who adopted these children. Although some other states followed the lead of New York, the programs cost the states a great deal of money; each bore the entire financial brunt of the adoption "subsidy."

In 1961 the federal government first offered financial help to the states for children in foster care through the Aid to Dependent Children of the Social Security Act. In 1980, P.L. 96–272 amended the Social Security Act. Since its implementation, many more children have found permanent adoptive homes instead of growing up in foster care.

The act established the Adoption Assistance Program through which the federal government partially subsidizes some adoptions. The federal share of adoption assistance varies from 50 to 80 percent. The program has provided monthly financial assistance, Medicaid coverage, and eligibility for Title XX social services for certain children.

The adoption assistance agreement must be signed before the finalization of the adoption. A subsidy may continue or be renegotiated before finalization of the adoption. A subsidy may also continue or be renegotiated until the child reaches the age of eighteen or, in some cases, age twenty-one.

Those adopting older or special needs children have the right to appeal an agency decision affecting subsidy benefits. In accordance with federal law, every state has established a "fair hearing" process to handle appeals.

An important amendment to P.L. 96–272 was the Tax Reform Act of 1986 (P.L. 99–154). This amendment required the states to reimburse adoptive parents for the "nonrecurring" expenses (such as a home study) incurred in the adoption of a child with special needs. Later, the Adoption and Safe Families Act of 1997 amended the original law by allowing children who were previously *not* eligible for Title IV-E adoption assistance to retain eligibility in a subsequent adoption, in the event of the death of an adoptive parent, or in a dissolution of an adoption.

On September 24, 2001, the Children's Bureau released a Child Welfare Policy Manual, which helps clarify many of the confusing aspects of the Title IV-E Adoption Assistance Program. For further information, parents and professionals can access "Adoption Subsidy in the United States" from the North American Council on Adoptable Children at http://www.nacac.org/subsidyusintro.html, contact NACAC's Adoption Subsidy Resource Center, (800) 470-6665 or (651) 644-3036, or e-mail adoption.assistance@nacac.org.

The Family Preservation and Family Support Services Program Provision of the Omnibus Reconciliation Act (P.L. 103–66)

On August 10, 1993, President Clinton signed the Omnibus Budget Reconciliation Act (OBRA). This act added several provisions of interest to adoption advocates. First, OBRA mandates health-care coverage for adopted children whose parents receive health-care benefits from their employers. The law requires employer group health plans covering dependent children to cover adopted children at *placement* with no restrictions for preexisting conditions. The act defines *child* as someone under the age of eighteen and *placement* as a legal assumption of responsibility in anticipation of a final adoption.

Second, the 1993 act added a new "capped" entitlement for family preservation and family support services to child welfare programs under Title IV-B. Congress also amended Section 479, a 1986 Title IV-E provision requiring the establishment of a data collection system for foster care and adoption. The amendment authorizes an enhanced federal matching rate related to costs of adoption data collection.

The Multiethnic Placement Act (P.L. 103–382)

Congress passed the Multiethnic Placement Act (MEPA) in October 1994 to (1) decrease the length of time children waited for adoptive and foster homes (especially those "other-than-Caucasian" children), (2) prevent discrimination on the basis of race, color, or national origin in the placement of children, and (3) facilitate the identification and recruitment of foster and adoptive families that could meet the children's needs. This was another controversial act (see Chapter2).

The Interethnic Adoption Provisions of the Small Business Job Protection Act of 1996 (P.L. 104–188)

The adoption-related provisions of this bill were initiated to eliminate discrimination on the basis of race, color, or national origin for the children who were waiting and for the parents who wanted to adopt them. It repealed the language of MEPA that allowed the consideration of "cultural, ethnic, or racial background" of a child, as well as the "capacity" of the prospective parents to meet the child's needs. In other words, the newer provisions are supportive of transracial adoption. States would be subject to penalties for noncompliance. Further information about transracial adoption is available from the Child Welfare Information Gateway at http://www.childwelfare.gov/pubs/f_trans.cfm.

The Adoption and Safe Families Act of 1997 (P.L. 105–89)

According to many experts, the Adoption and Safe Families Act (ASFA) was a landmark piece of legislation with provisions to help children, many of whom were waiting several years for permanent placements. "Reasonable efforts" to reunite children with their birth families had often been counterproductive. The act gave the states stricter guidelines and forced more accountability. Important provisions are detailed here.

Acceleration of permanent placements meant that (with some exceptions) states must initiate court proceedings to free a child for adoption if the child had been waiting in foster care for at least fifteen of the most recent twenty-two months.

Implementation of shorter time limits for making decisions about permanent placements meant that permanency hearings would be held no later than twelve months after the child entered foster care (six months earlier than previously required). The law also clarified that states could use concurrent planning, in which they would work toward reunification with birth parents while simultaneously seeking potential adoptive families if reunification did not work out.

Safety for abused and neglected children meant that the words "safety of the child" would be included in every step of the case plan and review process and that criminal record checks for foster and adoptive parents would be a part of the approval process.

Promotion of adoptions meant that states would get incentive funds for increases in adoptive placements, that states must use "reasonable efforts" to move children toward permanence, that special needs children would get healthcare coverage, that placements would not be denied on the basis of geographic location of the prospective adoptive parents, and that states would document and report child-specific adoption efforts.

Increased accountability meant that the Department of Health and Human Services would establish new outcome measures to monitor and improve the performance of the states, and that the states would have to document child-specific efforts to move children into adoptive homes.

For a retrospective view of the benefits of the Adoption and Safe Families Act, see "Testimony of Wade F. Horn, PhD, Assistant Secretary for Children and Families, U.S. Department of Health and Human Services before the Committee on Ways and

Means, Subcommittee on Human Resources, U.S. House of Representatives, April 8, 2003," available on the Committee on Ways and Means website at http://waysandmeans.house.gov/hearings.asp?formmode=detail&hearing=71 or at http://cbexpress.acf.hhs.gov/articles.cfm?article_id=713.

The Intercountry Adoption Act of 2000 (P.L. 106–279)

The Intercountry Adoption Act of 2000 (IAA) is the implementing legislation for the Hague Convention on the Protection of Children and Cooperation in Respect of Intercountry Adoption throughout the United States. As mentioned in Chapter 1, the Hague Adoption Convention sets minimum standards and procedures for adoptions between the countries that are parties to the convention. This act provides for full implementation of the convention in the United States. Provisions include the following: *Establishment of the U.S. Central Authority.* This entity within the Department of State will have general responsibility for U.S. implementation of the convention and will provide annual reports to the U.S. Congress. *Accrediting entities.* These groups or persons will (1) process applications, (2) be responsible for oversight and enforcement of compliance, and (3) perform information-collection activities. *Case registries.* Every intercountry adoption will have a case registry. *Responsibilities of the Department of State:* (1) Will monitor each accrediting entity's performance and its compliance with the convention, the Intercountry Adoption Act, and the applicable regulations, and (2) will issue certificates to cover convention adoptions/placements. *Recognition.* Convention adoptions finalized in other countries that are also parties to the convention will be recognized by the United States, and the procedures and requirements must be followed for the adoption of a child in the U.S. by persons who live in other countries and who are parties to the convention. *Verification.* State courts will be prohibited from finalizing convention adoptions or granting custody for a convention adoption unless the court has verified that the country of origin and the receiving country have verified the required determinations. *Amendment.* The Immigration and Nationality Act is amended to provide for a new category of children adopted, or to be adopted, under the Hague Adoption Convention and meeting other requirements to qualify for immigrant visas.

The text of the Intercountry Adoption Act of 2000 is available at http://www.acf.hhs.gov/programs/cb/laws/index.htm.

The Promoting Safe and Stable Families Amendments of 2001 (P.L. 107–133)

One of the provisions of the Promoting Safe and Stable Families Amendments of 2001 that affected adoption was the amending of the definition of *family preservation services* to include infant safe haven programs. When Congress reauthorized the Promoting Safe and Stable Families program, the new law included $305 million per year in mandatory or guaranteed funding for state programs that assist in family reunification and preservation, family support, and adoption assistance. The law also allows Congress to appropriate an additional $200 million per year to a possible total of $505 million.

The Adoption Promotion Act of 2003 (P.L. 108–45)

Among other provisions, this act reauthorized the adoption incentive program under Title IV-E of the Social Security Act. The act, primarily aimed at achieving permanency for children nine years of age and over, authorized $43 million per year for five years to states who are successful in increasing the number of children adopted from foster care. As part of the passage of this act, Congress included the requirement for a report presenting challenges and strategies to improve permanency outcomes for children.

Challenges included not enough families willing to provide permanency; lack of services for birth parents, children, and prospective adoptive families; inadequate permanency planning; youth resistance; staff issues; and court/legal issues. Strategies to address these challenges included ways of recruiting permanent families, such as general recruiting, targeted recruiting, and child-specific recruiting. The full report is available online through the Children's Bureau.

Testimony and Statements

In a democracy, voting is only a small part of the action. Although elected state and national representatives pass laws that affect the lives of children, they expect to hear from professionals in adoption and those on the "front lines," such as adoptive parents and former foster children who have grown up with or without a "forever family." This testimony often is filled not only with facts but also emotion. The testimony of one person may contradict the testimony of another. But the opinions expressed help form the basis for future laws.

U.S. Senate Hearing on the "Barriers to Adoption," 1993

On July 15, 1993, the Subcommittee on Children, Family, Drugs, and Alcoholism of the Committee on Labor and Human Resources of the U.S. Senate heard testimony on "Barriers to Adoption"; some of these statements preceded the passage of the Multiethnic Placement Act of 1994. The purpose of the hearing was to explore ways to find permanent, nurturing homes for children with special needs. (A similar hearing, as part of the oversight of the Adoption Opportunities Act, had been held six years earlier.)

During his opening statement, Senator Christopher J. Dodd (D-CT), chairman of the Subcommittee on Family, Drugs, and Alcoholism, testified that:

> For children of color, foster care placements have reached epidemic proportions, with rates of placement three times those for the U.S. population as a whole. More than half the children awaiting adoption nationally are children of color. Today, in seeking ways to open the doors to permanent homes for these children, we will hear about programs that recruit minority parents, particularly African American parents, for minority children.

In his opening statement, Senator Howard M. Metzenbaum (D-OH), of the committee on Labor and Human Resources, said the following:

> As a person who has fought for civil rights all my life, going back to my college days, even my high school days, I simply could not believe that in this day and age, we still have formal policies against transracial adoptions. That is unbelievable to me, incredible!
>
> The testimony at the PBS hearing of a white foster mother who encountered numerous obstacles in trying

to adopt her black foster children summed up my feelings with her statement that she did not spell love, "c-o-l-o-r."

Since that hearing, I have made no secret of the fact that I believe it is illegal, I believe it is unfair, cruel and destructive to deny a child a caring and stable adoptive home with parents of a different race when appropriate parents of the same race are not available.

Yesterday Senator Carol Moseley-Braun and I introduced legislation, the "Multi-Ethnic Placement Act," S. 1224, that reaffirms basic civil rights principles that race should not be the controlling factor in making foster care and adoptive placements.

I believe that same race placement is always desirable if the prospective parents are appropriate. For that reason, our bill also states that "race, color or national origin may be one of the many factors to consider in determining placement that is in the best interest of the child."

Among those speaking on behalf of same-race placements were Sidney Duncan from Homes for Black Children in Detroit, Michigan, and the Reverend Wilbert Talley of One Church, One Child.

The remarks of these and other senators were followed by a statement read by Sidney Duncan, representing Homes for Black Children in Detroit, Michigan:

As you know, I am from Homes for Black Children in Detroit, and Homes for Black Children stands as an example of what can happen when the African American community is given the opportunity to solve the problem of its children in need of families.

When we started in 1969, adoption was not available as an opportunity to most black children, and in our first full year of operation, we placed more black children in adoptive homes than the 13 existing local agencies combined. What had never occurred to me until this morning when Senator Levin was speaking of this is that it was also more black children in adoptive homes than all of the agencies in the state of Michigan combined for that time period.

Since our beginning, we have placed 1,049 children ranging in age from newborns as young as 3 days old, to 15 years of age. They have been all kinds of children—children who were abused, children who were abandoned, children who were neglected, children who had physical and emotional handicaps. The majority of them were simply children who needed a family.

I should also note that the children were placed with working class families, middle class families, two-parent families. Sometimes we assume that when black families come forth in large numbers, that in some way the standards have been altered. That is not true in terms of Homes for Black Children's experience.

Within 3 years of our beginning, the problem of not enough families for Detroit's black children was solved. The private agencies were learning by that time from our experience. The public agency instituted a specialized adoption program called Project 72 that was also successful in placing black children.

Detroit had become a community that could provide adoptive homes for its waiting children, and Homes for Black Children was the catalyst for that change. Having solved that problem, we reduced our adoption program significantly in 1974 and moved into family preservation. And for very nearly 20 years, we were minimally involved in adoption. However, in very recent years, adoption in Detroit has reemerged as a serious community problem, so Homes for Black Children has now refocused its energies on adoption. We have increased our adoptive placements, and we are providing leadership to the adoption community in planning and increasing the adoption opportunities for black children. . . .

I want to just very quickly say that one of the main problems in terms of African American children is that they are in the care of and being planned for by agencies that have traditionally served white children. Many of them do not know the African American community; they do not respect the African American community; they don't know of our diversity; they don't have any idea that there are families there who will take the children.

There are other factors that are part of it. My main

point is that the African American community, if given the opportunity, can offer a solution to the needs of black children.

The Reverend Wilbert Talley represented One Church, One Child, an organization that has been finding homes for African American children since 1981. He provided the following testimony:

> What I'd like to say is that for years, the myth existed that African American families did not adopt. The myth has been proven false through concentrated efforts by agencies and organizations such as One Church, One Child that are culturally focused and culturally sensitive. With the initiation of recruitment efforts geared toward the African American community, African American families have responded in record numbers.
>
> It is our contention that transracial adoption is not the issue. It is the availability in the pool of potential adoptive parents of African American families. . . . Our position is that we want our children to be with families of the same race, and we can find families for these children.
>
> Prior to implementing the legislation that would encourage multiethnic placement of children, consideration should be given by Congress to providing financial incentives to encourage States to implement concentrated recruitment efforts geared toward minority communities such as the examples that are funded in Virginia.

Following is an excerpt from the testimony of former foster child and current adoptive parent Shane Salter of Washington, DC:

> I'd like to begin by letting you know that my mother was 15 years old when I was born and 18 when she gave birth to my brother Keith. When I was about 4 years old, Keith and I were abandoned by my mother and left in a basement apartment alone. When the police discovered our situation, we were placed in an emergency foster home for approximately 1 year, after which we were

moved and placed in another foster home, where we remained for over 7 years.

Although my mother was unable to recover from her addictions, she was unwilling to relinquish her rights as a parent. However, courts concerned with parental rights allow parents who abandon their children to leave them in a system supported by tax dollars indefinitely while they make marginal attempts to demonstrate an interest in regaining custody. Consequently, many children like my brother and me live in uncertainty for most of their childhood.

Foster care is supposed to be and should only be temporary. So can you imagine what it feels like to grow up without a permanent home? Let me tell you first-hand—it destroys your self-esteem and creates another painful obstacle for little ones to overcome.

Well, after 7 years in our foster home, the courts finally decided to terminate my mother's rights and release my brother and me for adoption. At this time, I was 11 years old, and Keith was about 7. We had to be classified as "hard to place," because we were two older black boys and most people who are interested in adopting prefer very young children. Therefore, an aggressive effort to find a permanent home for us was launched.

In other words, while my mom was struggling for years with the hope of succeeding at rehabilitation, her children were getting older and older, and fewer people wanted them. With each year, our chances of getting a permanent home decreased significantly. A family was eventually found, but because of our ages and the difficulty of adjusting to a new family when you are older, this adoption was met with problems that resulted in a traumatic disruption for Keith and me. We were left in the lobby of the foster care agency, abandoned again, while the family sped off in their car to resume their lives.

Support services were not available to this family once they received us, and consequently problems that I believe could have been resolved escalated to a point of no return.

Before my childhood was complete, I lived in a total of nine different foster, adoptive, and group homes. I don't think this would have happened if the courts had terminated parental rights of my parents within one or 2 years after I was removed. It is a miracle, Senators, that I am able to speak before this distinguished body as a functioning adult. The system that was supposed to protect me when my parents could not, did not.

This does not have to keep happening to innocent children if we enact the following. Foster children who are dependent on adults, especially legislative adults, to act on their behalf must be given a fair shot at a permanent home within the second year of foster care. Whether that permanent home becomes an alternative relative or an adoptive home, they deserve the security of a loving, permanent home.

The rights of parents should not come before the rights of children who have no control over their destinies. It is this warped concept that increases the probability of next generation dependence on child welfare systems and creates barriers to adoption.

Second, when families adopt children, they must have access to federally funded support services such as respite care to assist in keeping the family together. Adopted children need access to support groups with other adopted children.

For example, I wish I could have sent my adopted son to a therapeutic camp this summer where he could have his unique emotional issues addressed while my wife and I recuperate and prepare for the upcoming school year and the challenges we will again face.

Adoption is a lifelong adjustment for both the adoptee and the adopting family. Therefore, therapeutic services should be available to these special families throughout the duration of these relationships.

Many more families would consider adoption of children who are "hard to place" if we allocated funds for subsidies that reflect the true cost of raising an additional child and held each local jurisdiction accountable for providing them to families.

Last, but certainly not of least importance, social service workers must be trained and be familiar with the culture of the children they wish to place. Only then will recruitment efforts succeed.

I thank you for the opportunity to share my experiences and thoughts with you. It is my hope that the countless numbers of children who are currently living the life that I escaped won't be destroyed by the system that was designed to protect them.

Lynn Gabbard, an adoptive parent from North Haven, Connecticut, provided similarly emotion-filled moments in her testimony:

During the past 18 1/2 years, my husband and I have adopted seven children, now ranging in age from 2 to 19 years, all of whom were placed from situations somewhat conducive to the development of special needs. . . . When I reflect on the "Barriers to Adoption" that we personally have faced with respect to the adoptions of our children, I think primarily of the societal, legislative and bureaucratic factors that magnify and exacerbate the physical and emotional injuries to children that actually result in their "special needs."

Our oldest son, now 17 years old, was born to a 13-year-old mother who, despite her young age, evident emotional instability, and clear ambivalence toward parenting, was encouraged to take her baby home from the hospital and assume the many responsibilities of parenthood. A birth defect that necessitated a full body cast made the care of her baby an even more difficult task. The extreme neglect and physical abuse that followed, while not to be condoned, could almost be explained when viewed from the perspective of the magnitude of daily parenting tasks demanded of a 13-year-old child.

The neglectful and abusive treatment of our son was to continue for nearly 2 years, interspersed with hospitalizations and foster placements, until the decision was made to terminate parental rights and let both of these children, mother and child, move on toward safer and more productive lives.

Another of our children, our daughter, now 11 years old, was born both heroin and methadone addicted, a victim of fetal alcohol syndrome, a 2.5-pound baby born at the bottom of a staircase following a domestic dispute. This child, medically and intellectually fragile

since birth, endured the disruption of 17 foster placements during the first 3 years of her life, and severe
physical and sexual abuse in the care of a mother struggling with substance abuse, family problems and her
own intellectual and emotional limitations in addition to
her child's. These factors add severe and permanent
emotional injuries to the burden of handicapping conditions which our daughter must struggle with daily.

Our youngest child, our baby's, permanency has been
successfully impeded for several years by an incarcer-
ated parent whose parental rights are protected despite
a sentence of 75 years' imprisonment for an extremely
violent crime. This man, who has lost the right to vote,
has not lost the right to further disrupt his child's life.

Our laws and certainly our practice continue to place
young children in continued jeopardy and ultimately
cause long-term, often permanent damage. Our son . . .
is plagued by a devastating inability to trust that per-
vades every aspect to his life. His self-esteem and self-
confidence are severely undermined, and impairments
in such areas as cause-and-effect thinking make it impossible for him to generalize from one situation to another, to learn from his mistakes, to grow and develop in
meaningful ways.

His relationships and interactions with others are impacted by his anger and mistrust, and he struggles in so
many aspects of day-to-day life that come so easily to
the rest of us.

Our daughter's emotional injuries appear to be even
more profound. While the physical effects of the drugs
and alcohol are difficult, they are correctable on some
level, and she has undergone frequent surgical and medical treatments. The neurological, intellectual, and emotional deficits are far more extreme. Intellectual retarda-
tion is a daily struggle. Seventeen foster placements and
numerous other disruptions appear to have permanently impaired her ability to form intimate, meaningful
relationships. At best her relationships are superficial,
and she is virtually unable to relate to others in anything
other than a self-focused way.

Our children and the growing population of children
for whom we seek adoptive placement are dramati-

cally and permanently affected by the significant traumas of their young lives. These traumas are becoming more far-reaching and more extreme as the years go on. A national call for standards of child care in each state may be a way to address such issues as how long substance-abusing parents can be allowed to place their children's immediate safety and future development at risk while they struggle to solve sometimes insurmountable problems.

Should we continue to allow drug-addicted mothers to leave the hospital with their drug-addicted babies? Standards may also want to address minimum age requirements for independent parenting. I believe that my son's life, and perhaps even his mother's, would have been positively affected if a system like this had been in place at the time of his birth.

It was a painful learning experience for us as parents to come to terms with the reality that there are some aspects of our children's development that no amount of love, nurturing and family stability can overcome. Since it is so profoundly difficult for our son to trust, he is absolutely unable to receive and therefore benefit from the positive feelings of others. Family occasions are difficult for him, as is communication and expression of affection. It is extremely painful to watch a child remain on the periphery of a family that wants desperately to welcome him inside.

We have had to learn, with the help of other families, not only to accept the inconsistent and minimal attempts at connection that he makes, but to validate them for him and to explain them to our other children. Each day we watch him struggle to conform, or to appear to conform, to the world's expectations of how a person needs to act and react. We watch him struggle to control his anger, to hide his mistrust of others, to build relationships that don't threaten and overwhelm him.

Too often, adoptive and foster families are viewed as part of the problem and not part of the solution when mental health issues arise. . . . We need to encourage schools and other institutions to develop healthy environments capable of accepting children who may never be capable of conformity. We need therapists who understand the dynamics of adoption; pediatricians and other practitioners who will accept Title XIX subsidy for medical care; coaches, teachers and community members who understand that our children's actions and reactions may be inappropriate. We need to help adoptive families to continue to emotionally and legally parent children who can no longer live within the family system.

If indeed we believe that children grow better in families, we need to nurture and respect those families. We need to involve them in every aspect of the planning for their children, understanding that they are not perfect and do not need to be, and that they cannot repair the injuries and damages that their children have sustained.

The following questions and comments occurred after the preceding testimony.

Senator METZENBAUM. "Did you have any feeling as a child as to whether it mattered to you if the adopting parents were white or black?"

Mr. SALTER. "As a child, I didn't even think about it. It really, honestly was just not—I was so concerned, I think probably more than others, but so concerned. I wanted my own parents. I wanted a mom and a dad. And I am still to this day very angry because I don't have a mom and a dad. And it is probably the driving force behind most of my life with my children. I wanted a mom and dad, and I didn't care who they were. I just wanted parents. I wanted someplace that was safe and loving for me, and it never happened."

Senator METZENBAUM. "Lynn, do you have any opinion on the question of allowing transracial adoptions where no appropriate same race placement is available?"

Ms. GABBARD. "Yes. Many of my children are adopted transracially, so I do feel strongly as Shane does, that children do need families, that that is what they need. And obviously, I think most people involved in adoption agree that same race placement is preferable and that we need to do more to try to achieve that, but we certainly should not be leaving children to wait for their whole lives while we look for that home."

Excerpt from Testimony by the Reverend Jesse Jackson, Rainbow Coalition, Washington, D.C.

The Reverend Jesse Jackson, representing the Rainbow Coalition, provided the following testimony at the "Barriers to Adoption" hearing:

> Senator Metzenbaum has introduced legislation, the "Multi-Ethnic Placement Act of 1993," which will serve as a tool to eliminate race, national origin, or color from being the only consideration in making foster care and adoptive placements. The Act is basically a reaffirmation of the Title VI ban on and remedies for discrimination. Transracial adoption, like intermarriage, must be protected by law and must be open as an option for everyone. Senators, I urge you to all support your colleague from Ohio and actively seek to see this Act become law.
>
> Because of the difficulties inherent in raising children, I think the majority of us feel that same race and color foster parenting and adoption must be the first choice. But if this type of placement is not possible or if transracial bonding has occurred, I believe that exceptions should be made. No child should ever be abandoned. There must be a firm commitment on the part of the adoptive or foster family to make sure there is no further loss of racial or ethnic identity. The prospective parent or parents must be capable of and willing to love them, for what they are, not for what they promise to be, in an environment free of constant fear and threat. An extra amount of effort should be waged within the African American, Asian and Hispanic communities to educate potential parents about the children needing homes and security, mental, physical and spiritual—not just a place to sleep.
>
> "Informal" adoption has always been common in these families. Rare is the family that has not seen one of its members raised by a grandmother or an aunt. I truly believe that with the passing into law of Senator Metzenbaum's Act, along with the re-education of social workers, adoption professionals and our own people, we will see far less warehousing and institutionalizing of children.

Source for the above section: Subcommittee on Children, Family, Drugs, and Alcoholism, U.S. Senate, *Barriers to Adoption,* 103rd Cong., 1st sess., 1993.

U.S. Senate Hearings on Clarifying the Adoption Assistance and Child Welfare Act, 1996

On November 20, 1996, the Committee on Labor and Human Resources of the U.S. Senate (104th Congress, 2nd session) continued testimony begun in the House on improving the well-being of abused and neglected children, exploring how the well-being of abused and neglected children could be improved by clarifying the reasonable efforts requirement of the Adoption Assistance and Child Welfare Act to make the child's health and safety the primary concern. The main issue under discussion was the question of birth parent rights versus children's safety.

In his opening statement, Senator Mike DeWine (R-OH) said, "We are sending too many children back to dangerous and abusive homes. . . . Every day in America, three children actually die of abuse and neglect at the hands of their parents or caretakers. That is over 1,200 children every year. And almost half of these children are killed after—after—their tragic circumstances have come to the attention of child welfare agencies."

Senator DeWine went on to say he believed some of the tragedies were the result of unintended circumstances caused by the misinterpretation of the 1980 Adoption and Child Welfare Act. "While the law has done a great deal of good, I have come to believe that the law is being frequently misinterpreted, with some truly unintended and undesirable consequences." The senator added he believed the authors of the 1980 act had in their minds the provision he would like to add: "In determining reasonable efforts, the best interests of the child, including the child's health and safety, shall be of primary concern."

Olivia A. Golden, acting assistant secretary for children and families for the Administration for Children and Families of the U.S. Department of Health and Human Services, agreed with Senator DeWine that child abuse and neglect was a tragedy of growing proportions. "The states report that in 1994, over one million children were victims of neglect or abuse, an increase of 27 percent over the number of children who were found to be victims in 1990. In recent years, the number of children in foster care has increased to more than 450,000 children and, although approximately 20,000 children are adopted from foster care each year, the number has failed to keep pace with the growing need." She suggested three means to reform the child welfare system: community-based prevention and early intervention efforts; increasing focus on permanence and timely decision making; and accountability with emphasis on safety, permanence, and the well-being of children.

After Golden's testimony, Senator DeWine posed a hypothetical situation. What if a family existed in which seven children had already been removed from the parents' care because of the father's active alcoholism and another child is born who tests positive for crack cocaine? How long would it take for that child to be eligible for adoption? The answers Senator DeWine received in his home state were from two to five years.

The following testimonies tell the stories behind the statistics quoted in the earlier testimony.

Richard J. Gelles, director of the Family Violence Research Program at the University of Rhode Island, Kingston, and author of *The Book of David* (about a fifteen-month-old boy suffocated by his mother), said that the crisis in the public welfare system "is a failure of inappropriate goals as well as a well-intentioned but improperly implemented federal law, . . . the Adoption Assistance and Child Welfare Act of 1980." He added that five factors contribute to society's inability to get vulnerable children out of harm's way. The first is the overselling of intensive family preservation services as a cost-effective and safe means of protecting children. The second is that in the Adoption Assistance and Child Welfare Act of 1980, the term *reasonable efforts* (to keep children with birth parents whenever possible) was not spelled out. The third erroneous belief is that children always do best when raised by their biological caregivers. Fourth is the belief in the fiction that one can actually balance family preservation and child safety. According to Gelles, "such a balancing act almost inevitably ends up tilting in the favor of parents and places many children at risk." The final myth is that it is easy to change parents who mistreat their children.

Gelles related the story of David:

David was a 15-month-old little boy who was smothered, suffocated, by his mother on one October morning. He himself had been the subject of two or three reports to the child welfare system in his state, but what was of greater concern to me as I did the review of his death was that his older sister had had her skull fractured, her ribs broken, her arms broken and her legs broken by the same mother when she was 6 weeks of age. And in that case, after many, many months of attempting to reunify, the mother actually gave up the parental rights to the older sister as she held David, who was then 1 week old, in her arms.

What concerned me as that story unfolded was that the case was closed, and the termination on the older daughter took place, and mom was allowed to take home this one-week-old baby without any further follow-up. And that clearly was a preventable death had we applied the most basic form of risk assessment in the child welfare system, and that is that parents generally behave tomorrow based on how they behaved yesterday.

And this was not a case that fell between little cracks. This was a case that fell between cracks large enough to serve as the Grand Canyon, and he should not have died; he should be 7 years old and in school today. We had him in our hands; we had the will, we had the ability. And the workers when we interviewed them said we could not have gotten a court to act on this because we had to make reasonable efforts to reunify David with his mother."

Helen Leonhart-Jones, executive director of the Montgomery County Children Services Board of Dayton, Ohio, offered among her remarks the following:

In its September 30, 1996 issue, *U.S. News and World Report* shared some statistics based upon data from Health and Human Services that talked about the numbers of children who are "suffering amid the breakdown of families and the abuse of drugs and alcohol." They have showed that children of single families have a 77 percent greater risk of being harmed by physical abuse and an 80 percent greater risk of suffering serious injuries than kids who are living with two parents. It went on to say that birth parents account for 72 percent of the physical abuse and 81 percent of the emotional abuse. I would say to you that we live in a country where more than 3 million children a year are being abused and neglected by the very people who should be ensuring their safety. These children are then being subjected to a lifetime of misery as a result of this maltreatment.

Finally, Sharon Aulton of Annapolis, Maryland, appeared before the committee to share her experiences as a grandmother attempting to gain custody of her own grandchildren:

My name is Sharon Aulton, and I would like to thank you for inviting me before the committee to share the tragedy of my granddaughters, Christina Lambert and Natalie Aulton.

My story begins with my daughter Rene. Rene has a low I.Q. and is emotionally unstable. This condition resulted in her receiving special education services as a student all of her life. She has never lived on her own. She has never been able to keep a job. She is an extremely needy person and gravitated toward boys and men who were just as dysfunctional as she.

She subsequently became pregnant and gave birth 12 weeks prematurely to my grandson, Mark. The baby was in a neonatal intensive care unit for 2 months, and during that time, she visited him maybe three or four times total. I visited him three or four times a week, plus called every day from work to inquire as to how he was doing.

Right from the beginning, I had to become this child's primary caretaker. I took Rene and the baby into my home with certain ground rules. She found those rules too restrictive and she did not like being told what to do. While she was home, though, social services, because of the baby's medical condition, sent a visiting nurse to the house a couple of times a week to check on the baby and to see how Rene was taking care of him. I would also come home from work at lunch time, as I work not far from where I live, and I would check on the baby and see how he was doing.

One afternoon, I came home to find Rene and Joe, the baby's father, packing up the baby's things and preparing to run off with him. This was a baby who was hooked up to an apnea monitor because of respiratory problems; he had just had emergency surgery and was still considered a medical risk because of complications of prematurity. Neither parent had a job, a place to live, or resources to take care of this ill baby. When I attempted to stop them, I was assaulted by Joe while being restrained by my daughter.

Until the deaths of Christina and Natalie, the hardest day that I ever had to face was deciding to press charges and have my daughter arrested and having to give my grandson to the custody of the department of social services. My heart was broken, and I was grief-stricken because I had to give up this baby that I had bonded with and considered my own.

Mark was placed in a foster care home until I could find day care, which was impossible because the child was ill, and I could not find an appropriate day care provider. When he was 9 months old, I found a day care facility that would take care of him. I then made visits to him on weekends. When he became a year old, I became his full-time permanent foster mother.

After many hearings and attempts by the court to re-unify the child with his parents with no success, I received legal custody and have been raising my grandson. He will be 9 years old in January.

After the custody of the baby was transferred to me, my relationship with his parents was strained and sporadic. The father received a sentence of 1 year, suspended except for 1 month, for the assault on me. The parents then moved from Anne Arundel County to Talbot County, where she became pregnant with Christina, the child with the red hair. It was only after Christina was born that I resumed a relationship with them.

I adored Christina the minute I laid eyes on her, but Rene and Joe were so dysfunctional that they could not parent properly. I visited when I could, but our relationship never got any better. If anything, it got worse, because I would tell them what they should do in order to take care of themselves and the baby. They did not want to hear it, and they hated me for "taking" their son. I tried to explain that I did not take their son, but that the court gave him to me because they did not meet any of the conditions of the plans to reunify the family. They absolutely would not take any responsibility for their actions. They perceived me as being the person who "took" their child.

Talbot County Social Services became involved when they became homeless and called me and asked me to take them all in—Rene, Joe and Christina. I said that I would take Christina, but I would not take the parents. They refused and said that they would not split up the family and put them up in a motel until they could find housing for them.

Joe was subsequently arrested for molesting three young girls and was sentenced to 10 years. . . . Since Rene could not or would not take care of herself, she moved to Baltimore County with another man. I did not know her whereabouts for 9 months and was frantic with worry about Christina.

One day, out of the blue, I got a phone call from Rene. "Guess what, Mom? I have another baby, and her name is Natalie. Would you like to see your new granddaughter?" There was no mention of the fact that I had not seen or heard from her for 9 months. She acted as if we were having a conversation about the weather. Natalie was already 1 month old.

I was overjoyed at seeing Christina again and seeing the new baby, but shocked to see the conditions that they were living in. She was living in a filthy slum. They slept on mattresses on the floor, and they also ate their meals sitting on the mattresses.

Natalie was a biracial child, and the only reason I mention that is because the man she was living with was white, so he was obviously not the father of the child.

Since I had not seen Christina for almost a year, I asked to take her home with me for the weekend. I then began a pattern where I would visit and play with Natalie and take Christina on weekends and vacations. I became very close to Christina, and she became extremely close to me and to her brother. Her personality would change from a sad, worried little girl to one who would smile, laugh and play.

I called Baltimore County protective services and told them the children were being neglected and related the parents' history to them. The girls were living in horrible conditions. When they investigated, they found the apartment filthy, but the children were well-nourished and appropriately clothed. The department was unable to substantiate any neglect in the case, and I was told that I was to blame because as long as I was rescuing and buying clothes and food for the children, they were not being totally neglected.

The man that she was living with kicked her out, and the children and she wound up in Baltimore City. She was living with a woman at that time who had two children. Social services was called to investigate that family, and those two children were removed from the home. I assumed erroneously that they were also looking at Rene and the children, but much to my surprise, much later, I found out that they were not. How can they remove one set of children from a home and not the other? When I inquired, I was told that no one had filed a formal complaint. I told them that there were complaints on file from Baltimore County, and Anne Arundel County had a record of me having custody of the first child. But I was told that Baltimore County was a different jurisdiction from Baltimore City. And did they follow up based on my conversations with them? No. I later found out that because I had not filed a formal complaint with the protective services people that they did not investigate further. Because she moved from place to place and from county to county, I had to start the process all over again.

Rene was eventually evicted from the house and became homeless again. She was on the street with the children and stayed wherever someone would take her in. She absolutely refused to let relatives take in the children. I called protective services and begged them to take the children. By this time, she was in a Salvation Army homeless shelter, and 1 month before their death, Baltimore City social workers told me that there was not enough proof of neglect to take the children from their mother. When I argued that they were living in a homeless shelter and that Christina had been ill for some time, the social worker told me that being homeless was not a reason to take the children, and that their mother was "trying" and loved her children. I never doubted that my daughter loved her children. She never abused them. She never physically did any harm to them. But she could not take care of herself. How did they expect her to know how to take care of two little girls?

Another resident of the homeless shelter filed a complaint with protective services as Rene was leaving them alone in the room, as did the day care center where the children went during the day. Eventually, somehow, Rene got some subsidy from an agency—I do not know what the agency was—and she was allowed to move into an unsafe building.

On November 15, the caseworker assigned to investigate the case arrived at the new address to find the fire engines at the house and received the news that the children had perished in the fire. This was 1 week after the complaints were filed.

My granddaughters are dead because of a law that says children should be reunified with their parents. Parents have all the rights and the children have none. My granddaughters are dead because of the many layers of bureaucratic bungling by the department of social services. My granddaughters are dead because of the inefficiency of an agency that employs unskilled and untrained social workers who did not seem to be able to make appropriate decisions, but kept quoting me the law. My granddaughters died 2 years and 5 days ago because the system failed to heed the warnings of responsible people who were trying to protect them.

My daughter was eventually convicted of two counts of first degree murder and is now serving two life sentences without the possibility of parole. It has been an agonizing 2 years for me when I know it should not have ended this way. I have buried two children, seen my daughter put in prison for the rest of her life, and my grandson, who is multihandicapped, is in a residential school for disabled children. My losses are many, and my grief is overwhelming—and it could have all been prevented.

Source for this section: Committee on Labor and Human Resources, U.S. Senate, *Improving the Well-Being of Abused and Neglected Children,* 104th Cong., 2nd sess., 1996, 1–61.

As a result of various testimonies, such as the ones above, Congress paved the way for transracial placements, when indicated, and has made and changed laws to allow children to move more quickly into permanent adoptive homes. But the battle for funding goes on, sometimes successfully and sometimes less so.

Litigation in Adoption

Finding homes for *children* who need them (rather than finding children for *people* who want them, although this can also work well for children) is the emphasis in adoption today. The classic book *Beyond the Best Interests of the Child* (Goldstein, Freud, and Solnit, 1973) was one of the first to call for recognition of the child's needs in adoption. Later, Andre Derdyn gave a detailed explanation of this subject (in David M. Brodzinsky and Marshall D. Schechter, eds., *The Psychology of Adoption,* New York: Oxford University Press, 1990).

A child who must leave a birth home because of abuse and neglect usually spends some time in a foster home. During that time, the child often develops a relationship with the foster parents; they become his "psychological parents," or de facto parents. A psychological parent is one who, through day-to-day interactions with a child, fulfills the child's needs for an "emotional parent." In other situations, the adoptive parents become the psychological parents. The birth parent may contest this situation, and the various parties involved call upon the courts to make decisions about the child's future. Sometimes the parties to a case appeal the lower courts' decisions all the way to the Supreme Court.

Because a combination of state, federal, and, in certain cases, international laws regulate adoption, various interpretations of the law are complex. A review of state-decided court cases involving adoption would fill several volumes; therefore, this chapter will highlight only a few important cases in which the U.S. Supreme Court reached a decision. These cases are in the categories of birth fathers' rights, birth parents' rights, foster parents' rights, protecting individual rights, and rights involving racial considerations.

In adoption cases, courts must consider the needs of all members of the triad (birth parents, adoptive parents, and the child/children); this not an easy task. There are many reasons why court rulings concerning adoption so often seem to contradict each other, but two stand out: First, courts consider "the best interests of the child" but must also consider the rights of other parties; judges must take into consideration constitutional rights that may appear to conflict in adoption—cases in which both birth families and adoptive families have "rights." For example, can a judge extend the due process clause of the Fourteenth Amendment to both a child's birth family and his adoptive family? Second, courts often base decisions on past legal precedents.

Birth Fathers' Rights

For many years, state law disregarded the rights of a father not married to the child's mother. Later, the courts gave birth fathers' rights equal consideration. Unmarried fathers' rights are at issue in the next four cases.

Stanley v. Illinois, 405 U.S. 645 (1972)

Although Peter Stanley was not married to the birth mother of their three children, he had lived with her off and on for eighteen years and had served as a father to the children. When she died, the state of Illinois denied Stanley a hearing and refused his rights as a parent. The state took custody of the children and put them in foster care.

The Supreme Court ruled that the state could not assume Stanley was an unfit parent simply because he had not married the children's mother. The Court awarded custody of the children to Stanley and returned them to his care because he had maintained a parental relationship with them, and because the birth father has rights under the due process and equal protection clauses of the Constitution.

Quilloin v. Walcott, 434 U.S. 246 (1978)

In this case, a birth father not married to the child's mother sought parental rights. More than ten years after the child's birth, Quilloin, the birth father, wanted to block the adoption of the child by the mother's current husband of ten years, who lived as family with the mother and the child. Although Quilloin had taken some responsibility for the child (he had visited and had made support payments), the Supreme Court granted the adoption as serving the best interests of the child.

In ruling against the birth father, the Supreme Court distinguished this case from *Stanley* (discussed above) because in that case the birth father had been a de facto member of the child's family; in other words, he was a "psychological parent" to the child.

Caban v. Mohammed, 441 U.S. 380 (1979)

An unmarried mother of two children had lived with the children's birth father (Caban) for five years. Subsequently, the mother moved with the children and married another man (Mohammed). Mohammed petitioned to adopt the children, and the petition was granted despite the objections of the birth father. According to New York law, a birth mother could block such an adoption by withholding her consent, but a birth father could not. The father of a child born out of wedlock could only block such an adoption if he could prove it was not in the best interests of the child or children.

On appeal, the Supreme Court ruled that the equal protection clause of the Fourteenth Amendment to the Constitution had been violated by a sex-based distinction between unmarried mothers and unmarried fathers. Caban was listed on the children's birth certificates, had supported the children, and had a relationship with them. The Supreme Court found the New York statute to be unconstitutional. In this case, Caban succeeded in blocking the adoption of his children by the prospective stepfather. The Court did, however, make a distinction between a birth father who has supported his children and one who has not.

Lehr v. Robertson, 463 U.S. 248 (1983)

The Supreme Court dealt with the issue of "notice" and whether notice of an adoption must be given to putative fathers. This case focused on the father's commitment and responsibilities toward the child. Lehr had not lived with the birth mother after the child's birth, had not provided financial support, his name was not on the child's birth certificate, and he had not registered with New York State's Putative Father Registry.

When Ms. Robertson later married and her husband sought to adopt the child, Lehr tried to block the adoption. The Court ruled that the father must have demonstrated commitment to parenthood and have been involved in child rearing. In this case, the birth father did not have an automatic constitutional right to block the adoption.

Birth Parents' Rights

The termination of parental rights is a difficult process. In termination cases the petitioning party, usually a public social service department, must prove the birth parents unfit because of neglect, abuse, abandonment, or other conduct endangering the child. States differ as to their definitions of these terms, the persons who may bring the action to the court, and the type of hearing. When birth parents oppose the action and appeal the rules, the process of termination of parental rights can take a long time.

Lassiter v. Department of Social Services, 452 U.S. 18, 68 (1981)

In 1981 the Supreme Court answered a question related to due process. In this case, a lower court had terminated the parental rights of Abby Gail Lassiter. She appealed the decision. The Court upheld the termination in spite of the fact that counsel had not been appointed for Lassiter. Among other things, the Court ruled that the presence of counsel would not have made a determinative difference for the petitioner.

Santosky v. Kramer, 455 U.S. 745 (1982)

The due process clause and the "liberty interest" of the birth parents took center stage in this case. (A liberty interest is an interest recognized as protected by the due process clauses of state and federal constitutions. Generally included are liberties guaranteed by the first eight amendments of the U.S. Constitution.) The Supreme Court struck down the "fair preponderance" of the evidence standard that had formerly been the rule for terminating parental rights. In this situation, due process required that allegations supporting termination of parental rights be proven by "clear and convincing evidence"; that is, the Court instituted the "enhanced evidentiary requirement"—a much higher standard of evidence. The case cites the liberty interest of natural parents, which does not go away because these people have not been model parents.

In this case, the children had not lived with their birth parents for four and a half years. Some say this decision, made on a four-to-three vote of the Supreme Court, was an unfortunate one for children in the foster care system, as many of these children have spent years developing a relationship with their "psychological parents," only to be wrenched from their current homes and returned to birth parents with whom they may have had little or no relationship.

Rights of Foster Families

Smith v. OFFER, 431 U.S. 816 (1977)

In 1976, after many years of tradition in which foster parents had few legal rights, a district court ruled as unconstitutional a provision of New York law authorizing the state to remove children from foster homes without a prior hearing. In 1977, however, the Supreme Court reversed the lower court's decision in *Smith v. Organization of Foster Families for Equality and Reform (OFFER)*.

In this case, the Supreme Court ruled that a full hearing is not necessary when a child is removed from a foster home to be returned to a birth home. In other words, the rights of the birth family outweigh those of the foster family.

The Court identified two distinctions between birth families and foster families. First, birth families' origins are not involved with state laws and contracts, whereas foster families do have a contract with the state. Second, this and subsequent Court decisions ruled that foster parents do not have constitutionally protected liberty interests. Therefore, foster parents still do not have the legal standing most of them would like.

Protection of Individual Rights

In 1923 the Supreme Court stated that the Constitution protects an individual's right "to marry, establish a home, and bring up children," among other freedoms. The rights of foster parents, who may after a number of years become a child's "psychological parents," are less clear. In other words, in the case of children who have been in the care of foster parents who would like to adopt them, whose "liberty" will be protected?

Meyer v. Nebraska, 262 U.S. 390 (1923)

Meyer had been convicted of teaching German to a ten-year-old child who was a pupil in the Zion Parochial School maintained by the Zion Evangelical Lutheran Congregation. Nebraska law stated that "languages, other than the English language, may be taught as languages only after a pupil shall have attained and successfully passed the eighth grade." The Supreme Court decided the law was unconstitutional and deprived individuals (teachers and parents) of liberty without due process of law in violation of the Fourteenth Amendment of the Constitution. As strange as it may seem to those unfamiliar with the law, this decision formed the basis of an interpretation of an individual's right as a parent.

May v. Anderson, 345 U.S. 528 (1953)

May v. Anderson was a case in which the Court upheld the rights of birth parents. In a divorce action, a Wisconsin court had awarded custody to the father. The mother's appeal reached the Supreme Court, which recognized that "a mother's right to custody of her children is a personal right entitled to at least as much protection as her right to alimony." (Because the mother did not live in the state in which the decree was issued, the court could not cut off her immediate right to custody of her children. A Wisconsin court did not have jurisdiction over a mother who lived in Ohio.)

Racial Considerations

Racial considerations in adoption have provided a subject for lively debate since the 1960s. In the late 1960s and early 1970s, white couples began (in significant numbers) to adopt black children who needed homes. In 1972 the National Association of Black Social Workers took a strong stand against transracial adoption. In 1994 the Multiethnic Placement Act banned discrimination in the placement of children for adoption on the grounds of race, color, or national origin.

Palmore v. Sidoti, 466 U.S. 429 (1984)

In this 1984 adoption case, the Supreme Court disallowed racial considerations. A white father attempted to take custody of a child from his ex-wife, who lived with (and later married) a black man; they lived in a black neighborhood. The Court's position was that race should not determine custody; the Court unanimously ruled that the state would not be justified in taking custody away from a fit mother just because she had married a man of another race. Private biases and the possible harm they might inflict were impermissible considerations under the equal protection clause of the Constitution.

Supporting Adoptive Families

Postlegal services (for families who have finalized an adoption) is a concept whose time has come. Figure 6.4 is a graphic depiction of an idea long recognized as a need in adoption services. The figure has five levels. The first level illustrates guiding principles in adoption. The second level puts adoptees, parents, peers, and professionals together as a team. This team (the third level) delivers needed services. (Not everyone needs every service, but most will benefit from some services.) The fourth level describes the qualities desired in the various services. The bottom tier of boxes shows the desired results.

A full narrative is available at http://www.childwelfare.gov/pubs/conceptmodel.cfm.

FIGURE 6.4
Concept Model for Post-Adoption Services

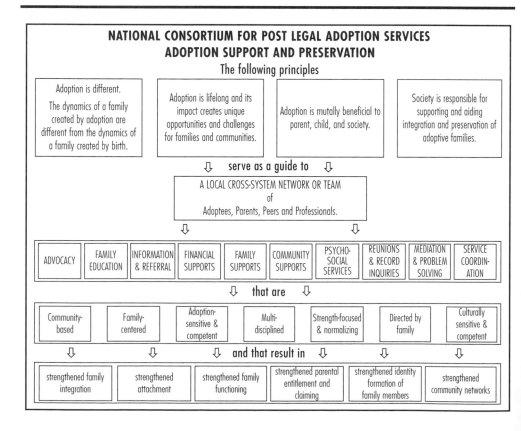

7

Directory of Organizations

Many organizations have formed around specialized concerns in adoption—intercountry adoption, special needs adoptions, open adoption, closed adoption, adopted persons' rights, the rights of "singles" or gays and lesbians to adopt, the rights of birth parents—to name a few. Some organizations work primarily as child advocates and for new policies to benefit children in adoption and foster care. Some offer training online. In addition, adoption "exchanges" network with individuals and agencies to help find homes for waiting children.

This chapter begins with an overview of agencies of the federal government concerned with adoption. Following this is a listing of national groups that take stands on issues, support adoptive parents, organize regional and national meetings, and inform their members through newsletters and other publications. Next is a listing of organizations in adoption concerned with legal issues. The final list gives an address, telephone number, and website for a central government office in each of the fifty states, Puerto Rico, and the Virgin Islands.

Federal Agencies
Concerned with Adoption

Picture a huge umbrella with a group of other umbrellas in descending order underneath. Be aware that each of the smaller umbrellas performs enormous jobs of its own.

The Department of Health and Human Services (HHS)

The U.S. Department of Health and Human Services is the biggest agency and the highest branch of the U.S. government concerned with adoption. Among the organizations under this head umbrella are the Food and Drug Administration (FDA), the Centers for Disease Control and Prevention (CDC), the Administration on Aging (AOA), the Indian Health Service (IHS), and the Administration for Children and Families (ACF).

The Administration for Children and Families (ACF)

The Administration for Children and Families brings together all of the federal programs concerned with the needs of children and families. It funds state, territorial, local, and tribal organizations supporting children. State, country, city, and tribal governments provide the direct services with the assistance of the ACF through funding, policy direction, and information services.

The Administration on Children, Youth, and Families (ACYF)

The Administration on Children, Youth, and Families administers the major *federal* government programs supporting children, youth, and families; protective services for children and young people in at-risk situations; child care for families; and adoption services for children with special needs. The ACYF is divided into several bureaus, each responsible for a different category of services to children, youth, and families. These are the Child Care Bureau, the Family and Youth Services Bureau, the Head Start Bureau, and the Children's Bureau. (Another bureau is responsible for research and evaluation of the work of the others.) In addition, ten divisions in the United States and its territories administer ACYF's programs in each of the regions.

The Children's Bureau (CB)

With an annual budget of more than $7 billion, the Children's Bureau undertakes many projects. It works with state, local, and tribal agencies to develop programs to prevent child abuse in troubled families, to protect children from all types of abuse, and to find permanent homes for children who cannot safely return to their birth families. It is responsible for programs under Titles IV-B and IV-E of the Social Security Act. The bureau also manages the AFCARS and SACWIS data collection systems and is responsible for the Child Welfare Information Gateway (which, as noted earlier, integrated the National Clearinghouse on Child Abuse and Neglect and the National Adoption Information Clearinghouse into one informational entity).

Another project of the CB (under the federal Department of Health and Human Services) is the Collaboration to Adopt-USKids. In October 2002 the Children's Bureau contracted with the Adoption Exchange Association and its partners to devise and implement a national recruitment and retention program for prospective adoptive parents. It operates the AdoptUSKids.org website, conducts a variety of adoption-related research projects, and works with adoptive family support organizations. The initial partners included:

The Adoption Exchange Association (AEA), the main contractor for the project. The AEA administers and supervises the subcontractors (below) and their projects. The website is http://www.adoptea.org.

The Child Welfare League of America (CWLA), which facilitates and reports on the workings of the National Adoption Advisory Board, manages an annual Partnership Summit, and conducts evaluations for the Collaboration to AdoptUSKids. The website is http://www.cwla.org.

The Northwest Adoption Exchange (NWAE), which manages, maintains, and enhances the AdoptUSKids.org website. For more information, the website is http://www.nwae.org.

The Adoption Exchange Education Center, which provides onsite training and technical assistance to the Collaboration to AdoptUSKids for recruiting and retaining adoptive families. The website is http://www.adoptex.org.

The University of Texas School of Social Work and the Center for Social Work Research (CSWR), which conduct research for the collaboration. Studies include identification of barriers to the completion of the adoption process (especially for families of color) and identification of factors affecting favorable long-term outcomes for families who adopt children with special needs. For further information, the website is http://www.utexas.edu/ssw.

Holt International Children's Services, which provides publication design and production for the collaboration, as well as assistance with media contact and cooperation. The website is http://www.holtintl.org.

The postal address of the Children's Bureau is:

Children's Bureau
Administration on Children, Youth, and Families
1250 Maryland Avenue SW, Eighth Floor
Washington, DC 20024

National Resource, Educational, Support, Advocacy, and/or Policymaking Organizations Concerned with Adoption

Adopt America Network (AAN)
1025 N. Reynolds Road
Toledo, Ohio 43615
(800) 246-1731
http://www.adoptamericanetwork.org

Founded in 1983 by Richard K. Ransom, Adopt America Network's mission is to find homes for waiting children in foster care. In addition to its headquarters in Toledo, Ohio, AAN volunteer specialists (parents of adopted children with special needs) are located across the United States to help recruit prospective adoptive parents and to help with the matching process. AAN also works with the agencies who have custody of children on behalf of prospective adoptive families, helps prepare families for adoption, and helps with postadoption services. Another mission is to increase public awareness of adoption.

The Adoption Exchange Association (AEA)
8015 Corporate Drive, Suite C

Baltimore, MD 21236
(410) 933-5700
Fax: (410) 933-5716
aedney@adoptuskids.org
http://www.adoptea.org

The Adoption Exchange Association (AEA) has served adoption in many ways over the years, always with the goal of finding permanent homes for children who need them. Currently it is the main contractor for the Collaboration to AdoptUSKids, a project of the Children's Bureau under the Department of Health and Human Services. AEA administers and supervises the subcontractors and their individual projects. The organization not only designs adoptive family recruitment and retainment strategies on a national level but also helps build support groups throughout the United States.

Publications: A variety of AEA publications are available at low or no cost (except postage), including *Standards for Adoption Exchanges, How to Make Adoption an Affordable Option, You Can Adopt! A Guide for Military Families, Adoption: A Guide for Military Family Service Center Staff and Civilian Social Workers, Overcoming Geographic Boundaries: A Guidebook for Families Pursuing Interstate Adoption, and Placing Children across Geographic Boundaries: A Step-by-Step Guide for Social Workers.*

The ALMA Society
Adoptees' Liberty Movement Association (ALMA)
P.O. Box 85
Denville, NJ 07834
(973) 586-1358
Fax: (973) 586-1358
Manderson@almasociety.com
http://almasociety.com

The Adoptees' Liberty Movement Association (ALMA) is an international organization founded in 1971 by Florence Anna Fisher, author of *The Search for Anna Fisher* (1986). The society is committed to helping adopted persons reunite with their birth parents and also helps birth parents find the children for which they made an adoption plan.

Publications: Available to members.

American Academy of Pediatrics Section on Adoption and Foster Care
141 Northwest Point Boulevard
Elk Grove, IL 60007
(847) 434-4000
adoption@aap.org
http://www.aap.org/sections/adoption

In June 2000 the American Academy of Pediatrics established its Provisional Section on Adoption. It is dedicated to improving the health and well-being of adopted children and those in foster care. In addition to offering input to the academy's board of directors on adoption and foster-care issues, it works with the AAP's Committee on Early Childhood, Adoption, and Dependent Care to influence official academy policy. Membership in the section is open to physicians, physicians' assistants, registered nurses, licensed practical nurses, speech and language pathologists, occupational and physical therapists, social workers, and educators.

Publications: Articles, policy statements, and books, such as *Caring for Your Baby and Young Child (Birth to Age Five).*

American Adoption Congress (AAC)
P.O. Box 42730
Washington, DC 20015
(800) 888-7970 or (202) 483-3399
Ameradoptioncong@aol.com
http://www.americanadoptioncongress.org

Founded in 1978 as a volunteer nonprofit organization, the American Adoption Congress (AAC) is an international education and advocacy network dedicated to promoting openness and honesty in adoption. Its membership is made up of adult adopted persons, birth parents, adoptive parents, professionals in adoption, and others wanting to explore adoption-related issues. The AAC holds regional and national conferences for all triad members.

Publications: Members receive *The Decree,* a quarterly publication highlighting adoption reform efforts.

American Humane Association (AHA)
National Headquarters
63 Inverness Drive East

Englewood, CO 80112
(818) 501-0123
Fax: (303) 792-5333
http://www.americanhumane.org

Many people would be surprised to know not only that the American Humane Association has existed since 1877 but also that it works to protect children from abuse and neglect, as well protecting animals. The organization offers consultation, training, research, evaluation, advocacy, and the dissemination of information on community, state, tribal, and national levels. Its programs include the promotion of best practice among child welfare professionals, a family group decisionmaking approach to working with families in the child welfare system, and programs for the prevention of child abuse and neglect.

Publications: The *Humane Review,* a quarterly newsletter; and two professional journals, *Protecting Animals* and *Protecting Children.* Reprints of individual articles from these journals are also available.

American Public Human Services Association (APHSA)
810 First Street NE, Suite 500
Washington, DC 20002
(202) 682-0100
Fax: (202) 289-6555
http://www.aphsa.org

The American Public Human Services Association is a nonprofit, bipartisan organization of individuals and agencies concerned with human services. It strives to develop, promote, and implement human service policies and practices that improve the health and well-being of families, adults, and children. Its members include state and territorial human services agencies, more than 150 local agencies, and thousands of individual members with an interest in human services. In addition, two important associations work under the umbrella of the APHSA. First is the Association of Administrators of the Interstate Compact on the Placement of Children (AAICPC), one of ten affiliates of the APHSA. The AAICPC was established in 1974 and is made up of members from all fifty states, as well as the District of Columbia and the U.S. Virgin Islands. (The Interstate Compact on the Placement of Children, discussed in Chapter 1, establishes uniform legal and administrative procedures that govern the placement of children across state lines.) The website of the AAICPC is http://icpc.aphsa.org. Second is the Association of Administrators of the Interstate Compact on Adoption and Medical Assistance (AAICAMA). This organization, established in 1986, though not an affiliate of the APHSA, has chosen the APHSA to provide its secretariat services. (The Interstate Compact on Adoption and Medical Assistance provides member states with technical assistance and support and helps coordinate the interstate delivery of services to children with special needs who are adopted with adoption assistance agreements in place.) The website of AAICAMA is http://aaicama.aphsa.org.

Publications: Magazines, books, periodicals, newsletters, surveys, and monographs, including *Policy & Practice,* the quarterly magazine of APHSA; the *Human Services Directory; This Week in Washington,* a weekly publication when Congress is in session; *Crossroads I & II,* dealing with directions in social policy; and *MMI Bulletin,* an electronic monthly newsletter dealing with the latest federal and state developments in Medicaid.

The Annie E. Casey Foundation
701 St. Paul Street
Baltimore, MD 21202
(410) 547-6600
Fax: (410) 547-6624
http://www.aecf.org

Since 1948 the Annie E. Casey Foundation, a philanthropic organization, has been devoted to improving the lives of disadvantaged children and families. The goals of one of its projects (designed in 1992) include developing a system of neighborhood-based foster care, reducing reliance on congregate or group care, increasing the number and quality of foster homes, and speeding reunification with birth families when possible. When not possible, the goal is to find permanent families (often the current foster or relative homes) in a timely manner.

Publications: A listing of the foundation's diverse publications is available online and on request.

Bastard Nation
P.O. Box 271672
Houston, TX 77277

(415) 704-3166
Fax: (415) 704-3166
bn@bastards.org
http://www.bastards.org

Bastard Nation is dedicated to full rights for adult adoptees. The organization advocates for the opening (on request of the adoptee at the age of majority) of any government documents pertaining to the adopted person's historical, genetic, and legal identity, including the unaltered original birth certificate and legal decree of adoption. (Bastard Nation does *not* support mandated mutual consent registries or intermediary systems in place of unconditional open records.)

Publications: The *Bastard Quarterly* is published four times a year for Bastard Nation members.

Black Administrators in Child Welfare (BACW)
1319 F Street NW, Suite 401
Washington, DC 20004
(202) 783-3714
Fax: (202) 783-7955
bacw@cwla.org
http://www.blackadministrators.org

Established in 1971 and incorporated in New York in 1975, Black Administrators in Child Welfare is a national nonprofit organization dedicated to improving the lives of African American children and their families in the child welfare system. It is an advocate for the employment of black executives in key administrative positions and serves as a resource for positive change. Membership is open to administrators and mental health and juvenile justice professionals who provide services to children and families. The organization has a long list of accomplishments, including policy statements on adoption and foster care, in-home services, day care, residential care, and child protective services, which serve as guidelines for agencies that serve African American children and families. It developed a Cultural Competence Training Seminar to train child welfare staff in agencies throughout the United States; an analysis of the "Federal Report to Congress on Kinship Foster Care"; one of the first family preservation models as a result of findings from the "Services to Families in Their Own

Homes" study; and cosponsored of the Twelfth National Conference on Child Abuse and Neglect.

Publications: The BACW quarterly newsletter; an analysis of the "Federal Report to Congress on Kinship Foster Care," which was published in the January 2000 *Federal Register* by the U.S. Department of Health and Human Services Children's Bureau; a monograph, "Children in Social Peril: A Community Vision for Preserving Family Care of African American Children and Youth"; and a special issue of the Child Welfare League of America's *Child Welfare Journal,* "Perspectives on Serving African American Children, Youth, and Families."

Center for Adoption Support and Education, Inc. (CASE)
4000 Blackburn Lane, Suite 260
Burtonsville, MD 20866
(301) 476-8525
Fax: (301) 476-8526
caseadopt@adoptionsupport.org
http://www.adoptionsupport.org

CASE, created in 1998 for postadoption support, is a national resource for families and professionals through its training, consultations, and publications. In addition it is a support center for families, educators, child welfare staff, and mental health providers in Maryland, Northern Virginia, and Washington, D.C. The center has developed several postadoption models as part of its mission to ensure the healthy preservation of adoptive families.

Publications: In addition to an e-newsletter, CASE provides Fact Sheets, articles, and books authored by CASE staff members. An online store offers the sale of these publications.

Center for Family Connections (CFFC)
350 Cambridge Street
Cambridge, MA 02141
(800) KINNECT or (617) 547-0909
Fax: (617) 497-5952
cffc@kinnect.org
http://www.kinnect.org

The goal of the Center for Family Connections is to help families touched by adoption, foster care, kinship care, guardianship, and other complex "blended" families. The organization offers clinical treatment, consultation, training, education, and advocacy. Training is generally done within the local area, but the CFFC has developed the Adoption Connections Training Institute: One World Network. In 2003 the organization collaborated with a British organization, After Adoption, to host an international conference, held in Dublin, Ireland, on adoption and postadoption. In 2004 CFFC formed an institute with plans to host an international conference every two years to discuss best practices in adoption and postadoption worldwide.

Child Welfare Information Gateway (CWIG)
Children's Bureau/ACYF
1250 Maryland Avenue SW, Eighth Floor
Washington, DC 20024
(800) 394-3366 or (703) 385-7565
info@childwelfare.gov
http://www.childwelfare.gov

The National Clearinghouse on Child Abuse and Neglect Information and the National Adoption Information Clearinghouse have now merged into the Child Welfare Information Gateway. By accessing the gateway website, professionals in adoption and child welfare, as well as the general public, can obtain information on all aspects of adoption. Various fact sheets on adoption issues, an online library of more than 48,000 documents, directories of adoption-related services, excerpts of state and federal laws on adoption, listings of agencies, information on children waiting for adoption, and much more information is available. Many of the publications and services are free. The CWIG is a service of the Children's Bureau, Administration for Children and Families, U.S. Department of Health and Human Services.

Child Welfare Institute (CWI)
111 East Wecher Drive, Suite 325
Chicago, IL 60601
(312) 949-5640
Fax: (312) 922-6736
http://www.gocwi.org

Since 1948 the Child Welfare Institute has put ideas into action to help state and local government agencies, as well as private child welfare agencies, administer systems that help children achieve safety, permanence, and well-being.

Publications: The CWI developed its Professional Communications Series to provide practical resources for child welfare administrators and practitioners. The complimentary publications that comprise the series include *Ideas in Action* (published monthly), *Commentary* (published bimonthly), and *Making a Difference That Matters* (an online series featuring brief practice articles by CWI staff and others). The publications examine the theory, practice, and implementation of child welfare services.

Child Welfare League of America (CWLA)
440 First Street NW, Third Floor
Washington, DC 20001
(202) 638-2952
Fax: (202) 638-4004
http://www.cwla.org

The Child Welfare League of America, founded in 1920, is the oldest and largest membership-based child-welfare organization in the United States. Concerned with setting standards and improving practice, the CWLA also advocates on behalf of children, conducts and encourages research on adoption, and provides consultations and training programs. This nonprofit organization unites approximately one thousand child-serving agencies throughout the United States, which serve more than two million abused and neglected children each year.

Publications: A large list of publications is available online; the CWLA also publishes a monthly journal, *Child Welfare: A Journal of Policy, Practice, and Programs.*

Children Awaiting Parents, Inc. (CAP)
595 Blossom Road, Suite 306
Rochester, NY 14610
(888) 835-8802 or (585) 232-5110
Fax: (585) 232-2634
info@capbook.org
http://www.childrenawaitingparents.org
or http://www.capbook.org

Children Awaiting Parents (CAP) is a national not-for-profit charitable organization that recruits foster and adoptive families for special needs children. A new CAP initiative, "A Right to be Heard," empowers waiting children to tell in their own words about themselves and their hopes for having a forever family. Videos are available online.

Publications: The CAP Book is a national photo listing of special needs children updated every two weeks and available on a subscription basis to interested families.

Circle of Parents
500 N. Michigan Avenue, Suite 200
Chicago, IL 60611
(312) 334-6837
http://www.circleofparents.org

Circle of Parents groups, which meet weekly and are free of charge, operate under different names across the country. They offer an exchange of ideas, support, information, and resources for individuals parenting children of all ages and for various reasons. The Circle of Parents national network represents a partnership of parent leaders and statewide and regional organizations in approximately half of the states. The organization was made possible by the Children's Bureau, Administration on Children, Youth, and Families, U.S. Department of Health and Human Services.

Concerned United Birthparents, Inc. (CUB)
P.O. Box 503475
San Diego, CA 92150
(800) 822-2777
Fax: (760) 929-1879
info@cubirthparents.org
http://www.cubirthparents.org

Concerned United Birthparents, Inc., is a national organization founded in 1976. Its mission is to provide support for all family members separated by adoption, to provide resources to prevent unnecessary family separations, to educate the public about the life-long impact of adoption, and to advocate for fair and ethical adoption laws, policies, and practices. Local branches are available in many cities throughout the United States.

Publications: Heather Lowe's booklet, "What You Should Know if You're Considering Adoption for Your Baby," is available online and as hard copies. CUB also offers other educational materials and a newsletter for members, *The Cub Communicator.*

Congressional Coalition on Adoption Institute (CCAI)
6723 Whittier Avenue, Suite 406
McLean, VA 22101
(703) 288-9700
Fax: (703) 288-0999
info@ccainstitute.org
http://www.ccainstitute.org

In 1985 members of Congress created the bipartisan Congressional Coalition on Adoption, dedicated to improving adoption policy and practice and to alerting the public to the benefits of adoption. In 2001 the active cochairs of the CCA created the current Congressional Coalition on Adoption Institute (CCAI) to more effectively raise public awareness of adoption issues. CCAI is a nonprofit, nonpartisan organization dedicated to eliminating barriers to adoption for the children in the United States and to those around the world who need permanent, safe, and loving homes. Working toward that goal, CCAI serves as an informational and educational resource for policymakers as they draft positive legislation having to do with adoption and foster care. CCAI educates members of Congress and their staff members about current domestic and international-related issues and needs. It hosts a number of public awareness events each year for members of Congress and other public leaders to do whatever they can for the world's most vulnerable children and to recognize those who have done similar work.

Dave Thomas Foundation for Adoption
4150 Tuller Road, Suite 204
Dublin, Ohio 43017
(800) ASK-DTFA or (800) 275-3832
Fax: (614) 766-3871
adoption@wendys.com
http://www.davethomasfoundationforadoption.org

Dave Thomas, founder of Wendy's International, created the Dave Thomas Foundation for Adoption. He believed that every child deserves a permanent home and a loving family. To that end, he devoted his nonprofit, public charity to increasing the number of children adopted from the foster-care system. The foundation give many grants to deserving adoption programs, underwrites a one-hour television special on adoption each December, sponsors a fund-raising professional golf tournament each year, launched a ground-breaking research project to measure attitudes to adoption in theUnited States, and promotes adoption through Wendy's restaurants.

Publications: The foundation supplies posters, educational videos, public service announcements, and other materials at no charge to adoption organizations. It also distributes *A Child Is Waiting . . . A Beginner's Guide to Adoption* to encourage adoption and raise public awareness about adoption.

Evan B. Donaldson Adoption Institute
525 Broadway, Sixth Floor
New York, NY 10012
(212) 925-4089
Fax: (775) 796-6592
info@adoptioninstitute.org
http://www.adoptioninstitute.org

Founded in 1996, the Evan B. Donaldson Adoption Institute is a national not-for-profit organization dedicated to promoting leadership to improve adoption laws, policies, and practice in order to better the lives of those touched by adoption. The institute also cohosts conferences throughout the year.

Publications: A comprehensive list of publications, presentations, books, conferences, press releases, and testimonies is available online. Most documents are available free in pdf format. A recent featured publication is *Expanding Resources for Children: Is Adoption by Gays and Lesbians Part of the Answer for Boys and Girls Who Need Homes?*

Family Pride Coalition (FPC)
P.O. Box 65327
Washington, DC 20035
(202) 331-5015
Fax: (202) 331-0080
http://www.familypride.org

The Family Pride Coalition is a national nonprofit organization dedicated to equality for lesbian, gay, bisexual, and transgender parents and their families. Members are formerly married, considering parenthood, considering or awaiting adoption, or currently parenting. Members also include grandparents, aunts and uncles, straight spouses, neighbors, coworkers, clergy, professionals, and companies that support this family movement. FPC is involved primarily in the areas of advocacy, education, and support. It works with state-based as well as local parenting groups to achieve family-friendly laws and to fight antifamily laws; it facilitates understanding among parents, teachers, and administrators to make schools safe and hospitable for all children; and it gathers families across the United States for special events throughout the year.

Hear My Voice: Protecting Our Nation's Children
1100 N. Main Street, Suite 201
Ann Arbor, MI 48104
(734) 747-9653 or (734) 747-9654
Fax: (734) 747-9559
http://www.hearmyvoice.org

Hear My Voice is a nationwide nonprofit network of child advocates, attorneys, mental health experts, and members of the media that works for children in contested adoption cases, long-term foster care, third-party placements, and de-facto parent situations. The organization works on local, statewide, and national levels to help children whose well-being is threatened by the lack of permanent, safe families. Hear My Voice began as the DeBoer Committee for Children's Rights in August 1993, on the day Jessica DeBoer was returned by the courts to her birth parents. In this case, back-and-forth legal battles ended with the child's court-ordered return to her birth parents at the age of two and a half. The organization lists many of its awards on the website.

Insight: Open Adoption Resources and Support
721 Hawthorne
Royal Oak, MI 48067
(248) 543-0997
Fax: (248) 543-0997
brenr@openadoptioninsight.org
http://openadoptioninsight.org

Insight is based on several beliefs: that adoption is a lifelong process; that efforts should be made to preserve birth families whenever possible; that in an adoption, maintaining relationships with birth families (when possible) serves children well; that adoption creates extended family relationships whether or not there is contact; that for open adoption to work well for children, all triad members need support and ongoing education; and that adults have the insight and ability to put the needs of the children above their own interests. Insight offers support for birth parents, adoptive parents, and adopted children.

Publications: Great Articles, Poetry, and Stories for Everyone! is a page on the website for all triad members.

Institute for Adoption Information, Inc. (IAI)

P.O. Box 4405
Bennington, VT 05201
(802) 442-2845
info@adoptioninformationinstitute.org
http://www.adoptioninformationinstitute.org

Founded in 1996 as Celebrate Adoption, the organization changed its name to reflect the educational aspects of its mission. One goal is to develop projects designed to dispel the myths and stereotypes about adoption and to advocate for balanced and accurate coverage by the media. The nonprofit IAI is made up of adopted persons, birth parents, adoptive parents, adoption professionals, and anyone else who shares its goals.

Publications: Guides to help with education about adoption include *An Educator's Guide to Adoption* and *A Guide to Adoption for Health Care & Counseling Professionals.*

International Social Service–United States of America Branch, Inc. (ISS-USA)

207 E. Redwood Street, Suite 300
Baltimore, MD 21202
(443) 451-1200
Fax: (443) 451-1220
iss-usa@iss-usa.org
http://www.iss-usa.org

ISS-USA is part of the International Social Service Network, which (under different names) has provided social work services internationally for many years. For decades, ISS had worked in intercountry adoption, most often assisting those who were friends or relatives of the children. With the passage of the Refugee Relief Act in 1953, the U.S. Department of State contracted with ISS-USA to help with the adoption process of children coming to the United States. In the 1950s that adoption expertise led to two research studies in collaboration with the Child Welfare League of America (CWLA). In 1957, ISS-USA conducted the first study, "Korean-American Children in American Adoptive Homes, which the CWLA published. In 1958 the organizations jointly sponsored "A Study of Proxy Adoptions." Over the years ISS-USA has continued to work with individuals and organizations to assist families, adults, and children. The organization also works with family courts, with the Interstate Compact on the Placement of Children, and with the U.S. government on aspects of intercountry adoption. The organization participated in meetings leading to the Hague Convention on International Adoption.

Publications: Annual reports are available online.

International Soundex Reunion Registry (ISRR)
P.O. Box 2312
Carson City, NV 89702
(775) 882-7755
http://www.ISRR.net

The International Soundex Reunion Registry, founded in 1975 by Emma May Vilardi, is a system for matching persons who have been separated by any number of reasons, including adoption. This is a nonprofit, tax-exempt corporation funded by donations. Those interested in registering may call for information.

Joint Council on International Children's Services (JCICS)
117 S. Saint Asaph Street
Alexandria, VA 22314
(703) 535-8045
Fax: (703) 535-8049
jcics@jcics.org
http://www.jcics.org

First organized in 1976, the Joint Council on International Children's Services is the oldest group of licensed nonprofit international adoption agencies in the world. Members include adoption agencies, child welfare organizations, parent support groups, and medical specialists. Member agencies, who must be located in North America, meet for an annual conference each year to share concerns and formulate policy. The organization advocates for moral and ethical standards in intercountry adoption and has worked for the adoption of the Hague Convention on Intercountry Adoption.

Publications: Members receive a quarterly newsletter, *The Bulletin.*

Latin American Parents Association (LAPA)

P.O. Box 339-340
Brooklyn, NY 11234
(718) 236-8689
info@lapa.com
http://www.lapa.com

The Latin American Parents Association (LAPA) is a national nonprofit support organization for those considering adopting from Latin America or for those who have already adopted from Latin America. It provides information and resources.

National Adoption Center (NAC)

1500 Walnut Street, Suite 701
Philadelphia, PA 19102
(800) TO-ADOPT
http://www.adopt.org

The National Adoption Center expands adoption opportunities throughout the United States, especially for children with special needs and those from minority cultures. In 1972 the NAC began as a volunteer organization to help social workers in the Philadelphia area find homes for waiting children. Although it still serves the region of southern Pennsylvania, New Jersey, and Delaware, NAC has expanded its national programs (with the sponsorship of the Dave Thomas Foundation for Adoption and the Freddie Mac Foundation) to include (1) increasing public awareness and recruitment for children waiting for permanent families, (2) information (online and by mail) on a wide variety of adoption topics, and resource lists of adoption agencies in all fifty states, Puerto Rico, and Canada, as well as international agencies, (3) a Wednesday's Child website, which can be accessed through http://www.adopt.org, and (4) a

Learning Center (funded by the Dave Thomas Foundation for Adoption) featuring an online parenting course.

Publications: The Adoption Update is printed twice a year and focuses on NAC activities, as well as highlighting waiting children and discussing current legislation and adoption practices that impact adoptive families. *NACzine* is an online magazine. The center also publishes brochures and booklets on a variety of adoption topics.

National Adoption Foundation (NAF)
100 Mill Plain Road
Danbury, CT 06811
(203) 791-3811
http://www.nafadopt.org

The National Adoption Foundation is a resource for financial assistance and support services to families who are adopting from a spectrum of adoption programs, including domestic infant, intercountry, or children from the foster care system. Besides providing financial help to families, the foundation attempts to educate the public and various policymakers about financial barriers to adoption.

National Association of Black Social Workers, Inc. (NABSW)
2305 Martin Luther King Avenue, SE
Washington, DC 20020
(202) 678-4570
Fax: (202) 678-4572
Nabsw.harambee@verizon.net
http://www.nabsw.org

The National Association of Black Social Workers, established in 1968, addresses and advocates for important social issues that affect the health and welfare of the black community. One of four task forces, the Task Force on Family, has addressed adoption issues. The NABSW considers adoption with nonrelated families the last option to be considered for African American children, preferring family preservation or kinship placement with supportive services.

National Child Welfare Resource Center for Adoption
Spaulding for Children

16250 Northland Drive, Suite 120
Southfield, MI 48075
(248) 443-0306
Fax: (248) 443-7099
nrc@nrcadoption.org
http://www.nrcadoption.org

This organization is a service of the Children's Bureau, U.S. Department of Health and Human Services, one of seven such resource centers. It assists states, tribes, and other federally funded child welfare agencies in improving their ability to help with the safety, well-being, and permanency of abused and neglected children. These services include program planning, policy development, and postlegal services. In addition, the center offers training and consultation services.

Publications: Include informational materials for parents, professionals, and organizations, as well as an e-newsletter.

National Council for Adoption (NCFA)
225 N. Washington Street
Alexandria, VA 22314
(703) 299-6633
Fax: (703) 299-6004
Membership e-mail: cjohnson@adoptioncouncil.org
http://www.adoptioncouncil.org

Founded in 1980, the nonprofit, nonsectarian NCFA seeks to promote the well-being of children, birth parents, and adoptive families by serving as a research, advocacy, and education organization. Its "Adoption First Principles" (available online) are: adoption should serve the best interests of children; making an adoption plan for a child is a loving act; growing up adopted is healthy and normal; adoptive parents are the real parents; there is no right to adopt, only the right of the child to be adopted; children's interests, not ideologies, should come first; preference in adoption placements should be given to families that offer married mother-and-father parenting; single-parent adoption is in the best interests of some children; and mutual consent should decide issues of privacy and openness. Among other activities, the organization holds an annual conference, an Adoption Hall of Fame Awards Banquet, and a Kids at Heart festival during National Adoption Month.

Publications: White papers, editorials, monographs, and National Adoption Reports, as well as a quarterly newsletter for members. The *Adoption Factbook* is available by order or online and reports on various aspects of adoption policy and practice and adoption data based on original research.

National Council of Birthmothers (NCOB)
P.O. Box 99769
Seattle, WA 98199
NCOBHdqtr@aol.com

Established in 1998, the National Council of Birthmothers supports the rights of birth mothers in regard to adoption issues. The council believes that everyone has the right to an unaltered birth record.

National Resource Center for Family-Centered Practice and Permanency Planning (NRCFCPPP)
Hunter College School of Social Work
129 E. 79th Street
New York, NY 10021
(212) 452-7053
http://www.hunter.cuny.edu/socwork/nrcfcpp

This National Resource Center, a service of the Children's Bureau, works in collaboration with the Child Welfare League of America and the National Indian Child Welfare Association, focusing on increasing the capacity and resources of tribal and other publicly supported child welfare agencies to promote family-centered practices and to keep children safe and in permanent families. The NRCFCPPP offers onsite training and technical assistance. Areas of training and technical assistance in regard to adoption include permanency planning and goal achievement, concurrent permanency planning, engaging fathers and paternal resources in permanency planning, trying to achieve permanency for older adolescents, helping to achieve placement stability, giving postplacement services, facilitating IV-E agreements between states and tribes, and providing linkages with courts and legal personnel.

Publications: The NRCFCPPP Weekly Update is an electronic newsletter published on Wednesdays for child welfare professionals, foster and adoptive parents, kinship providers, and other interested parties. *Permanency Planning Today* is published twice a year and addresses key issues in permanency planning, family-centered practice, and foster care. Training curricula in English and Spanish are available free online.

North American Council on Adoptable Children (NACAC)
970 Raymond Avenue, Suite 106
St. Paul, MN 55114
(651) 644-3036
Fax: (651) 644-9848
info@nacac.org
http://www.nacac.org

Founded in 1974 by a group of adoptive parents, the North American Council on Adoptable Children is committed to meeting the needs of waiting children and the families who adopt them. NACAC divides its services into four general areas: *advocacy* includes supporting groups for waiting children and adoptive families, offering testimony at congressional hearings and communicating with policy makers, and identifying ways to help foster children find adoptive families. *Education* includes hosting an annual comprehensive training conference with over one hundred accredited workshops; publishing its quarterly newsletter, *Adoptalk;* and providing numerous training sessions and workshops throughout the year on adoption subsidy, child welfare reform, transracial adoption, and other issues related to special needs adoption and foster care. *Leadership* includes offering leadership training to adoptive, foster, and kinship families so that they can create and operate support groups for families in their communities. *Adoption support* includes publications and telephone consultations, especially having to do with questions about adoption subsidies in the various states.

Publications: Quarterly newsletter, *Adoptalk,* and educational publications covering such topics as adoption subsidies, transracial adoptive parenting, and concurrent planning.

PACT, An Adoption Alliance
4179 Piedmont Avenue, Suite 330
Oakland, CA 94611
(800) 750-7590 (Birth Parent Line)
(510) 243-9460
Fax: (510) 243-9970

info@pactadopt.org
http://www.pactadopt.org

A nonprofit organization begun in 1991 by two adoptive parents, PACT serves all members of the adoption triad. It offers educational events and provides free crisis consultations to birth parents and also counsels and supports prospective adoptive parents. It specializes in adoptive services to children of color, their birth parents, and their adoptive parents. It offers extensive post-placement services.

Publications: PACT specializes in articles regarding adopted children of color. The Internet site offers links to other Internet resources and has a book reference guide with a searchable database. The site also provides reprints of past *Pact Press* issues.

Parents Network for the Post-Institutionalized Child (PNPIC)
P.O. Box 613
Meadow Lands, PA 15347
(724) 222-1666
thais1@earthlink.net
http://www.pnpic.org

Founded in 1993, this international network works to connect families whose children came from maternity hospitals, orphanages, and institutions in economically disadvantaged countries. It helps parents deal with a variety of problems, such as learning disorders or aggressive behaviors, that an early history of deprivation can cause.

Publications: The Post, a newsletter, was published between 1995 and 2001 but has been discontinued. Some past issues are available for purchase through an online listing. Also available is a book, *International Adoption: Challenges and Opportunities.* The website provides links to other recommended books and articles.

RESOLVE
7910 Woodmont Avenue, Suite 1350
Bethesda, MD 20814
(301) 652-8585
Fax: (301) 652-9375
info@resolve.org
http://www.resolve.org

RESOLVE is the national infertility association. The organization provides information on adoption and offers member-to-member contacts.

Publications: Members receive *Family Building*, an infertility magazine, and many other educational and supportive publications about infertility. Registered users can receive RESOLVE's e-updates online.

Stars of David International, Inc.
3175 Commercial Avenue, Suite 100
Northbrook, IL 60062
(800) 782-7349 or (847) 274-1527
info@starsofdavid.org
http://www.starsofdavid.org

Founded in 1984, this is a nonprofit support, information-sharing, and advocacy network for Jewish and interfaith adoptive families, as well as extended families, clergy, adoption agencies, and professionals in adoption. Stars of David provides a wide range of services, from helping to establish and support local chapters to international mailings.

Publications: Provides online resources (e.g., articles and book reviews) for school-age adoptees, teens and young adults, and adult adopted persons, as well as a quarterly newsletter for members.

National Legally Oriented Organizations with Adoption Connections

American Academy of Adoption Attorneys (AAAA)
P.O. Box 33053
Washington, DC 20033
(202) 832-2222
info@adoptionattorneys.org
http://www.adoptionattorneys.org

The American Academy of Adoption Attorneys is made up of approximately 330 attorneys who work in adoption law. This work includes promoting adoption law reform and distributing information related to ethical practice in adoption. The AAAA holds educational seminars and an annual meeting. It is also a resource for locating and choosing an adoption attorney.

Publications: A newsletter and a printable brochure are available through the website.

American Bar Association (ABA)
321 N. Clark Street
Chicago, IL 60610
(800) 285-2221 or (312) 988-5000
http://www.abanet.org

With more than 400,000 members, the ABA is the largest voluntary professional organization in the world. The ABA Center on Children and the Law, established in 1978, is a program of the American Bar Association's Young Lawyers' Division. It aims to improve the lives of children through advances in law, justice, knowledge, practice, and public policy. An associated resource is the National Child Welfare Resource on Legal and Judicial Issues, which is funded by the Children's Bureau and is part of the ABA Center on Children and the Law. The latter organization helps agencies, courts, and bar organizations with information on child maltreatment, foster care, permanency planning, and adoption.

Publications: ABA Journal, as well as many articles and publications related to adoption.

Children's Rights
330 Seventh Avenue, Fourth Floor
New York, NY 10001
(212) 683-2210
http://www.childrensrights.org

This watchdog group is dedicated to reforming child welfare services in the United States. As such, it is one of the country's leading child advocacy organizations, and attempts to hold state-run welfare agencies accountable for providing quality services to abused and neglected children. In addition to legal advocacy, the organization does research and analysis to ensure improved policies and practices, and it uses public education to promote and protect the rights of children. It aims to create meaningful and lasting reforms in government systems so that all children can be safe and grow up in loving families. A link to its online adoption section provides easy-to-digest statistics, such as the fact that two-thirds of children waiting to be adopted are six years of age or older, that the average length of time a child in foster care waits to be adopted is 44 months, and that only 18 percent of children who left foster care in 2003 were adopted.

Publications: Include those written and/or produced independently by Children's Rights or in collaboration with other child welfare professionals and organizations. Recent publications in adoption include *Ending the Foster Care Life Sentence: The Critical Need for Adoption Subsidies* (2006), *Lasting Impressions: A Guide for Photolisting Children* (2004), and *Post Permanency Services* (2003).

Legal Advocates for Permanent Parenting (LAPP)
3182 Campus Drive, Suite 175
San Mateo, CA 94403
(650) 712-1441
Fax: (650) 712-1637
info@lapponline.org
http://www.lapponline.org

LAPP was founded in 2003 by experienced dependency attorneys who have cared for foster children in their own homes; many have become permanent adoptive or kinship parents. The organization addresses the need for legal information, training, referrals, and support for kinship parents, foster parents, adoptive parents, and those with whom they work in the child welfare system. LAPP also works to improve communication among all of the parties associated with the children. Although the organization works mostly in California, members are often asked to speak at conferences and training sessions throughout the nation.

National Association of Counsel for Children (NACC)
1825 Marion Street, Suite 242
Denver, CO 80218
(888) 828-NACC or (303) 864-5320
Fax: (303) 864-5351
advocate@naccchildlaw.org
http://www.naccchildlaw.org

Founded in 1977, the National Association of Counsel for Children is a nonprofit advocacy and professional membership organization dedicated to representing and protecting children involved with the legal system. In addition to its home base in the Kempe Children's Center on the campus of the Children's Hospital in Denver, Colorado, it has a policy representative in Washington, D.C. Members include those who work with children, such as attorneys, physicians, therapists, social workers, teachers, law-enforcement officers, and other concerned citizens.

Publications: A quarterly newsletter/magazine is free to members; subscriptions are also available to others. A 2005 book, published by the Bradford Press and the NACC, is *Child Welfare Law and Practice: Representing Children, Parents, and State Agencies in Abuse, Neglect, and Dependency Cases.*

National Center for Adoption Law and Policy (NCALP)
Capital University Law School
303 E. Broad Street
Columbus, OH 43215
(614) 236-6730
Fax: (614) 236-6958
adoption@law.capital.edu
http://www.law.capital.edu/adoption

The mission of the National Center for Adoption Law and Policy is to improve the policies, laws, and practices associated with the systems that govern child protection and adoption in order to help the children have safe, healthy, and permanent homes. Changes in the law and the way the law is implemented are part of the advocacy efforts. Education is aimed toward passing along strategies for making the laws work to judges, attorneys, social workers, and government managers.

Publications: The Weekly Adoption News and *CASE Services.*

National Center for Youth Law (NCYL)
405 14th Street, 15th Floor
Oakland, CA 94612
(510) 835-8098
Fax: (510) 835-8099
Info@youthlaw.org
http://www.youthlaw.org

Founded in 1970, the nonprofit National Center for Youth Law aims to improve the lives of poor children. It acts as a resource (on a pro bono basis) for attorneys, legal services programs, social

service organizations, community groups, healthcare professionals, teachers, and others who work with poor children. NCYL employs three attorneys who have expertise in the areas of adoption,
foster care, abuse, and neglect. The organization supports the advocacy of others by providing training, technical assistance, and
published legal analyses and information.

Publications: A quarterly journal, *Youth Law News,* which
helps keep youth advocates throughout the United States abreast
of new developments in the law as well as key policies. The organization also publishes the national *Foster Care Reform Litigation
Docket,* which tracks foster care reform litigation throughout the
country. Many other publications are listed on the NCYL website.

**National Council of Juvenile and Family Court Judges
(NCJFCJ)**
P.O. Box 8970
Reno, NV 89507
(775) 784-6012
Fax: (775) 784-6628
staff@ncjfcj.org
http://www.ncjfcj.org

In 1937 a group of judges dedicated to improving the effectiveness
of the juvenile courts in the United States founded the National
Council of Juvenile and Family Court Judges. The mission of the
nonprofit organization is to improve court practices and raise
awareness of the core issues that affect the lives of many of the nation's families and children. These core issues related to adoption
practice include child abuse and neglect, termination of parental
rights, custody and visitation, adoption and foster care, domestic
violence, substance abuse, juvenile delinquency, and victims of
juvenile offenders. Since 1969 the NCJFCJ has had its headquarters on the campus of the University of Nevada in Reno. It provides up-to-date training, technical assistance, and research to
help the nation's courts, judges, and staff. Working with the University of Nevada and the National Judicial College, the NCJFCJ
participates in advanced degree programs for judges and other
court professionals.

Publications: Resources including monographs, journals,
benchcards, bulletins, briefs, and CDs (catalogued online by
topic). Also available: NCJFCJ's weekly electronic newsletter,
Brevity on the Net. Members and subscribers receive the monthly

Juvenile and Family Law Digest, the quarterly *Juvenile and Family Court Journal,* and the quarterly *Family Justice Today* magazine.

National Court Appointed Special Advocate (CASA) Association
100 West Harrison
North Tower, Suite 500
Seattle, WA 98119
(800) 628-3233
Fax: (206) 270-0078
inquiry@nationalcasa.org
http://www.nationalcasa.org

The mission of the National CASA Association (with its state and local chapters) is to support and promote court-appointed volunteer advocacy for abused and neglected children and to help these children do well in safe and permanent homes. A judge in Seattle came up with the idea of using trained community volunteers to work with state or local judges and courts on behalf of children. Today more than nine hundred CASA program offices across the country train volunteers to work with and for children. The National CASA Association helps start new CASA programs and gives ongoing assistance to established programs. It also organizes an annual conference.

Publications: A quarterly newsletter, *The Powerful Voice.*

State Offices

Because adoption is largely regulated by state laws and policies, individuals with questions about licensing may need to contact one of the fifty state offices (plus Puerto Rico and the Virgin Islands) listed below. A state licensing specialist maintains a record of the licensed child-placing agencies in each state and territory. (This record is available through the Child Welfare Information Gateway, http://www.childwelfare.gov.)

Alabama Department of Human Resources
50 N. Ripley Street
Montgomery, AL 36130
(334) 242-9500
Fax: (334) 242-0939
http://www.dhr.state.al.us

Alaska Department of Health and Social Services
404 Spruce Street
Craig, AK 99921
(907) 826-3433
http://www.hhs.state.ak.us

Arizona Department of Economic Security
Office of Licensing Certification & Regulation—
Child Welfare Licensing
1951 W. Camelback Road, Suite 400
Phoenix, AZ 85015
(602) 347-6346, (602) 347-6340, or (888) 229-1814
Fax: (502) 336-9603

Arkansas Department of Health and Human Services—
Division of Child and Family Services
Child Welfare Agency Licensing Unit
P.O. Box 1437, Slot 570
Little Rock, AR 72203
(501) 683-4322

California Department of Social Services
Community Care Licensing
744 P Street, MS 17-17
Sacramento, CA 95814
(916) 657-2346
Fax: (916) 657-3783
http://ccld.ca.gov/default.htm

Colorado Department of Social Services
Division of Child Care
1575 Sherman Street
Denver, CO 80203
(800) 799-5876 or (303) 866-5958
Fax: (303) 866-4453
http://www.cdhs.state.co.us/childcare/licensing.htm

Connecticut Department of Children and Families
505 Hudson Street
Hartford, CT 06106
(860) 550-6306
Fax: (860) 566-6726

Delaware Department of Services for Children, Youth, and Their Families
Office of Child Care Licensing
Barrett Building
821 Silver Lake Boulevard, Suite 103
Dover, DE 19904
(800) 822-2236 or (302) 739-5487
Fax: (302) 739-6589

Delaware Youth and Family Center
1825 Faulkland Road
Wilmington, DE 19805
(302) 892-5800
Fax: (302) 633-5112
http://www.state.de.us/kids/occl.htm

District of Columbia Department of Health—Licensing and Regulatory Administration
Human Social Services Facility Division
825 N. Capital Street NE
Washington, DC 20002
(202) 442-5929
Fax: (202) 442-9430

Florida Department of Children and Families
Office of Family Safety
1317 Winewood Boulevard, Building 6
Tallahassee, FL 32399
(850) 921-1928

Georgia Department of Human Resources
Office of Regulatory Services
2 Peachtree Street NW
Atlanta, GA 30303
(404) 657-9644
Fax: (404) 657-5708
http://www.ors.dhr.state.ga.us

Hawaii Department of Human Services
810 Richards Street, Suite 400
Honolulu, HI 96813
(808) 586-5698

Fax: (808) 586-4806
http://www.state.hi.us/dhs

Idaho Department of Children and Family Services
Division of Family and Community Services
450 W. State Street
P.O. Box 83720
Boise, ID 83720
(208) 334-5534
Fax: (208) 334-6699

Illinois Department of Children and Family Services
Division of Foster Care and Permanency Services
406 E. Monroe Street
Springfield, IL 62701
(217) 785-2688
http://www.state.il.us/dcfs

Indiana Department of Child Services
402 W. Washington Street
Room W-364
Indianapolis, IN 46204
(317) 232-3476
Fax: (317) 232-4436
http://www.state.in.us/dcs/protections/lcpa.html

Iowa Department of Human Services
Adult, Children, and Family Services
Hoover State Office Building, Fifth Floor
Des Moines, IA 50319
(515) 281-6802 or (515) 281-6220
Fax: (515) 281-4597
http://www.dhs.state.ia.us/dhs2005/dhs_homepage/chil-
dren_family/adoption/index.html

Kansas Department of Health and Environment
Child Care Licensing and Regulation
Curtis State Office Building
1000 SW Jackson, Suite 200
Topeka, KS 66612
(785) 296-8892
Fax: (785) 296-7025

Kentucky Cabinet for Health and Family Services
Division of Regulated Child Care
275 E. Main Street 6E-B
Frankfort, KY 00004
(502) 564-7962
Fax: (502) 564-9350
http://chfs.ky.gov/dcbs/dpp/permanency+services+branch.htm

Louisiana Department of Social Services
Bureau of Licensing
P.O. Box 3078
Baton Rouge, LA 70821
(225) 922-0015
Fax: (225) 922-0014
http://www.dss.state.la.us/departments/os/Licensing_.html

Maine Department of Health and Human Services
Bureau of Child and Family Services
221 State Street, Station 11
Augusta, ME 04333
(207) 287-5060 or (207) 287-4139
Fax: (207) 287-5282
http://www.afamilyforme.org/foster.html

Maryland Department of Human Resources
311 W. Saratoga Street
Baltimore, MD 21201
(410) 767-7382
Fax: (410) 333-0566
http://www.dhr.state.md.us/ssa/privadop.htm

Massachusetts Department of Early Education and Care
Central Office
600 Washington Street, Suite 6100
Boston, MA 02211
(617) 988-6600
http://www.eec.state.ma.us

Michigan Department of Human Services
Office of Child and Adult Licensing

7109 W. Saginaw
P.O. Box 30650
Lansing, MI 48909
(517) 335-6124
Fax: (517) 335-6121
http://www.cis.state.mi.us/brs_cwl/sr_cwl.asp

Minnesota Department of Human Services
Division of Licensing
Human Services Building
444 Lafayette Road North
St. Paul, MN 55155
(651) 296-3971
Fax: (651) 297-1490

Mississippi Department of Human Services
Division of Family and Children Services
750 N. State Street
Jackson, MS 39202
(601) 359-4599 or (601) 359-4656

Missouri Division of Family Services
Department of Social Services
P.O. Box 88
Jefferson City, MO 65103
(573) 751-4247
http://www.dnss.mo.gov

Montana Department of Public Health and Human Services
P.O. Box 8005
Helena, MT 59604
(406) 444-5919
Fax: (406) 444-5956
http://www.dphhs.mt.gov

Nebraska Department of Health and Human Services
Child and Family Services Division
301 Centennial Mall South
P.O. Box 95044
Lincoln, NE 68509
(402) 471-9331

Fax: (402) 471-9034
http://www.hhs.state.ne.us/chs/adp/adpindex.htm

Nevada Department of Human Services
Division of Child and Family Services
4220 S. Maryland Parkway
Building B, Suite 300
Las Vegas, NV 89119
(702) 486-7633
Fax: (702) 486-7626
http://www.dcfs.state.nv.us/DCFS_Adoption.htm

New Hampshire Department of Health and Human Services
Division of Children, Youth, and Families
129 Pleasant Street
Brown Building
Concord, NH 03301
(603) 271-4711
Fax: (603) 271-4729
http://www.dhhs.state.nh.us/DHHS/FCADOPTION/default.htm

New Jersey Department of Human Services
Office of Licensing—Youth and Family Licensing
P.O. Box 707
Trenton, NJ 08625
(609) 987-1985
http://www.state.nj.us/humanservices/adoption/resource/
frame.html

New Mexico Department of Children, Youth, and Families
PERA Building
P.O. Drawer 5160
Santa Fe, NM 87502
(505) 476-0343
Fax: (505) 827-8480
http://www.cyfd.org

New York State Office of Children and Family Services
Riverview Center, Sixth Floor
52 Washington Street
Rensselaer, NY 12144

(800) 345-5437 or (518) 474-9406
Fax: (518) 486-6326
http://www.ocfs.state.ny.us/adopt/agcymenu.asp

North Carolina Division of Social Services
Regulatory and Licensing Services
932 Old U.S. 70 Highway, Building 17–Black Mountain Center
Black Mountain, NC 28711
(828) 669-3388
Fax: (828) 669-3365

North Dakota Department of Human Services
Children and Family Services Division
State Capitol, Department 325
Bismarck, ND 58505
(800) 245-3736 or (701) 328-4805
Fax: (701) 328-3538
http://www.staate.nd.us/humanservices/services/childfam-ily/adoption

Ohio Department of Job and Family Services
Office for Children and Families
255 E. Main Street, Third Floor
Columbus, OH 43215
(614) 466-1213
Fax: (614) 466-6185
http://jfs.ohio.gov/oap/index.htm

Oklahoma Department of Human Services
Division of Child Care
P.O. Box 25352
2400 N. Lincoln Boulevard
Oklahoma City, OK 73125
(800) 347-2276 or (405) 521-3561

Oregon Department of Human Services
Treatment Services and Licensing Unit
500 Summer Street NE, E83
Salem, OR 97310
(503) 947-5140
Fax: (503) 947-5084

http://www.dhs.state.org.us/children/adoption/inadoptions/l
icensedag.htm

Pennsylvania Department of Public Welfare
Office of Children, Youth, and Families
P.O. Box 2675
Harrisburg, PA 17105
(717) 705-2908
Fax: (717) 346-9663
http://www.dpw.state.pa.us/Child/AdoptionFosterCare

Puerto Rico Department of the Families
P.O. Box 11398
Santurce, PR 00910
(787) 722-7450
Fax: (787) 723-1223

Rhode Island Department of Children, Youth, and Families
101 Friendship Street, Fourth Floor
Providence, RI 02906
(401) 528-3605
Fax: (401) 528-3650
http://www.dcyf.ri.gov/licensing.htm

South Carolina Department of Social Services
1535 Confederate Avenue
P.O. Box 1520
Columbia, SC 29202
(803) 898-7254
http://www.state.sc.us/dss/adoption/index.html

South Dakota Department of Social Services
Child Protection Services
700 Governor's Drive
Pierre, SD 57501
(605) 773-3227
Fax: (605) 773-6834
http://www.state.sd.us/social/cps/services/licensing.htm
District Office

Division of Child Protective Services
811 E. Tenth Street, Department 10
Sioux Falls, SD 57103

(605) 367-5600
Fax: (605) 782-3149
http://www.state.sd.us/social/cps/services/licensing.htm

Tennessee Department of Children's Services
1272 Foster Avenue
Nashville, TN 37210
(865) 594-2836
http://www.state.tn.us/youth

Texas Department of Family and Protective Services
P.O. Box 149030, E-550
Austin, TX 78714
(512) 438-3269
Fax: (512) 438-3848
http://www.dfps.state.tx.us

Utah Department of Human Services
Office of Licensing
120 N. 200 West, #303
Salt Lake City, UT 84103
(801) 538-4242
Fax: (801) 538-4553
http://www.hslic.utah.gov

Vermont Department for Children and Families
103 S. Main Street
Waterbury, VT 05671
(802) 241-2159
http://www.projectfamilyvt.org/adoption.html

Virgin Islands Department of Human Services
1303 Hospital Ground
Building A–Knud Hansen Complex
St. Thomas, VI 00802
(340) 774-0930, ext. 4243
Fax: (340) 774-0082

Virginia Department of Social Services
7 N. Eighth Street
Richmond, VA 23219
(804) 726-7137
http://www.dss.virginia.gov/family/ap/index.html

Washington Department of Social and Health Services
Division of Licensed Resources
P.O. Box 45700
Olympia, WA 98504
(360) 902-7967

West Virginia Department of Health and Human Resources
Bureau for Children and Families
350 Capitol Street, Room 691
Charleston, WV 25301
(304) 558-8839
Fax: (304) 558-4563

Wisconsin Department of Health and Family Services
Bureau of Regulation and Licensing
1 W. Wilson Street
P.O. Box 8916
Madison, WI 53708
(608) 266-0415
Fax: (608) 267-7252
http://www.dhfs.state.wi.us/licensing.htm

Wyoming Department of Family Services
851 Werner Court, Suite 200
Casper, WY 82601
(307) 473-3924
Fax: (307) 473-3967
http://dfsweb.state.wy.us/certlist.htm

The Child Welfare Information Gateway assisted in the preparation of these listings.

8

Selected Print and Nonprint Resources

The list of resources on adoption topics (of which the following is only a part) seems never-ending. This "wealth" may be the result of the various perspectives (e.g., birth parent, adoptive parent, adopted person), programs (e.g., domestic infant, special needs/older, intercountry), and methods (e.g., open, closed) from which adoption can be viewed. The following selective list includes both recent information and classic/historical works.

In this chapter, students of adoption will find a listing of books, journals, websites, videos/DVDs, CD-ROMs, software, and databases having to do with adoption.

Books

For ease of locating information, books are listed in alphabetical order by subject in the following categories: Adopted Persons, Attachment/Bonding, Birth Parents, Communication/Understanding, Controversy, Infant Adoption, General, Infertility, Intercountry/International, Open Adoption, Special Adoptive Parent Categories/Special Needs Children/Older/From Foster Care/ and Transracial/Transcultural. Most of the books are still in print; a few are out of print but readily available.

Adopted Persons

Fisher, Florence. *The Search for Anna Fisher.* New York: Fawcett Books, 1986. 224 pages.

This is the story of a woman's twenty-year search to find her birth parents, which culminated in the founding of a national organization for adopted persons, the Adoptees' Liberty Movement Association.

Lifton, Betty Jean. *Journey of the Adopted Self: A Quest for Wholeness.* New York: Basic Books, 1994. 336 pages.

In trying to explain the psychological complexity of being adopted, Lifton pleads for more openness in the adoption process. She uses the phrase *cumulative adoption trauma* to explain the "injury" and attempts (sometimes unhealthy) that the adopted person may make to justify his or her existence and identity.

Lifton, Betty Jean. *Lost and Found: The Adoption Experience,* rev. ed. New York: Harper and Row, 1988. 320 pages.

Lifton has written this book for adoptees and "brave new babies," those conceived with the help of the latest reproductive technologies. With real-life stories from adopted persons, the author continues the quest begun in her earlier book to answer such questions as: Who is my real mother? Who is my real father? Who is the authentic mother or father? Although most people consider themselves alienated from others in some ways, the author considers an adopted person "cut off" from others in many ways and "different" from the nonadopted person.

Lifton, Betty Jean. *Twice Born: Memoirs of an Adopted Daughter,* rev. ed. New York: St. Martin's Press, 1998. 288 pages.

Lifton describes her life as an adopted person: her doubts, questions, and fantasies; her search and reunion; and her anger about the closed adoption process.

Paton, Jean. *The Adopted Break Silence: Forty Men and Women Describe Their Search for Their Natural Parents.* Philadelphia: Life History Study Center, 1954.

The author began this classic work by publishing a notice in the *Saturday Review of Literature:* "Were you adopted before 1932? Your experience may assist research in adoption from the point of view of the experienced adult." Paton, an adopted person herself, was one of the first to realize that adults who have been adopted not only have something to say but also have unfinished business.

Attachment/Bonding

Bowlby, John. *Attachment.* 3 vols. New York: Basic Books, 1983. 464 pages.

Bowlby's classic trilogy (*Attachment,* 1969; *Separation,* 1973; and *Loss,* 1980) addresses the role attachment (or the lack of it) plays in the life of any child. In commemoration of its fiftieth year, Basic Books reissued a selection of the most influential and distinguished books by its authors. John Bowlby's trilogy focuses on the mother-child bond and what happens when it is broken (for one reason or another). In this new edition, Allen Schore, a neurobiologist/attachment theorist, shows how the recent research validates many of Bowlby's ideas.

Eyer, Diane E. *Mother-Infant Bonding: A Scientific Fiction.* New Haven, CT: Yale University Press, 1992. 237 pages.

The author disputes widely held beliefs about maternal-infant bonding. Eyer claims that research on goats, who reject their babies if separated from them after birth, is not necessarily applicable to humans. She seeks to relieve the guilt of women who for reasons such as adoption, maternal illness, or infant prematurity cannot spend the requisite amount of "bonding" time with their infants.

Gray, Deborah D. *Attaching in Adoption: Practical Tools for Today's Parents.* Indianapolis, IN: Perspectives Press, 2002. 400 pages.

This book provides practical tips for dealing with the challenges presented by children who have to leave one home (e.g., a birth parent's, a foster family's, or an orphanage) and adjust to another.

James, Beverly. *Handbook for Treatment of Attachment-Trauma Problems in Children.* New York: Free Press, 1994. 290 pages.

James discusses how to assess attachment difficulties and how to treat them. She describes the role of trauma in attachment disorders, gives a "brief treatise" against coercive therapies, and includes chapters on dynamic play therapy. She ends by suggesting to prospective adoptive parents that if they do not want the "ride of their life," they should consider getting a pet instead of a child. Those who have "been there" with attachment-disordered children may find themselves nodding in recognition at the case histories added (by thirty-five contributors) to the text of this book.

Welch, Martha G. *Holding Time.* New York: Simon and Schuster, 1989. 254 pages.

Written by a psychiatrist who specializes in attachment, the book's central message is that regular sessions of mother-child holding decrease anger, conflict, temper tantrums, and sibling rivalry while increasing self-esteem, self-confidence, and contentment in infants through the preteen years.

Birth Parents

Collins, Pauline. *Letter to Louise: The Story of the Daughter She Gave for Adoption More Than Twenty-Five Years Ago.* New York: HarperCollins, 1992. 224 pages. (Also available on audiocassette.)

British actress Pauline Collins (*Upstairs Downstairs*) relinquished her daughter for adoption in 1964. This is the story of the next twenty-two years, ending in a happy reunion.

Fessler, Ann. *The Girls Who Went Away: The Hidden History of Women Who Surrendered Children for Adoption in the Decades before Roe v. Wade.* New York: Penguin Press, 2006. 355 pages.

Through an audio and video installation project, Ann Fessler began interviewing women who had made an adoption plan for their children. (Fessler is a professor of photography at the Rhode Island School of Design.) The book is filled with anecdotes and true stories of women caught up in a "revolution" in which birth control was restricted and abortion was illegal in many states. At the same time, in those post–World War II years, families shunned single pregnant women, schools expelled them, and they were sent away to "maternity homes" to have their babies, where they were told that "surrendering" their babies was their best option and that they would soon "forget." But they didn't forget; the majority of the women Fessler interviewed were haunted by their loss for the rest of their lives. An adopted person herself, Fessler ends the book with her own successful search for her birth mother.

Finnegan, Joanne. *Shattered Dreams—Lonely Choices: Birthparents of Babies with Disabilities Talk about Adoption.* Westport, CT: Bergin and Garvey, 1993. 183 pages.

The author shares her personal experiences (giving birth to a baby with Down syndrome), the process of "making a plan," and life after the decision. She includes stories of others with similar experiences.

Gritter, James L. *Lifegivers: Framing the Birthparent Experience in Open Adoption.* Washington, D.C.: Child Welfare League of America, 2000.

Although this is a book about open adoption, it is also a book about birth parents. Society tends to either ignore birth parents or marginalize them, Gritter writes. A strong advocate of open adoption, Gritter gets into the minds and emotions of birth parents and says that children's interests are best served when birth parents and adoptive parents work together to keep birth parents part of the children's lives.

Perkins, Ann, and Rita Townsend. *Bitter Fruit: Women's Experiences of Unplanned Pregnancy, Abortion, and Adoption.* Alameda, CA: Hunter House, 1992. 286 pages.

This is a collection of true stories (some in poetry) of women "in a bind," forced to make what appears to be at the time a no-win decision. Perkins and Townsend allow the women—some now grandmothers, some still very young—to speak for themselves about what it means to face an unwanted pregnancy.

Communication/Understanding

Keefer, Betsy. *Tell the Truth to Your Adopted or Foster Child: Making Sense of the Past.* Westport, CT: Bergin and Garvey, 2000. 256 pages.

Most parents today understand the importance of telling the truth to children. As hard as that rule may be to live by, foster and adoptive parents must also tell the truth to *all* of their children—biological, foster, or adoptive—even if the truth is confusing, complicated, and/or painful. Various chapters discuss principles and strategies for telling the truth, as well as communication with adolescents and talking to the child's teachers. The book also presents developmental stages, useful to know when trying to figure out *what* to say and *when*. (The authors are both training consultants in human services.)

Kumar, Miriam. *Communicating with the Adopted Child.* Lincoln, NE: iUniverse, 1978. 300 pages.

With assistance help of stories and anecdotes, the author tries to help adoptive parents understand the meanings behind an adopted child's words and actions. In addition, she points out how adoption colors ongoing events in a child's life, such as discipline, independence, and sexuality.

Lanchon, Anne. *All About Adoption: How to Deal with the Questions of Your Past.* New York: Amulet Books, 2006. 104 pages.

Anyone who is a teenager or who wonders what a teen may be thinking about adoption would likely learn something from this book, originally published in French. With lively illustrations by Monike Czarnecki and edited by Tucker Shaw, the book tackles common and not-so-common questions young people may have, such as "Who am I?" and "Where did I come from?"

Riley, Debbie, with John Meeks, MD. *Beneath the Mask: Understanding Adopted Teens: Case Studies and Treatment Considerations for Therapists and Parents.* Silver Spring, MD: CASE Publications, 2005. 260 pages.

Being a teenager can be difficult, but adding adoption issues to the mix can be hard on parents and children alike. Issues such as rejection, depression, and identity confusion arise, and help is needed. The authors give clinical examples and case studies that show how professionals can work successfully with parents and their children.

Watkins, Mary, and Susan Fisher. *Talking with Young Children About Adoption,* rev. ed. New Haven, CT: Yale University Press, 1995. 270 pages.

The authors, both adoptive parents, believe that to communicate effectively with young children, the adults must do some psychological work first. Knowing how to interpret past and current research is an important first step. The bulk of the book gives accounts of conversations between adoptive parents and their children regarding adoption. The book also documents changes in adoption practices and how these changes affect adoptive parents and their children.

Controversy

Bartholet, Elizabeth. *Family Bonds: Adoption and the Politics of Parenting.* Boston: Houghton Mifflin, 1994. 276 pages.

Considered controversial by some, this book takes a careful look at adoption policies that leave waiting children without parents and waiting parents without children. The author discusses infertility treatments and surrogate parenting, as well as transracial and transnational families, single and same-sex parents, and older parents.

Cahn, Naomi, and Joan H. Hollinger. *Families by Law: An Adoption Reader.* New York University Press, 2004. 282 pages.

The authors cover much diverse ground in this volume, which presents various perspectives on adoption law and practice. Included is a historical overview of adoption in American law and society. The authors then explore "new frontiers" in adoption, such as transracial and intercountry adoption, the adoption of children with special needs, adoption by same-sex couples, a trend toward openness with records, and continued postadoption contact between birth families and adoptive families. Not omitted is a presentation of the relationship between adoption and assisted reproductive technologies, as well as feminist, economic, and philosophical perspectives on adoption. Also included are statutes and legal cases, statements from advocacy organizations, and a great deal of information about contemporary controversies in adoption.

Dudley, William, ed. *Issues in Adoption: Current Controversies.* Farmington Hills, MI: Greenhaven Press, 2004. 208 pages.

Various experts on "both sides of the question" explore such issues as "Should adoption be encouraged?" "Does America's adoption system need more government regulation?" "Should adoptees be given open access to adoption and birth records?" and "Should adoption by gays and lesbians be permitted?"

Harnack, Andrew, ed. *Adoption: Opposing Viewpoints.* San Diego, CA: Greenhaven Press, 1995. 306 pages.

As part of the Opposing Viewpoints series, this book offers chapters from adoption writers and experts such as Elizabeth Bartholet, Annette Baran, Reuben Pannor, Arthur Sorosky, and Kenneth Watson. It also presents opinions from organizations such as the North American Council on Adoptable Children and Concerned United Birthparents. Some of the subjects that elicit differing viewpoints are: "Should the orphanage system be reestablished?" "Should intercountry adoptions be discouraged?" "Should transracial adoption be forbidden?" and "Is an open adoption policy best?"

Liptak, Karen. **Adoption Controversies.** Danbury, CT: Franklin Watts, 1993. 160 pages.

There are at least two sides to every story. This book provides those two sides in relation to such issues as search and reunion, which may be faced by all members of the adoption triad—birth parents, adoptive parents, and adopted children.

Pertman, Adam. *Adoption Nation: How the Adoption Revolution Is Transforming America.* New York: Basic Books, 2000. 349 pages.

As executive director of the Evan B. Donaldson Adoption Institute, Pertman knows his subject from a professional viewpoint. He also understands it from the viewpoint of an adoptive parent; he and his wife have two adopted children. Although this book is packed with historical facts, it does not shrink from current controversies. Pertman's book advocates for reforms in confusing and sometimes conflicting rules, regulations, and laws. He looks at adoption from the perspective of birth parents, adoptive parents, and children. He examines international, transracial, domestic infant, and special needs adoption, as well as adoption by same-sex couples and single persons. Pertman's message is that adoption touches much of society, not just the 80 million Americans with adoption in their immediate families. Adoption today is a revolution that is transforming society.

Smith, Jerome. *The Realities of Adoption.* Lanham, MD: Madison Books, 1997. 158 pages.

Acknowledging that the adoption of a child can be a joyous experience, the author (a former professor of social work and the father of two adopted children) discusses the many controversies in adoption. Smith tackles such issues as openness in adoption, children's rights, the role of the birth father, and transracial adoption. He uses case examples, including the Baby Jessica case in which he was an evaluator of the parent-child bond.

Infant Adoption

Adamec, Christine. *There Are Babies to Adopt: A Resource Guide for Prospective Parents,* rev. ed. New York: Citadel Press, 2002. 288 pages.

This book covers territory for all adoptive parents but focuses on adopting infants and young children. Information for U.S. families living overseas who want to adopt as well as use of the Internet in an adoption process are useful sections not always included in other books.

Johnston, Patricia I. *Launching a Baby's Adoption: Practical Strategies for Parents and Professionals.* Indianapolis, IN: Perspectives Press, 1998. 257 pages.

Written for single parents as well as for couples, this book covers everything the new adoptive parents of an infant need to know—the extended family's reactions, society's reactions, how to encourage bonding and attachment, the impact of infertility, the relationship with birth parents, and much more.

General

Adamec, Christine A. *Complete Idiot's Guide: Adoption,* 2nd ed. New York: Penguin Group, 2005. 432 pages.

This comprehensive resource (updated) includes new listings for adoptive parent support groups, adoption attorneys, adoption agencies, and adoption publications. It also includes information on cyber adoption, financial considerations in adoption, and the latest in adoption laws.

Adamec, Christine A. *The Encyclopedia of Adoption,* 3rd ed. New York: Facts on File, 2006. 432 pages.

From A (abandonment) to Z (zygote adoption) the author, an adoptive parent herself, includes entries on every conceivable adoption topic, including a history of adoption.

Beauvais-Godwin, Laura, and Raymond Godwin. *The Complete Adoption Book: Everything You Need to Know to Adopt a Child,* 3rd ed. Avon, MA: Adams Media, 2005. 690 pages.

The expertise of an adoption agency director joins with that of an adoption attorney to provide adoption professionals and those who wish to adopt with a comprehensive range of information about the adoption process. The stories of experienced adoptive parents add to the updated information regarding court/legal processes and the latest resources.

Blau, Eric. *Stories of Adoption: Loss and Reunion.* Portland, OR: New Sage Press, 1994. 132 pages.

With black-and-white photographs and first-person accounts of adoption, this book is similar to *How It Feels to Be Adopted,* by Jill Krementz. Unlike Krementz's book, which explores feelings about adoption from the perspective of children, this volume explores the viewpoints of adults—adopted persons, adoptive parents, and birth parents.

Bothun, Linda. *Dialogues about Adoption: Conversations between Parents and Their Children.* Chevy Chase, MD: Swan Publications, 1994. 216 pages.

This book uses true-life conversations in a chapter for each developmental stage of the adopted child's life to illustrate questions the children may ask. Sometimes there is no "pat" answer, but parents will find support and good ideas in other parents' answers.

Bothun, Linda. *When Friends Ask about Adoption: A Question and Answer Guide for Non-Adoptive Parents and Other Caring Adults.* Chevy Chase, MD: Swan Publications, 1996. 96 pages.

Questions and answers for friends, relatives, neighbors, teachers, coaches, counselors, and others who are friends of the adoptive family fill the pages of this book.

Brodzinsky, David M., and Marshall D. Schechter, eds. *The Psychology of Adoption.* New York: Oxford University Press, 1990. 416 pages.

Adoption cuts across many disciplines (social work, psychology, psychiatry, sociology, special education, and the legal system, to name a few); the editors bring together thirty experts to discuss theory, research, clinical issues, and social policy as they relate to adoption. One question the book raises is this: Are adopted persons more vulnerable to emotional difficulties than those who have not been adopted? If so, what is the reason or reasons? The book may be of interest to adoptive parents, psychologists and psychiatrists, social workers, and other social service providers.

Brodzinsky, David M., Marshall D. Schechter, and Robin M. Henig. *Being Adopted: The Lifelong Search for Self.* New York: Doubleday, 1993. 224 pages.

The authors use anecdotes from adopted persons to explore the effects of adoption throughout the life cycle. Erik Erikson's seven stages of life serve as a focus for observations having to do with the ways adoption affects a person's life and relationships.

Canape, Charlene. *Adoption: Parenthood without Pregnancy,* rev. ed. New York: Avon Books, 1988. 320 pages.

The author says it took seven years to write this book because it took that long for her to become a mother by adoption. Starting with infertility and its heartbreak, the book ends with ideas for improving the adoption process. In between are chapters on the search for an agency, the adoption process itself, and various categories of adoption, such as independent adoption, intercountry adoption, the adoption of older children and those with special needs, and adoption by single parents.

Fahlberg, Vera I., MD. *A Child's Journey through Placement.* Indianapolis, IN: Perspectives Press, 1991. 432 pages.

With abundant case examples, the author attempts to show how attachment develops, what normal child development consists of, and some of the effects of separation and loss. Dr. Fahlberg suggests ways to minimize the trauma of children's moves in the child welfare system. Subsequent chapters look at children's common behavior problems and their coping skills. Fahlberg includes a section on the "life book," which is a pictorial and written representation of a child's life history.

Gilman, Lois. *The Adoption Resource Book: All the Things You Need to Know and Ought to Know about Creating an Adoptive Family,* 4th ed. New York: Morrow/Avon, 1998. 592 pages.

This edition is a comprehensive guide to all types of adopting, including agency and independent adoption, intercountry adoption, special needs adoption, and open adoption. It features a state-by-state guide to agencies and a discussion about raising an adopted child with all of the necessary adjustments.

Kirk, H. David. *Adoptive Kinship: A Modern Institution in Need of Reform,* rev. ed. Port Angeles, WA: Ben-Simon Publications, 1985. 200 pages.

The culmination of three decades of research, Kirk bases *Adoptive Kinship* on his earlier pioneering work, *Shared Fate.* This later book attempts to prove that some of the difficulties of adoptive family life are caused by mistaken laws and administrative practices. For example, "Why can't adopted siblings marry?" is one of the fascinating questions this book poses.

Kirk, H. David. *Shared Fate: A Theory and Method of Adoptive Relationships,* rev. ed. Brentwood Bay, BC: Ben-Simon Publications, 1984. 215 pages.

This classic book studies family relationships from a sociological/psychological point of view. To fully appreciate Kirk's contribution, it helps to realize that before this book's publication, people considered families by birth and those formed by adoption to be basically the same. Kirk points out that there are differences, and that those who acknowledge the differences are likely to have a more successful adjustment than those who don't.

Kruger, Pamela, and Jill Smolowe, eds. *A Love Like No Other.* New York: Penguin Group, 2006. 272 pages.

Some well-known and other not-so-well known adoptive parents discuss their parenting experiences with the children placed in their families through adoption. These are not "pie-in-the-sky" stories with fairy-tale endings, but stories of real life by twenty essayists who have "been there."

McColm, Michelle. *Adoption Reunions: A Book for Adoptees, Birth Parents, and Adoptive Families.* Toronto: Second Story Press, 1993.

McColm, an adoptee from Canada, gives advice on searching for birth families and what to do after the reunion. She is nonjudgmental as she considers the feelings of each member of the adoption triad.

Melina, Lois R. *Making Sense of Adoption: A Parent's Guide.* New York: HarperPerennial, 1989. 288 pages.

This book for adoptive families gives helpful tips on how, when, and what to say when children ask the inevitable questions about adoption. It includes situations, role-plays, conversations, and activities not only for families formed by traditional adoption but also for those formed by in vitro fertilization, donor insemination, and surrogacy. Melina maintains that children conceived through such methods as donor insemination share issues and questions with those adopted in more "traditional" ways.

Melina, Lois R. *Raising Adopted Children: A Manual for Adoptive Parents.* New York: HarperPerennial, 1986. 288 pages.

This handbook for adoptive parents gives practical advice on such topics as adjustment, attachment, talking with children about adoption, dealing with sexuality, and coping with adolescents, birth relatives, and behavior problems.

Mewshaw, Michael. *If You Could See Me Now: A Chronicle of Identity and Adoption.* Denver: Unbridled Books, 2006. 225 pages.

In this memoir, Michael Mewshaw, a travel writer, novelist, and investigative reporter, tells the story of a quest for identity and an obsession with the past. In a look at the culture of the early 1960s, he tells of his involvement in a baby's birth and adoption and, years later, in her search for her biological parents.

O'Halloran, Kerry. *The Politics of Adoption: International Perspectives on Law, Policy, and Practice.* New York: Springer, 2006. 334 pages.

This scholarly work provides a comparative analysis of adoption law, policy, and practices in England, Wales, Ireland, the United States, and Australia. It explores both intercountry adoption and open adoption.

O'Hanlon, Tim, and Rita Laws. *Adoption Digest: Stories of Joy, Loss, and the Journey.* Westport, CT: Bergin and Garvey, 2001. 216 pages.

These stories illustrate the saying that adoption is a life-long process that changes the lives of those involved. The narrative tells of young children and older ones, their families, and the professionals who work with them. Written for anyone who has worked in adoption, who has been adopted, who has thought of adopting, or has adopted.

Rosenberg, Elinor B. *The Children and Their Families through the Years,* 2nd ed. Philadelphia: DIANE Publishing, 2000. 209 pages.

Rosenberg uses case examples to show what adoption means to all members of the adoption triad *throughout the lifespan.* She gives examples in which the lives of birth parents, adoptive parents, and children interact and affect each other, and gives practical advice on how to handle conflicts if they arise. A distinctive feature of the book is the outline of developmental tasks for each member of the triad.

Schooler, Jayne, and Betsie Norris. *Journeys after Adoption: Understanding Lifelong Issues.* Westport, CT: Greenwood Publishing, 2002. 312 pages.

With help from birth parents, adoptive parents, and adopted persons, the authors explore lifelong issues in adoption such as search, reunion, and postreunion. From these triad members, insights arise about the joys and pains and concerns of anyone who has a connection with adoption.

Siegel, Stephanie E. *Parenting Your Adopted Child: A Complete and Loving Guide,* 2nd ed. SES Publishers, 1997. 242 pages.

The author, a family therapist and mother of three adopted children and one birth child, begins the book with a couple's discovery of infertility and a decision to adopt. She tackles the stages of a child's life and the ways parents can help guide their children. Next, she deals with identity issues that are certain to arise in the adopted child's teenage years. Finally, she touches on relationships and concerns about birth parents, as well as how it feels to be a grandparent.

Smith, Eve P., and Lisa A. Merkel-Holguin, eds. *A History of Child Welfare.* New Brunswick, NJ: Transaction Publishers, 1996. 313 pages.

The chapters that make up this book were originally published in the January/February 1995 issue of *Child Welfare,* a special volume commemorating the Child Welfare League of America's seventy-fifth anniversary. Themes recycle throughout history, say the editors, and society is currently experiencing a recurrence of the social and economic conditions that lead to child abuse, neglect, and out-of-home care. Chapter titles include "Factors and Events Leading to the Passage of the Indian Child Welfare Act," "Adoption and Disclosure of Family Information: A Historical Perspective," "From Family Duty to Family Policy: The Evolution of Kinship Care," "A History of Placing-Out: The Orphan Trains," and "Bring Back the Orphanages? What Policymakers of Today Can Learn from the Past."

Infertility

Bartholet, Elizabeth. *Family Bonds: Adoption, Infertility, and the New World of Child Production.* Boston: Beacon Press, 1999. 286 pages.

Explores how adoption and treatments for infertility fit together. While fertility treatments are expensive, increasingly complex, and often frustrating, children are waiting to be adopted.

Johnston, Patricia I. *Adopting after Infertility.* Indianapolis, IN: Perspectives Press, 1992. 320 pages.

For couples with infertility problems, this book provides a guide through three stages of the adoption process. Part One (The Challenge) explores the losses that accompany infertility. Part Two (The Commitment) discusses decisions and choices. Part Three (Adoption through a Lifetime) presents ongoing issues for adoptive parents and their children.

Intercountry/International

Alperson, Myra. *The International Adoption Handbook: How to Make an Overseas Adoption Work for You.* New York: Henry Holt, 1997. 208 pages.

The author, who has adopted from China, focuses on procedural issues in adopting from that country as well as intercountry adoption procedures when adopting from Eastern Europe or Latin America. The book provides information on useful resources and interviews from adoptive families.

Dodds, Peter F. *Outer Search/Inner Journey: An Orphan and*

Adoptee's Quest. Puyallup, WA: Aphrodite Publishing, 1997. 280 pages.

This is a story of an international adoption but also a story of a search. The author, adopted at age three from Germany by an American couple, describes his lifelong search for a sense of identity. Returning to his country of birth to find his birth mother proves disappointing. His conclusion is not supportive of intercountry adoption.

Erichsen, Jean, and Heino R. Erichsen. *Butterflies in the Wind: Spanish-Indian Children with White Parents.* The Woodlands, TX: Los Ninos International Adoption Center, 1992. 355 pages.

This is one family's story involving the adoptions of Rosana and Tatiana, infant twins from Colombia, and later of Omar at age nine from the same country. Through their own story, the authors offer tips to others wanting to adopt from Latin America.

Erichsen, Jean, and Heino R. Erichsen. *Butterflies in the Wind: The Truth about Latin American Adoptions.* Lincoln, NE: iUniverse, 2004. 387 pages.

This book follows the Erichsens' children into young adulthood. Although told from the point of view of the parents, the authors explore the emotions of the young people and what they have to face in and out of school, including culture clashes, gang problems, and school dropout.

Erichsen, Jean, and Heino R. Erichsen. *How to Adopt Internationally: A Guide for Agency Direct and Independent Adoptions,* rev. ed. Fort Worth: Mesa House Publishing, 2003. 296 pages.

The authors take readers through every phase of the intercountry adoption process, from choosing an agency to adjusting to a life changed by a child. The book covers possible costs and provides samples of forms and documents. This updated version provides in-depth information on laws and requirements for adopting in sixty-eight countries. In addition it provides Internet addresses for use in finding sites for various necessary forms, how to contact an embassy, finding country-specific adoption support groups, and travel information.

Miller, Laurie C. *The Handbook of International Adoption Medicine: A Guide for Physicians, Parents, and Providers.* New York: Oxford University Press, 2004. 464 pages.

This book gives an overview of specialized medical and developmental conditions that may affect children adopted from other countries. In addition to serving as a guide for physicians, it offers advice and support to adoptive families before and after the adoption. The text gives information on how to perform an initial assessment of the new child and how to manage special developmental issues if they arise.

Register, Cheri. *Beyond Good Intentions: A Mother Reflects on Raising Internationally Adopted Children.* St. Paul, MN: Yeong and Yeong, 2005. 183 pages.

This is a collection of essays about the joys and risks of raising children adopted internationally. Each essay begins with an exaggerated version of words or practices adoptive families often use that may not serve their best interests or those of the children. Examples are "believing adoption saves souls," " judging our country superior," and "believing race doesn't matter." One of the author's goals is to help readers look at practices that they may not previously have questioned.

Reid, Theresa. *Two Little Girls: A Memoir of Adoption.* New York: Berkeley Books, 2006. 297 pages.

The author, who spent years working with abused and neglected children, tells the story of Natalie and Lana and their entry into the Reid family, as well as the "before" and the "after." Infertility, decisions to adopt, and "adventures" in orphanages in Russia and Ukraine are among the topics discussed.

Open Adoption

Caplan, Lincoln. *An Open Adoption.* New York: Houghton Mifflin, 1991. 160 pages.

As a personal history, this book tells of one couple's experience with open adoption. It also includes a history of the open adoption movement. Included are aspects of the debate over how much adoptive families and birth parents should know about each other.

Gritter, James L. *The Spirit of Open Adoption.* Washington, DC: Child Welfare League of America, 1997. 314 pages.

After showing that children of open adoption have done well, the author decries the apparent growth of commercialism in infant adoption. He is concerned about the high costs that threaten to turn infant adoption from a professional service into a high-priced business. Unlike many other books on adoption, this one deals with spiritual and philosophical questions.

Gritter, James L., ed. *Adoption without Fear.* San Antonio, TX: Corona Publishing, 1989. 176 pages.

Seventeen families tell of their experiences with open adoption.

Melina, Lois, and Sharon K. Roszia. *The Open Adoption Experience: A Complete Guide for Adoptive and Birth Families—From Making the Decision through the Child's Growing Years.* New York: HarperPerennial, 1993. 416 pages.

This comprehensive guide begins with an explanation of the concept of open adoption and the reasons the authors believe it works. The two adoption veterans then take the reader through the stages of an open adoption—before, during, and after the birth—then on through the adopted child's adolescent years.

Rappaport, Bruce M. *The Open Adoption Book: A Guide to Making Adoption Work for You,* 2nd ed. Hoboken, NJ: John Wiley and Sons, 1998. 208 pages.

In this updated version of an earlier classic, Rappaport, founder of the Independent Adoption Center in California, discusses the reasons for open adoption and the ways in which birth parents and adoptive parents can develop positive relationships.

Sorosky, Arthur D., Annette Baran, and Reuben Pannor. *The Adoption Triangle: Sealed or Open Records: How They Affect Adoptees, Birth Parents and Adoptive Parents,* 2nd ed. San Antonio, TX: Corona Publishing, 1989. 236 pages.

This book, which sees adoption as a lifelong process, sounds a call for more openness in adoption. The authors studied the particular needs of adult adoptees (e.g., issues such as search and reunion), the long-term effects of relinquishment of a child on birth parents, and the effects of sealed records on adoptive parents.

Stephenson, Mary. *My Child Is a Mother: A True and Happy Story of Open Adoption.* San Antonio, TX: Corona Publishing, 1994. 253 pages.

This is the true story of a young woman's unplanned pregnancy, her decision to relinquish her child, and her experiences with open adoption.

Special Adoptive Parent Categories

Bozett, Frederick W., ed. *Gay and Lesbian Parents.* New York: Greenwood Publishing, 1987. 263 pages.

This book poses the following questions: Is homosexuality compatible with effective parenting? Can homosexuals establish healthy family units? Does the sexual orientation of a parent affect a child's sexual orientation? Bozett presents answers to these types of questions on many contemporary gay and lesbian parenthood issues. These include mental health considerations of lesbian mothers, counseling gay husbands and fathers, legal issues in gay and lesbian parenting, children of gay fathers, and children of lesbian mothers. Chapter 6, "The Adoptive and Foster Gay and Lesbian Parent," will be of special interest to students of adoption. In an epilogue, the editor discusses future perspectives for gay and lesbian parents. Since Bozett edited this book, many more authors and editors have weighed in on this subject. And now that "the future" is here, Bozett's observations are even more interesting than they were when he wrote them.

Hauschild, Myra, and Pat Rosier. *Get Used to It! Children of Gay and Lesbian Parents.* Christchurch, New Zealand: Canterbury University Press, 1999. 128 pages.

The authors interviewed and photographed young people between the ages of fifteen and thirty-four, each of whom had grown up with a gay or lesbian parent.

Miller, Naomi. *Single Parents by Choice: A Growing Trend in Family Life.* New York: Plenum Press, 1992. 239 pages.

In an objective manner, Miller examines the many ways single persons, male as well as female, have chosen to be (or find themselves being) parents, not just in the United States but in countries such as Sweden, Israel, and the United Kingdom. She describes the joys and frustrations of single parenthood and raises the question as to how children fare in single-parent families.

Morrissette, Mikki. *Choosing Single Motherhood: The Thinking Woman's Guide.* New York: Be-Mondo Publishing, 2005.

Morrissette calls women who choose to become parents on their own "Choice Moms." She estimates that more than 50,000 single women choose each year to become mothers. For this book, she interviewed more than one hundred of them. Domestic and intercountry adoption are two of the options for single women who want to become parents. Morrissette tries to answer as many of their questions as possible. She also looks at the stereotype of single mothers as "less able" to parent than married ones. She observes that studies showing single moms in a negative light are often looking at women from "disrupted" relationships or very young women. Morrissette also gives a history of the single motherhood "movement."

Varon, Lee. *Adopting on Your Own: The Complete Guide to Adopting as a Single Parent: A How-To for Single Parents.* New York: Farrar, Straus & Geroux, 2003. 432 pages.

This book covers the wide range of issues unmarried women and men face when they want to adopt. Using exercises and actual experiences, the book tries to answer the equally wide range of questions these prospective parents might ask. The author, codirector of the Adoption Network, an agency that helps single parents adopt, attempts to help prospective singles decide if adoption is the right choice for them and a good choice for their prospective child.

Special Needs Children/Older/From Foster Care

Babb, L. Anne; Rita Laws; and Bruce I. Gudmundsson. *Adopting* and *Advocating for the Special Needs Child: A Guide for Parents and Professionals.* Westport, CT: Bergen and Garvey, 1997. 280 pages.

The authors, adoptive parents of older special needs children, are advocates for adoption who know whereof they speak. They wrote the book because of a desire to help bridge the gap between a prospective adoptive parent's desire to help a waiting child and the realities of the U.S. adoption system, which can be as frustrating as the child himself may be at times.

Barth, Richard P., David Brodzinsky, and Madelyn Freundlich, eds. *Adoption and Prenatal Alcohol and Drug Exposure: Research, Policy, and Practice.* Washington, D.C.: Child Welfare League of America, 2000. 302 pages.

National and international experts in adoption and in the effects of prenatal substance abuse contribute to this book, which adds much to the understanding of the complexities of the subject. The research section presents information about children exposed to drugs, alcohol, or both, some of whom are being raised by relatives. The bottom line is that all of these children and families need support services, but that children raised in kinship homes may get less support. This is a book that adoptive parents, adoption professionals, judges, and medical personnel will find useful.

Bartholet, Elizabeth. *Nobody's Children: Abuse and Neglect, Foster Drift, and the Adoption Alternative.* Boston: Beacon Press, 2000. 304 pages.

Bartholet examines the prevailing view of children as the "property" of their parents. Sometimes, she writes, family preservation ideology ignores the facts of severe child abuse and neglect. Bartholet not only presents the problems but offers some suggestions for change.

Blank, Joseph P. *19 Steps Up the Mountain: The Story of the DeBolt Family.* New York: Penguin Group, 1982. 234 pages.

This book tells of the experiences of the DeBolt family. After their marriage, Bob and Dorothy DeBolt added thirteen children of various races and handicapping conditions to Dorothy's original group of children. Through a combination of tenderness and toughness, the DeBolts prepared all of their children for independent living. In addition, they started a nonprofit foundation, Aid to the Adoption of Special Kids (AASK), later changed to AASK America (Adopt a Special Kid), to find homes for physically and/or mentally handicapped children of all races.

Capper, Lizanne. *That's My Child: Strategies for Parents of Children with Disabilities.* Washington, DC: Child Welfare League of America, 1996. 208 pages.

This book contains information on coparenting, healthcare professionals, rights and services under federal law, school programs and systems, how to get started in special education, recreational opportunities, daycare providers, family, and friends—in other words, where to get informal, as well as formal, support.

Carney, Ann. *No More Here and There: Adopting the Older Child.* Chapel Hill: University of North Carolina Press, 1976. 88 pages.

In this adoption classic, Carney interweaves her own family's experiences with the adoption of a five-year-old son with practical advice on such issues as the phases of an adoption, sibling rivalry, talking about the past, dealing with feelings, relationships with the "outside world," and the effects of a special needs adoption on a marriage.

Dorris, Michael. *The Broken Cord.* New York: Harper Trade, 1990. 320 pages.

Like a novel but actually a true story, this book tells of a father's devotion to his adopted son, a Native American child with fetal alcohol syndrome.

Edelstein, Susan B., et al. *Children with Prenatal Alcohol and/or Other Drug Exposure: Weighing the Risks of Adoption.* Washington, DC: Child Welfare League of America, 1995. 320 pages.

The decision to adopt a child with prenatal drug or alcohol exposure adds an extra dimension to the already big decision to adopt. This book, designed mostly for professionals, gives practical suggestions and recommendations for counseling preadoptive parents about children with these conditions.

Gelles, Richard. *The Book of David: How Preserving Families Can Cost Children's Lives.* New York: Basic Books, 1996. 200 pages.

David, a boy suffocated by his birth mother, changed Richard Gelles's mind about the preservation of birth parents' rights at the expense of children's lives. Gelles offers suggestions for changes in the system that include making child safety a priority.

Goldstein, Joseph, Albert J. Solnit, Sonja Goldstein, and Anna Freud. *The Best Interests of the Child: The Least Detrimental Alternative.* New York: Free Press, 1996. 311 pages.

Combining their three classic works into one volume, the authors address the question, What is the least detrimental alternative for assuring continuity of the psychological parent-child relationship in any child custody case? (The earlier groundbreaking works, each available in a separate edition published by the Free Press, are *Beyond the Best Interests of the Child*, rev. ed., 1979; *Before the Best Interests of the Child*, 1979; and *In the Bests Interests of the Child*, 1986.) The authors maintain that continuity of care is the most important factor in the promotion of a child's well-being.

James, Beverly. *Treating Traumatized Children: New Insights and Creative Interventions.* New York: Free Press, 1989. 269 pages.

The author, a specialist in evaluating and treating traumatized children, believes that counselors must help children "work through" their trauma so that the children can move on with their lives. In addition to case examples, James presents a variety of exercises and techniques (including art, play, and drama) for "joining" with the children. Some of the exercises may be useful for adults traumatized as children.

Jewett, Claudia L. *Adopting the Older Child.* Cambridge: MA: Harvard Common Press, 1978. 320 pages.

Using the stories of four hypothetical families and the older children they adopt, the author describes problems potential adopters are likely to encounter and ways to solve them.

Jewett, Claudia L. *Helping Children Cope with Separation and Loss,* rev. ed. United Kingdom: B. T. Batsford, 1994. 230 pages.

This book gives advice on identifying short-term and long-term behaviors resulting from loss and for helping a child through the grief process.

Keck, Gregory C., and Regina M. Kupecky. *Adopting the Hurt Child: Hope for Families with Special Needs Kids: A Guide for Parents and Professionals.* Falls Church, VA: NavPress Publishing, 1998. 256 pages.

The authors use case studies to show the toll that impermanence takes on children. Also included are symptoms of attachment disorder, discussions of phases in the adoption process, the use of psychological therapy, ways families can make sure that their children have a "history," and stories of successful and unsuccessful adoptions. Includes a bibliography and information on intercountry adoptions.

Keck, Gregory C., and Regina M. Kupecky, with Lynda G. Mansfield, ed. *Parenting the Hurt Child: Helping Adoptive Families Heal and Grow.* Falls Church, VA: NavPress Publishing, 2004.

Suggestions for parents who wonder after they bring a "hurting" child into their home, Can they can manage to raise that child into a healthy adult? The authors believe that with stability, wisdom, tenacity, and love, everyone can "make it."

Kempe, C. Henry, MD, and Ray E. Helfer, MD, eds. *The Battered Child,* 4th ed. Chicago: University of Chicago Press, 1987. 440 pages.

This classic text, first published in 1968, helped alert the public to the problems of child abuse and neglect. Part I includes historical aspects of child abuse, psychodynamic factors, and the influence of parental drug and alcohol abuse. Part II includes chapters by various authorities on neglect, failure to thrive, child abuse by burning, and incest. Part III details efforts at intervention and treatment with a chapter on guidelines for placing a child in foster care. Part IV focuses on prevention of child abuse.

Kleinfeld, Judith, and Siobhan Wescott. *Fantastic Antone Succeeds! Experiences in Educating Children with Fetal Alcohol Syndrome.* Anchorage: University of Alaska Press, 1993. 380 pages.

"Bathing the fetal brain in alcohol is a lot like spilling a drink on a computer," says Judith Kleinfeld. "The electrical circuitry gets scrambled in unpredictable ways." Nevertheless, children with fetal alcohol syndrome can learn. When the adoptive mother of nine-year-old Antone asks if he knows the meaning of the initials FAS, he says "Fantastic Antone Succeeds!" Hence the title of the book, which the authors divide into four parts: How Prenatal Alcohol Exposure Affects Children and Their Families, Parents' Know-How, Teachers' Techniques, and Working with Families of Alcohol-Affected Children.

Laws, Rita, and Tim O'Hanlon. *Adoption and Financial Assistance: Tools for Navigating the Bureaucracy.* Westport, CT: Bergin and Garvey, 1999. 288 pages.

Putting the federal Title IV-E adoption assistance program to work for families can be a challenge to all involved. This book guides parents and professionals through the state adoption maze, so that everyone can deal with an adoption assistance contract and be prepared for administrative hearings and adoption subsidy appeals.

Lindsay, Caroline. *Nothing Good Ever Happens to Me: An Adoption Love Story.* Washington, DC: Child Welfare League of America, 1996. 107 pages.

This is one family's story of the adoption of an older child, an adoption that took ten years to complete. Lee Ann joined the Lindsay family at age seven after bouncing from one foster home to another. The book describes her struggle to "grow" and to become secure with her adoptive parents, siblings, friends, counselors, teachers, lawyers, and judges.

Merkel-Holguin, Lisa. *Children Who Lose Their Parents to AIDS:*

Agency Guidelines for Kinship Care and Adoption Placement. Washington, DC: Child Welfare League of America, 1996.

Topics include outreach to HIV-positive birth parents, education and training of professionals, and services to prospective adoptive parents, birth parents, and extended family members. Also included are practice and policy issues related to the recruitment of adoptive families, preparation of children and families, and support for families after placement.

O'Hanlon, Tim. *Accessing Federal Adoption Subsides after Legalization.* Washington, DC: Child Welfare League of America, 1995. 67 pages.

This is a guide to help adoptive families of special needs children to go back and apply for adoption assistance after finalization, if necessary, so that they may receive retroactive assistance regardless of their state of residence.

Transracial/Transcultural

Comer, James, MD, and Alvin Toussaint, MD. *Raising Black Children.* New York: Penguin Books, 1992. 448 pages.

Using a question-and-answer format, two psychiatrists confront educational, social, and emotional issues in each developmental stage, from infancy through adolescence. A short adoption section addresses inracial, as well as transracial, adoptions.

Lander, Joyce. *Mixed Families: Adoption across Racial Boundaries.* Lincoln, NE: iUniverse, 1978. 300 pages.

This is a book for those who want to delve more deeply into the reasons people adopt across racial lines, what their expectations are, and what the reactions of relatives, friends, and neighbors will be. For this work the author interviewed more than one hundred couples who adopted transracially, as well as their relatives. The author, an adoptive mother, sociologist, and African American, presents an objective view of the issues involved in transracial adoption, with a focus on black social workers' concerns about the black child's identity.

Pohl, Constance, and Kathleen Harris. *Transracial Adoption: Children and Parents Speak.* Danbury, CT: Franklin Watts, 1992. 128 pages.

Stories of families involved in transracial adoptions make up the "meat" of this book. Those involved tell of their difficulties and their joys.

Rothman, Barbara K. *Weaving a Family: Untangling Race and Adoption.* Boston: Beacon Press, 2006. 288 pages.

As the white mother of a black child, Rothman brings a personal perspective as well as a sociological and historical perspective to the subjects of race and family.

Simon, Rita, and Howard Alsteins. *Adoption: Serving the Children in Transracial and Intercountry Adoptions.* Lanham, MD: Rowan and Littlefield Publishers, 2000. 176 pages.

The book summarizes (and compares with other studies) the findings of these researchers who have studied transracial and transcultural adoptions for thirty years.

Steinberg, Gail, and Beth Hall. *Inside Transracial Adoption: Strength-Based, Culture-Sensitizing Parenting Strategies for Intercountry or Domestic Adoptive Families That Don't "Match."* Indianapolis, IN: Perspectives Press, 2000. 405 pages.

The codirectors of PACT: An Adoption Alliance put forth some of their agency's tools for fostering honesty in race and adoption and give tips for helping with issues that arise from infancy to young adulthood.

Journals and Other Periodicals

Listed below are some of the more well-known journals and other periodicals to help students of adoption stay current on adoption issues. Entire journals devoted to adoption are rare. However, journals in related fields, such as sociology, social work, medicine and nursing, psychology, and law, occasionally publish articles on adoption topics. Because of the overwhelming number of adoption-related articles appearing in professional journals and periodicals, they are not listed here.

Most of the organizations listed in Chapter 7 will send sample newsletters free of charge, and many others are available online. The journals listed here will be of interest to members of the adoption triad, professionals in foster care and adoption, and those doing research in these areas. Subscription information, such as the current price, is usually available online or by telephone.

In addition, the Child Welfare Information Gateway, a service of the Children's Bureau, offers information on the latest child welfare publications, as well as free subscriptions online and free monthly e-mail services. The subscriptions page on the Child Welfare Information Gateway website is http://www.childwelfare.gov/admin/subscribe/index.cfm. One of the choices under My Child Welfare Librarian is "adoption." As web addresses and journal titles change, the library keeps the list updated. Also available free of charge are the Child Welfare Information Gateway E-lert! and the *Children's Bureau Express.*

Adoptalk. This quarterly newsletter contains articles on a wide variety of subjects related to adoption and foster care, including information on policy issues, postadoption support, recruitment of adoptive families, parenting techniques, and more. Subscriptions are available to members of the North American Council on Adoptable Children. Web address: http://www.nacac.org.

Adoption & Fostering. The British Association for Adoption & Fostering has published this journal for more than fifty years. Since 1953, when it was first published as *Child Adoption*, the quarterly peer-reviewed journal has given practitioners, academics, and others concerned with adoption a forum in which to share discussion on current research and practice from the United Kingdom and overseas. Subscribers can also receive the journal online. Web address: http://www.baaf.org.uk.

Adoption Quarterly: Innovations in Community and Clinical Practice, Theory, and Research. This academic and scholarly journal focusing on adoption has been published by Haworth Press since its inception. It is an international multidisciplinary forum featuring conceptual and empirical work, commentaries, and book reviews from the social sciences, humanities, biological sciences, law, and social policy. Web address: http://www.haworthpress.com.

Adoption Today. This publication presents issues and answers to questions about international and domestic adoption. It is written by adopted persons, adoptive parents, and adoption professionals in medicine, law, education, social work, and child development. Web address: http://adoptinfo.net.

Child and Adolescent Social Work Journal. This journal (one volume, six issues) focuses on clinical social work with children, adolescents, and their families, addressing problems affecting specific populations in specific settings. Web address: http://www.springerlink.com.

Child and Youth Care Forum. This bimonthly, international, peer-reviewed journal is committed to articles focusing on improving child and youth care practices, early childhood education, and youth development policy, practice, and research. It is an interdisciplinary channel of communication, including debate on issues in child welfare, child and youth services, and mental health. Web address: http://www.springerlink.com.

Child Welfare Journal. Begun in 1921, this scholarly bimonthly journal published by the Child Welfare League of America highlights problems and possible solutions for children who are homeless, abused, disabled, and new to the country. For child welfare and associated professionals, it links the latest findings in child welfare with related research on best practice, policy, and program development. Web address: http://www.cwla.org/pubs/periodicals.htm.

Children's Voice. A magazine for foster and adoptive parents, frontline professionals, agency executives, and child and family advocates, this publication of the Child Welfare League of America offers practical news and special features. Web address: http://www.cwla.org/pubs/periodicals.htm.

The Future of Children Journal. The journal is published twice a year by the Woodrow Wilson School of Public and International Affairs at Princeton University or the Brookings Institution. It offers comprehensive cross-disciplinary articles on a variety of issues related to children. Web address: http://www.futureofchildren.org.

Journal of Child and Family Studies. This is an international forum (one volume, six issues) for problems having to do with the mental well-being of children, adolescents, and their families. Original papers deal with child abuse and neglect, respite care, foster care, mental health care financing, homelessness, family stress, AIDS, substance abuse, and other issues of topical interest. Web address: http://www.springerlink.com.

Social Work. Published quarterly in January, April, July, and October, this is the official journal of the National Association of Social Workers (NASW) and is provided to members as a membership benefit. The journal's major emphasis is on social policy and the solutions to serious human problems. Web address: http://www.naswpress.org.

Websites

The websites listed here are adoption-related sites that were not included with the organizations listed in the previous chapter.

About.com
http://adoption.about.com/parenting/adoption

A "full service" site with up-to-the minute stories and articles on adoption and foster care. About.com is part of the New York Times Company.

Adopting.com
http://www.adopting.com

This site helps prospective adoptive parents find a path to adoption that fits them. It offers information on how to get started in adoption, links to adoption agencies and attorneys, letters to birth parents from families hoping to adopt an infant, support groups, information on the rights of adopted persons, e-mail lists, news groups, bulletin boards and chat rooms, and photo listings of waiting children.

Adoption Advocates—Adoption Policy Resource Center
http://www.fpsol.com/adoption/advocates.html

This service provided by Adoption Subsidy Advocates helps adoptive families with subsidy questions and provides technical assistance to organizations and professionals.

Adoption: A Gathering
http://www.pbs.org/weblab/adoption

This site is a safe place for anyone touched by adoption to gain a sense of community from shared experiences. It is a project of Web Lab in cooperation with PBS Online.

Adoption . . . Assistance, Information, Support
http://www.adopting.org

Features information, education, and profile presentations on-line for prospective adoptive parents and support for those who have already adopted. Also assists birth parents considering placing a child and provides resources for professionals working in adoption.

The Adoption History Project
http://darkwing.uoregon.edu/~adoption/about.html

This website, launched on June 1, 2003, by Ellen Herman, faculty member of the Department of History at the University of Oregon, is a digital public history resource. It covers individuals, organizations, issues, and studies that shaped adoption in theory and practice in the twentieth century.

Adoption.com
http://www.adoption.com

In existence since 1996, this website is committed to helping as many children as possible both in the United States and throughout the world find loving, permanent homes. The site also provides information for women facing crisis pregnancies and helps prospective adoptive parents find children. It features an adoption site search with more than 500,000 pages of content, daily adoption news and blogs, message boards and chat rooms, adoption resources by location, a photo listing of thousands of waiting children, profiles of waiting parents, more than a thousand adoption products, an adoption registry for finding birth families, support from others of the same faith, searches for professionals (e.g., attorneys), and a weekly e-magazine.

Gift of Adoption
www.giftofadoption.org

Gene and Lucy Wyka cofounded this 501(c)(3) charity in 1996 to give grants in the form of subsidies to help prospective adoptive parents cover the costs associated with adopting a child.

Homes4Kids
http://www.homes4kids.org

Adoption issues can be found under "parenting" in the lifestyle category. This site offers related links to a variety of adoption-related organizations.

Thomas—Legislative Information on the Internet
www.http://thomas.loc.gov

For following bills in Congress, this is an official source of U.S. federal legislation.

U.S. State Department—International Adoptions
http://www.travel.state.gov/family/adoption/adoption_485.html

Offers a guide for U.S. citizens interested in adopting a child from another country and applying for an immigrant visa for the child to come to the United States. The site tells what the State Department *can* and *cannot* do and offers a full text of the *International Adoption Booklet* online.

The Urban Institute
http://www.urbaninstitute.org

A nonpartisan economic and social policy research organization, the Urban Institute has links to *Child Welfare* and offers many publications on this subject and its relationship to adoption, including several publications on kinship care.

Videos and DVDs

The list below, compiled with assistance from the Child Welfare Information Gateway, is a sampling of the many videos and DVDs available on all aspects of adoption.

AdoptUSKids Public Service Announcement: Bruce Willis and Jamie Foxx: Change a Child's Life
Videotape
Copyright 2003
To view: http://www.onthescene.com/wm/+6

Actors Bruce Willis and Jamie Foxx encourage prospective adoptive parents to adopt children from foster care. Contact information for AdoptUSKids is provided.

Caring for Caregiver Families
KinNET (Project) Generations United and Richfield Productions
Videocassette
Copyright 2003
Length: 10 minutes
Generations United
1333 H Street NW, Suite 500 W
Washington, DC 20005
(202) 289-3979
http://www.gu.org
Sponsoring organization: The Children's Bureau

This videotape comes from KinNET, a national initiative that has established a network of support groups for relatives who care for kin in foster care. KinNET focuses on the unique needs of kinship providers, who receive education on topics relative to the goals of the Adoption and Safe Families Act with special emphasis on permanency options. The videotape emphasizes care of caregiver families through support groups.

"The Caseworker Files" and "A National Dialogue," **Failure to Protect**
PBS *Frontline* and WGBH (a Boston TV station)
Videocassette
Copyright 2003

WGBH
125 Western Avenue
Boston, MA 02134
http://www.pbs.org/wgbh/pages/frontline/shows/foster-care/

Parts 2 and 3 of a *Frontline* series about the child protective system tackles the process of removal of a child from the home and/or custody of his or her birth parents. Part 2 features child protective workers in Bangor, Maine, as they manage several cases in which these difficult decisions must be made. Caseworkers, supervisors, and parents reveal their different perspectives. Television crews also filmed meetings between supervisors and caseworkers and between caseworkers and birth parents. Part 3 features a panel discussion with child welfare professionals and news journalists.

The Indian Child Welfare Act of 1978: A Child Welfare Professional Training Video
Loyola University of Chicago, School of Social Work
Videocassette
Copyright 2002
Length: 75 minutes
Loyola University of Chicago
School of Social Work
820 N. Michigan Avenue
Chicago, IL 60611
(312) 915-7005
http://www.luc.edu/socialwork
Sponsoring organization: The Children's Bureau

A 233-page curriculum guide designed to educate child-welfare professionals accompanies this videotape. The focus of the curriculum is on training professionals to understand and be able to work with urban Native American communities. A young adult tells his story of being placed in a non–Native American home and learning of his Native American heritage later.

Is Anyone in There?: Adopting a Wounded Child
Videocassette
Copyright 2004
The Infant-Parent Institute

328 N. Neil Street
Champaign, IL 61820
(217) 352-4060
http://www.infant-parent.com

Presents a mother's thoughts as she meets her adopted baby and has concerns about the lack of eye contact. The text and pictures show the mother's sense of rejection, guilt, and shame. Along with her expectations of raising a child who may have difficult behaviors, she hopes that "love will always triumph." The video package includes a booklet about reactive attachment disorder and its prevalence in children adopted from Eastern Europe. The videotape also discusses characteristics of children with reactive attachment disorder and the effects on adoptive families. Included are thirty-four references.

Is This Job for ME?
DVD
Copyright 2005
Michigan Department of Human Services, Personnel Services
235 S. Grand Street, Suite 708
Lansing, MI 48909

Contains interviews with child protective services workers and foster care workers. Introduces the viewer to child welfare work by giving a sense of the type of interactions that go on in a typical caseworker's day.

Listening to Birth Families: Forming Kinship
DVD
Copyright 2003
Length: 80 minutes
Northwest Media, Inc.
326 W. 12th Avenue
Eugene, Oregon 97401
(541) 343-6636 or (800) 777-6636
http://www.sociallearning.com

Dr. Vera Fahlberg stresses the importance of social service agencies helping to facilitate the formation of relationships between birth parents and foster parents. For foster parents, birth parents, and social workers, this training DVD shows a panel discussion with a birth mother, her oldest daughter, and the two foster mothers who are part of their kinship care group. A viewer's guide includes questions for discussion, exercises for foster parents and birth parents, strategies for working with birth parents, and a review questionnaire with answer key.

Making Your Support Group Work for You
Professional Association of Treatment Homes, National Foster Parent Association, and FosterParentNet
Videocassette
Copyright 2003
Length: 24 minutes
Professional Association of Treatment Homes
2324 University Avenue West, Suite 120
St. Paul, MN 55114
(612) 259-1600
http://www.pathinc.org
Sponsoring organization: The Children's Bureau

This videotape provides information on how foster and adoptive parents can strengthen their social support network and support groups while at the same time positively impacting the lives of their foster or adoptive children.

Parent Leadership/Circle of Parents
Videocassette
Copyright 2004
Length: 7 minutes
Circle of Parents
200 S. Michigan Avenue, 17th Floor
Chicago, IL 60604
(312) 334-3520
http://www.circleofparents.org
Sponsoring organization: The Children's Bureau

This videotape features national parent leaders from Circle of Parents, a support group, as well as parent leaders from a local parent support group in Illinois. The participants discuss how parents can become leaders in parent support groups, why parents *should* become leaders, opportunities for becoming leaders, and the challenges parents face in becoming leaders.

Partners in Permanency: Achieving Permanency for Children
Socios en Permanencia: logrando permanencia para los ninos

DVD or VHS
Copyright 2004
Philadelphia Department of Human Services
1515 Arch Street
Philadelphia, PA 19102
(215) 633-4DHS
http://www.phila.gov/dhs

Designed to show the importance of clear and consistent communication among all partners about the options available to those who have children in foster care, as well as families caring for children in foster care. The goal is to convey that the future of children depends on collaboration with families. Available in English and Spanish and includes a facilitator's guide.

Reeducation of Foster and Adoptive Children: Prospects for a Healthy Life
DVD
Copyright 2003
Length: 70 minutes
Northwest Media, Inc.
326 W. 12th Avenue
Eugene, OR 97401
(541) 343-6636 or (800) 777-6636
http://www.northwestmedia.com

Social workers, foster and adoptive parents, and birth parents will learn how they can help foster and adopted young people overcome negative behavioral and emotional patterns in adult-child relationships. Needing work are the acceptability of feelings opposed to the unacceptability of certain behaviors, the worth of the child as a person, the reciprocity of relationships, taking care of oneself physically and emotionally, caring for and about others, and how to have fun. A viewer's guide includes a discussion of the topics addressed on the DVD, a list of negative parent messages, and an answer key to the review questionnaire.

Separation and Loss Issues for Foster and Birth Families
DVD
Copyright 2003
Length: 80 minutes
Northwest Media, Inc.
326 W. 12th Avenue

Eugene, OR 97401
(541) 343-6636 or (800) 777-6636
http://www.sociallearning.com

For social workers, foster parents, and birth parents, this DVD explores the feelings of loss and rejection experienced by children in foster care. It begins with the journey of three children through the foster care system. The stages of grief include shock and denial, anger, bargaining, sadness, despair, and finally acceptance. Next, Dr. Vera Fahlberg talks with three teenagers about the feelings they had when they entered foster care. The next segment features three adults who spent many of their teen years in foster care. Fahlberg then interviews foster parents who discuss grief and loss in young children and point out the importance of maintaining contact with foster children even when they move. Finally, a birth mother who had three of her children in foster care in three separate homes shares her experiences. Includes a viewer's guide with a synopsis of the DVD, discussion questions, a fact sheet on separation and loss, and a review questionnaire.

Understanding Childhood Trauma: A Parent's Guide to Identifying and Responding to Childhood Trauma
Videocassette
Copyright 2002
Length: 45 minutes
Child Trauma Academy, Linkletter Media
Distributed by Magna Systems, Inc.
95 W. County Line Road
Barrington, IL 60010
(800) 203-7060
http://www.maganasystems.videos.com

Dr. Bruce Perry describes the neurobiological impact of child neglect and the effect of loss of experience on a child's normal development. He defines neglect as sensory deprivation or the lack of stimulation at key points in a child's developmental stages. Related videos (also available on DVD) are, *Understanding Childhood Trauma: Identifying and Responding to Trauma, Ages 0-5 Years Old* and *Understanding Childhood Trauma: What Is Childhood Trauma?*

Unlocking the Heart of Adoption
Videocassette plus booklet (discussion guide)
Copyright 2003

Length: 56 minutes
Pandora's Box Productions
1546 Great Highway, Suite 44
San Francisco, CA 94122
(415) 564-3691
http://www.unlockingtheheart.com

Combining the history of adoption with personal stories, this
video describes the impact of adoption on birth parents, adoptive
parents, and adopted persons. Those interviewed share feelings
of loss, pain, shame, guilt, abandonment, and identity confusion.
Some adoptees share feelings about their adoption by parents of
a different race. Searching for birth relatives presents a range of
challenges and outcomes.

In addition to the above sampling of videos and DVDs available from a variety of sources, Adoption.com has a link to audio
and video (under "adoption products"), which presents more
than 400 audio and video resources arranged under such head-
ings as Adoption Support and Preservation, Adoptive and Parent Support Groups, Advocacy and Public Policy, Agency
Issues and Concerns, Documentaries & Instructional, International Adoption, Kinship Care, Openness in Adoption, Parenting Children with Challenges, Permanency Options, Preparing
Parents for Adoption, Race and Culture in Adoption, Recruiting Permanent Families, Search & Reunion, and Supporting
Children.

CD-ROMs

The Child Welfare Information Gateway assisted in the preparation of this list.

*All in the Family: Achieving Excellence in Adoption, November
8–10, 2004*
Copyright 2004
Child Welfare League of America
440 First Street NW, Third Floor
Washington, DC 20001
(202) 638-2952
http://www.cwla.org

Prepared for the Child Welfare League of America's Achieving Excellence in Adoption conference, November 2004, this CD-ROM contains proceedings papers and PowerPoint presentations. Sessions address topics such as legal services for adoptive parents, postadoption support, clinical interventions, assistance for relatives caring for children, cultural competency, and subsidized guardianships. A workshop by Casey Family Services identifies federal, state, and other sources of funding for various types of adoption support projects.

Child Abuse, Child Welfare, and Adoption 1965–2002
Copyright 2002
Child Welfare Information Gateway
1250 Maryland Avenue SW, Eighth Floor
Washington, DC 20024
(800) 394-3366 or (703) 385-7565
http://www.childwelfare.gov

This CD-ROM, produced by the National Clearinghouse on Child Abuse and Neglect Information, contains the Child Abuse and Neglect Documents Database, a searchable database of resources about child abuse and neglect and adoption. Records include abstracts, distributor information, and links to the online full text (when available). It also includes a thesaurus of terms used to index documents, a User's Guide, and a Quick Guide.

Fifteenth National Conference on Child Abuse and Neglect: Supporting Promising Practices and Positive Outcomes; A Shared Responsibility Resource Guide
Copyright 2005
Source: U.S. Department of Health and Human Services, Administration for Children and Families; Administration on Children, Youth, and Families; Children's Bureau; and the Office on Child Abuse and Neglect
Available from: Child Welfare Information Gateway
1250 Maryland Avenue SW, Eighth Floor
Washington, DC 20024
(800) 394-3366 or (703) 385-7565
http://www.childwelfare.gov

Provides summaries of more than 450 papers, posters, seminars, and workshops presented at the Fifteenth National Conference on Child Abuse and Neglect. It also gives contact information for the presenters, websites of the federal partners, and the conference national sponsors and cosponsors.

When Love Takes You In: A Music Video for the 2004 Adopt-USKids Summit
Copyright 2004
Adoption Exchange Association
8015 Corporate Drive, Suite C
Baltimore, MD 21236
(888) 200-4005
http://www.adoptuskids.org
Sponsoring organization: The Children's Bureau

Presents a slideshow of photos of adoptive families, as well as children waiting for adoption. The accompanying song, "When Love Takes You In," by Steven Curtis Chapman, tells of the importance of love and belonging. Viewers can visit the Adopt-USKids website for information about waiting children.

Software

Adoption Information and Reporting Software (AIRS)
Powered by Pinnacle Development Group
18 Common Street
Waterville, ME 04901
(207) 873-7540
http://www.adoptsoft.com

This system was developed for adoption case management and related purposes in adoption at the request of Maine Adoptive Placement Services (MAPS). Version 6 was released in May 2006. AIRS helps track and manage an array of management issues in domestic and intercountry adoption as well as foster-care activities.

Databases

Adoption: Public Agency Adoptions
Child Welfare League of America, National Data Analysis System

50 F Street NW, Sixth Floor
Washington, DC 20001
(202) 638-2952
http://ndas.cwla.org

Provides access to statistics on public agency adoptions in the United States from 1998–2001. Links to information on the Multiethnic Placement Act, the number of children waiting to be adopted, the number of children adopted, the number of public agency adoptions from 1995–2000, the mean and median months between the time of termination of parental rights and adoption, the number of children adopted who receive any kind of adoption subsidy, the number of children who receive Title IV-E adoption subsides, adoption subsides by age, specialized adoption subsidy rates, reimbursement rates for nonrecurring adoption expenses, and state use of subsidized guardianship. The information is provided by state and year and also nationally.

Adoption Dynamics: The Impact of the Adoption and Safe Families Act
Source: U.S. Department of Health and Human Services, Office of the Assistant Secretary for Planning and Evaluation
Distributed by: U.S. Department of Health and Human Services Office of the Assistant Secretary for Planning and Evaluation
Humphrey Building, Room 404
E. 200 Independence Avenue SW
Washington, DC 20201
(202) 619-0257 or (877) 696-6775
http://aspe.hhs.gov

Adoptions from foster care were studied using data from the Multistate Foster Care Data Archive, which is a database containing administrative information about children in foster care from a number of states. Children in the study were admitted to foster care for the first time between 1990 and 1999. The goal of the study was to try to understand what effects, if any, the federal Adoption and Safe Families Act had on the proportion of children admitted to foster care who were later adopted and the time needed to complete these adoptions.

Children in America/First Star
First Star

1666 K Street NW, Suite 700
Washington, DC 20006
(202) 293-3703
http://www.firststar.org

The First Star website presents statistics on reports of child abuse
or neglect (and child fatalities) in the United States. Statistics are
presented by state and include the rank of the state in number of
child abuse and neglect reports, child fatalities, child victims with
court action, children in foster care, the type of the child's representation in court, whether the court hearings were closed or
open, whether court records were open or sealed, the number of
child victims by age and race, outcomes of investigations, the
number of cases in which parental rights were terminated, and
the number of children waiting for adoption.

Database of Parent Support Groups
North American Council on Adoptable Children
970 Raymond Avenue, Suite 106
St. Paul, MN 55114
(651) 644-3036
http://www.nacac.org/pas_database.html

This parent group database contains approximately nine hundred
adoption-related support groups across the United States and
Canada. The database is searchable by state or province, by the
type of group, or by the group's activity. Group types include
preadoption, postadoption, foster care, transracial/transcultural,
international, single parent, special needs, and infertility.

Kids Count State-Level Data Online
Annie E. Casey Foundation
701 St. Paul Street
Baltimore, MD 21202
(410) 547-6600
http://www.aecf.org

Contains state-level data for more than seventy-five measures of
child well-being, including those used in the Annie E. Casey
Foundation's KIDS COUNT Data Book. This online database allows searchers to generate custom reports for geographic areas

(profiles) or to compare various geographic areas on a certain topic (ranking, maps, and line graphs).

NASW Practice Snapshot: Promising Practices in Foster Care for Recruiting and Retaining Resource Families
National Association of Social Workers
705 First Street NE, Suite 700
Washington, DC 20002
(800) 227-3590
http://www.socialworkers.org

This "brief" summarizes the findings of a study that investigated promising practices in recruitment and retention of foster (and adoptive) families. The study found that few of the materials used to recruit families were culturally and/or linguistically specific, which might partially explain why families of various cultural backgrounds did not respond to publicity messages. Changes and their outcomes were entered into a searchable database; the need for more professional training in cultural competence is emphasized.

Preserving Adoption Support Programs: Parents Can Make a Difference
North American Council on Adoptable Children
970 Raymond Avenue, Suite 106
St. Paul, MN 55114
(800) 470-6665 or (651) 644-3036
http://www.nacac.org

To alleviate budget shortfalls, many states are reducing allocations for adoption assistance. What can adoptive parents do to protect financial supports for adopted children with special needs? NACAC's fact sheet urges parents to respond immediately to proposed cuts by obtaining information about legislation, contacting other concerned families, and communicating with legislators. The database tracks volunteers as well as legislators.

Summaries of State Legislation Enacted in Response to the Adoption and Safe Families Act
National Conference of State Legislatures
444 N. Capitol Street NW, Suite 515

Washington, DC 20001
(202) 624-5400
http://www.ncsl.org

This searchable database provides links to summaries of state legislation enacted in response to the Adoption and Safe Families Act. The database gives information for each of the states on legislation that addresses permanency hearings, adoption across state lines, assurances of child safety, clarification of reasonable efforts, termination of parental rights, criminal record checks, health insurance for children with special needs, notice requirements, and effective date of implementation.

Glossary

Most of the terms used to describe various facets of adoption have their origins in psychology, sociology, law, and social work. In addition, the field of adoption has "coined" some of these terms. This glossary lists some of the words that might need clarification for students of adoption.

Adoptee An adopted person. Some adopted persons object to being called an "adoptee" because it seems to distinguish an adopted child from a birth child in the same family (a parent does not say, "This is my birth son, Johnny"), and it implies that adoption is the central fact of the adopted person's life. (It may or may not be.)

Adoption A court action in which an adult assumes legal and other responsibilities for another person, usually a minor.

Adoption agency An organization that helps birth parents, adoptive parents, and children in need of homes with placement in an adoptive home. Agencies may be public or private, secular or religious, for profit or nonprofit.

Adoption assistance Generally refers to monthly subsidy payments to help adoptive parents raise children with special needs. These payments were made possible by the passage of the Adoption Assistance and Child Welfare Act of 1980. In a larger sense, "adoption assistance" could refer to any help given to parties in an adoption.

Adoption disruption The interruption of an adoption prior to finalization, usually within a year of placement. A "disrupted adoption" is sometimes called a "failed placement."

Adoption dissolution   When an adoption fails after finalization; in this circumstance, court action is required.

Adoption exchanges   Organizations that help find homes for waiting children by getting out the word on children available for adoption. Adoption exchanges use all types of media plus adoption "parties," which bring together waiting parents and waiting children in a child-focused setting. Adoption exchanges may be local, state, regional, national, or international.

Adoption plan   The preferred terminology for the decision of the birth parents to allow their child to be placed for adoption.

Adoption triad   The three major parties in an adoption: birth parents, adoptive parents, and the adopted child. Also called "adoption triangle" or "adoption circle."

Artificial insemination   A procedure leading to pregnancy by other than the usual means.

Attachment   The process of emotional connection that occurs (or does not occur) between parents and their children. Some say the word *attachment* is synonymous with the word *bonding* and can happen at any age; others make a distinction, reserving *bonding* for a process that occurs in infancy between biological parents and their babies.

Attachment disorder   A situation, usually resulting from breaks in the early connection with the mother figure, in which children have problems accepting parents and other authority figures; sometimes called *reactive attachment disorder* or *RAD*.

Attention deficit disorder (ADD)   A neurological condition of unknown cause that may reveal itself in inattentiveness (not listening), distractibility (difficulty concentrating), impulsivity (acting quickly without prior thought), and disorganization.

Attention deficit disorder with hyperactivity (ADHD or ADDH)   A condition that includes the problems of attention deficit disorder (see above) plus hyperactivity (relatively speaking, the inability to sit still).

Birth parent A child's biological mother or father.

Black-market adoption An independent adoption in which someone makes an unearned profit from an adoptive placement.

Boarder babies Infants abandoned in hospitals because of the parents' inability to take care of them. These babies may be born HIV-positive or drug addicted.

Certification The process that takes place to ensure (insofar as possible) that adoptive parents (or foster parents) are suitable, dependable, and responsible.

Closed adoption An adoption that involves total confidentiality and sealed records.

Concurrent planning A process used in some adoptions involving foster-care case management. In this case, professional staff works to reunify the child with birth family (if possible) while at the same time giving the child a permanent family if efforts at reunification fail. The rationale is to decrease the time a child spends in foster care.

Confidentiality The process of keeping identifying information secret.

Consent to adopt or **consent to adoption** Legal permission by whomever has custody of the child.

Co-parenting A situation in which there are community-based alternatives, such as extra caregivers, for parenting adopted (or foster) children with special needs such as developmental disabilities. In some cases the term is used to describe any arrangement in which a number of caregivers share the duties of parenting a child with whom they have a signifiant relationship.

Decree of adoption A legal order finalizing an adoption.

De facto In fact; actually. Refers to a situation that is "reality based" even if it is not based on the law. A de facto family is a "psychological family" in which members have ties to each other even though they are not blood relatives and do not have a legal document recognizing their relationship.

Dossier   A file of legal documents used in an intercountry adoption to process the child's assignment to an adoptive family.

Eugenics   A "science" concerned with improving a species, especially the human species, by such measures as influencing reproduction by persons thought to have desirable genetic traits.

Extended family   A child's relatives, other than birth parents; includes such relatives as aunts, uncles, grandparents, and sometimes even close friends.

Fetal alcohol spectrum disorder (FASD)   A range of disabilities, usually not as severe as FAS, that may have resulted from a mother's alcohol use during pregnancy.

Fetal alcohol syndrome (FAS)   A developmental disability caused by a mother's use of alcohol during her pregnancy.

Finalization   The legal process of making an adoption permanent.

Foster-adoption   A child's placement in which birth parents' rights have not yet been completely severed by the court or in which birth parents are appealing the court's decision. Social workers place the child in a foster-adopt home (sometimes called a "fost-adopt" or "permanency planning" home) when they believe the foster-adopt parents will adopt the child when the child is available for adoption. The main reason for making such a placement (also called a "legal-risk" adoption) is to spare the child another move.

Genealogy   A family's genetic line or a record of such ancestry.

Group home   A homelike setting in which a number of unrelated children live for varying periods. Group homes may have one set of house parents or may have a rotating staff.

Guardian ad litem   A person, often an attorney, appointed by the court to represent the child's best interests.

Home study   Another name for the certification process that determines if a potential adoptive family will be a good home for a child. Because it is not a study of the home per se, some professionals have substituted other terms, such as *family assessment.*

Independent adoption   An adoption facilitated by those other than caseworkers associated with an adoption agency. Facilitators may be attorneys, physicians, or other intermediaries. In some states, independent adoptions are illegal.

Infertility   The inability to produce birth children. Sometimes one person in a couple has problems with infertility; sometimes both do.

Interstate Compact on the Placement of Children (ICPC)   An agreement to which all of the states and U.S. territories have subscribed. Its aim is the safe placement of children across state lines.

Kinship care   The full-time nurturing of a child by someone related to the child by family ties or earlier relationship.

Legal-risk adoption   See foster-adoption.

Life book   Any child who moves into an adoption has a history. Social workers and foster parents can help the older child make this book, a pictorial and written representation of the child's life before adoption.

Nonidentifying information   Facts about the birth parents or adoptive parents that would *not* lead to their discovery by another person.

Nonrecurring adoption costs   One-time adoption expenses, such as the cost of a home study, which through provisions of the Adoption Assistance and Child Welfare Act of 1980 may be at least partially reimbursed to families who adopt children with special needs.

Open adoption   An arrangement with varying degrees of ongoing contact (usually decided upon by the involved parties) among birth parents, adoptive parents, and adopted child.

Parens patriae The state is the protector of its people. In other words, the state has a legal duty to protect children who cannot take care of themselves. For example, if birth parents cannot take care of their children, the state must step in to protect those children.

Permanency planning Efforts to allow a child to stay in his birth family, if possible, or to return him to his birth family as soon as possible, and if neither plan works, to find him a permanent family. This latter step, finding a legally permanent family, often involves adoption.

Placement date The time at which the child comes to live with the adoptive family.

Post-traumatic stress disorder A condition in which victims of overwhelming and uncontrollable experiences are psychologically affected by feelings and fears of loss of safety, loss of control, helplessness, and extreme vulnerability.

Psychological parent A person who (although not biologically related to a child) takes care of the child on a daily basis; a person the child considers his parent; sometimes called a de facto parent.

Putative Generally regarded as true.

Relinquishment Voluntary termination of parental rights; sometimes referred to as "making a plan" for one's birth child.

Respite care For parents who need a rest, this short-term care is given (usually for pay) on a voluntary basis.

Semi-open adoption Usually, an adoption in which the birth family and the adoptive family communicate in a confidential manner through an intermediary.

Substitute care In general, any kind of sanctioned care in which the child does not live with the birth parents.

Surrender "Making a plan" for a child, "relinquishing" a child, or "giving up" a child for adoption.

Surrogate mother   A woman who carries another's child by pre-arrangement.

System   Often referred to as "the system." Refers to the governmental organization of facilities for foster care and/or child welfare.

Termination   The legal ending of birth parents' rights.

Traditional adoption   Most often used to refer to a domestic infant adoption in which confidentiality is preserved.

Transracial adoption   Generally refers to the adoption of a black or biracial (e.g., black/white) child by white parents; the adoption of an Asian child by white parents would be considered both transracial and transcultural. Hispanic/Latino children are not, technically speaking, a racial group. However, the term *transracial* is often used (rightly or wrongly) to describe any adoption crossing racial or ethnic lines.

Index

About the Author

Barbara Moe, MSW, is a consultant to Adoption Alliance, a private nonprofit agency in Denver, Colorado, where she directed the Special Needs Program for sixteen years. She is the author of twenty-four books, including the first edition of *Adoption: A Reference Handbook*. She and her husband have two adopted children.